LEVITICUS AS LITERATURE

Leviticus as Literature

MARY DOUGLAS

OXFORD
UNIVERSITY PRESS

OXFORD

UNIVERSITY PRESS

Great Clarendon Street, Oxford OX2 6DP

Oxford University Press is a department of the University of Oxford.
It furthers the University's objective of excellence in research, scholarship,
and education by publishing worldwide in

Oxford New York

Auckland Cape Town Dar es Salaam Hong Kong Karachi Kuala Lumpur
Madrid Melbourne Mexico City Nairobi New Delhi Shanghai Taipei Toronto

With offices in

Argentina Austria Brazil Chile Czech Republic France Greece
Guatemala Hungary Italy Japan South Korea Poland Portugal
Singapore Switzerland Thailand Turkey Ukraine Vietnam

Oxford is a registered trade mark of Oxford University Press
in the UK and in certain other countries

Published in the United States
by Oxford University Press Inc., New York

© Mary Douglas 1999

First published in paperback 2000

British Library Cataloguing in Publication Data
Data available

Library of Congress Cataloging in Publication Data
Data available

ISBN 0-19-815092-X (hbk)
ISBN 0-19-924419-7 (pbk)

7 9 10 8 6

Typeset by in Imprint
By Hope Services (Abingdon) Ltd.
Printed in Great Britain
on acid-free paper by
Biddles Ltd., King's Lynn, Norfolk

PREFACE

Like Abraham holding his ground against God (Gen 18: 30), I ask how I can take it upon myself to speak. Without qualifications for interpreting an ancient text, I am presuming to tell the Bible scholars about Leviticus. A friendly professor of Hebrew finding my style uncomfortable (a mixture of grovelling and truculence), advised me to get on with the job in all simplicity. So this is it.

To study the book of Leviticus as an anthropologist has been a project very dear to my heart. It seemed far beyond my reach. Yet not to do it would be to leave dangling a number of threads from early work. Let me explain some things about my training which have influenced my attitude to the Bible. Young anthropologists in Oxford in the late 1940s and 1950s were heirs to an old debate about human rationality, a debate provoked by the experience of science and biased by the experience of empire. Nineteenth-century rationalists centred on what they thought of as the natives' intellectual problems. Gross superstitions, naïve magic, and immoral gods, were explained by reference to moral evolutionism. The mind of the primitive in aeons past had been hampered by illogical mental habits and proneness to letting emotions govern reason, and the same handicaps were thought to afflict present-day backward peoples. However, in reaction, for the students of my generation the main text was Evans-Pritchard's *Witchcraft, Oracles and Magic* (1937). From this we learnt that people from alien traditions, trusting in their gods and ancestors and fearing their witches, were every bit as logical as we (or just as illogical). It is actually no more 'logical' to believe in a divinely created moral universe than to believe in an amoral self-generating universe. Foundational beliefs stand beyond the operations of logic. Our researches were framed by an interest in the moral construction of the universe and the nature of belief.

In those days it was axiomatic for anthropologists that, however peculiar they might seem to us, the strange beliefs of a foreign tradition make sense. Explanations of other minds based on mystery, mystique, native credulity or mysticism, were out. Moral evolution was replaced by a down-to-earth approach to alternative ways of living and dying. We took on a hardy scepticism and a nuts-and-bolts demand for evidence. The point about doing fieldwork was to learn how a world-view was adapted to what the people were trying to achieve, especially to what they were doing towards living together in society. Hence our attention to ritual and symbolism. Rain rites, for example, would be a collective act of affirmation. The rite did not attempt to prove the priests' control of meteorology, it was done to affirm publicly the moral aspect of the natural order. Spectacular ceremonials to appease the gods were also performed for the sake of influencing each other's minds.

I would never have felt impelled to attempt an anthropological reading of Leviticus if during African fieldwork I had not been confronted by local dietary rules, and so thought of looking up the passage in chapter 11 on the forbidden animals. I actually cited Leviticus and the parallel passage in Deuteronomy in my 'Animals in Lele religious symbolism' (1957). What I wrote ten years later about uncleanness and pollution in *Purity and Danger* (1966) was driven by fieldwork experience, stiffened by training in Oxford anthropology and enriched with some reading about the psychology of perception. But before looking up those baffling chapters, I had never read the Bible, either at school or at university or subsequently. When I came eventually to read the scholarly commentaries on the Mosaic dietary laws I was surprised to find so much disagreement on such an important subject. Though with some minor variations scholars almost unanimously associated the forbidden animals with unpleasant characteristics, there was no agreement and no satisfactory explanation either in the book or outside it about why each particular species should have been selected and not others which might equally be abominated.

Reflecting on these animals I was drawn to focus on the class of unclassifiable things. The forbidden land animals

were certainly described as such a class, and I extended it
with some confidence to water creatures and speculatively to
those in the air that could not be identified. I proposed a
theory of anomaly, a universal feeling of disquiet (even of
disgust) on confrontation with unclassifiables. Taking the
Levitical classification system as it revealed itself, the said
abominable species failed to show the taxonomic requirements of inhabitants of the three environmental classes, land,
air, water, and the abominability of species that 'go upon the
belly' in all environments went by the same rule: the forbidden animals were species that escaped being classified.
Consistently with the main thrust of social anthropology of
my period, the argument explained abominability, but
denied magicality and favoured the rationality of the Mosaic
dietary code. It was gratifying to find that some Bible scholars accepted the idea that the puzzles of the abominable animals in Leviticus and Deuteronomy could be laid to rest, the
prohibitions being part of the process of tidying up the
classifications of the environment (see Levine's *JPS
Commentary, Leviticus* (1989), 243). But a puzzle remained.

The central argument of *Purity and Danger* was that classifications are not otiose. They do something, they are necessary in organization. The pollution theory that I have seen
develop over the last thirty years shows that where lines of
abominability are drawn heavy stakes are at issue. The classification of the universe is part and parcel of social organization, and the categories are useful in defining who can be
admitted where, and who comes first and who comes second
or nowhere at all. This works so effectively elsewhere that I
was implicitly waiting for it to be found true of biblical pollution (see my 'Sacred contagion' (1996)). It applies well
enough, in fairly obvious ways, for the cult of the tabernacle
and the dignity of the priesthood, but for the organization of
society the doctrine of pollution did nothing except draw a
boundary round the people of Israel against outsiders.
Nothing happens at the level of action to explain the selection
of forbidden animals. Against everything I believe, the
cognitive scheme which left these creatures unclassified hung
in the air uselessly. If chapter 11 of Leviticus was a case
for pollution theory the classifying of the animals should

correspond to some important classifying for the internal organization of society. But the more that pollution theory developed, and the more that pollution was seen as the vehicle of accusations and downgradings, the more I was bound to acknowledge that it does not apply to the most famous instance of the Western tradition, the Pentateuch. All of this volume is an attempt to explain why. General pollution theory still stands, but its application to the Bible is limited. The forbidden animals turn out to have a much more interesting role than ever I imagined.

M.D.

London
September 1998

ACKNOWLEDGEMENTS

So many people have helped me with the Leviticus project, it is impossible to thank them all, yet it is a great pleasure to remember them. Some had already retired from teaching almost as long as I have (yet I think I am older than the oldest of them). Some started guiding and encouraging me when they were still students, who now are distinguished members of Bible departments all over the world. For example, Ronald Hendel was a student at a summer school in 1983 when he insisted that I should try what I so much wanted to do, and has kept his promise to help me at all stages. Kate Cooper, Richard Lim, Diane Sharon, Michael Hildebrand, and Jonathan Klawans were all graduate students under the usual pressures to finish dissertations when this started, and I am moved to remember how much they did then and still do now to help me.

As I got into the work I had to take note that Israel was in the midst of powerful empires. My woeful ignorance of Greek history and philosophy embarrassingly blocked the way, which I was forced to confess to classical scholars. Marcel Detienne, Geoffrey Lloyd, and Richard Sorabji gave so generously that I do not know how to thank them. The most fruitful ideas on archaic literary styles came from Kathryn Gutzwiller, Aditya Behl, and specially from Simon Hornblower. In divinity schools and departments of religion I drew on friends who were not primarily Bible specialists, Wendy Doniger, Paul Morris, and Simon Weightman, for relevant aspects of Indian religions. I am grateful for the insights of some remarkable Israeli anthropologists who do work on the Hebrew Bible, especially Harvey Goldberg and Don Handelman. Mark Geller, at my own college, is an unfailing source of support and advice on the relation of the Bible to Mesopotamian religions. I am also grateful to Stephanie Dalley in Oxford for the same. A European trying to understand the Bible is likely to find the wholesale rejection of images a stumbling-block, so I was fortunate to make friends with art historians, Moshe Barasch and Lionel Kochan, who have given deep thought to the aniconic tradition. I thank them and also Miriam Hansen, who has brought her knowledge of modern German philosophy to bear so interestingly on film history.

Of course the heaviest debt is to Bible scholars. I could well have expected to be patronized, openly spurned, or subtly excluded, but instead I felt welcomed into a gracious confraternity. The obvious person to start and to end with is Jacob Milgrom. The text acknowledges his work and I will say more below. Another friend who towers over Leviticus studies is Baruch Levine, whom I only met the once in New York but who has helped me many times since. Robert Murray I have known since he was a young scholastic at Campion Hall at the close of the 1940s. His originality and his insight into the relation of humans and animals in Genesis have been crucial for this study. He is cited in the text, so also are Peter Schafer and Joseph Dan, but I need also to thank them for editorial support in the *Jewish Studies Quarterly*, and similarly, David Klein, in the *Journal of Old Testament Studies*. Others not mentioned in the writing have been indispensable as friends and as scholarly resources ever since I started to work on the Book of Numbers. Graeme Auld, my host for the Gifford Lectures on Numbers in Edinburgh in 1989, has continued to host me with great courtesy through biblical controversy. Rolf Rendtorff whenever I came to Frankfurt used to spread Hebrew works of reference over the tables and chairs in the airport lounge so that he could speedily check his remarks without interrupting a privileged commentary on what needed to be done. Hyam Maccoby, whose book on purity started after I had started on this, but which will be out first, is a good friend who has given me much help. Philip Davies, Giovanni Garbini, and Joseph Blenkinsopp have quickened my interest in the controversies surrounding the history of the Bible. Walter Houston and Gordon Wenham as Leviticus commentators have even been so good as to give expert comments on draft chapters. I must also thank Bernard Jackson for a sustained correspondence on biblical law.

For some time I had realized that Leviticus was not as much in the forefront of current biblical research as it deserved, and had been longing for a seminar that I could attend in which the hoary old problems could be discussed anew. In 1995 John Sawyer and Paul Morris organized a conference on Leviticus at Lancaster University. For anyone trying to make up for a life not spent on Bible studies it was the undreamed of, perfect, gift. I want to thank everyone who came to it, and for their very original and stimulating papers which were subsequently published by John Sawyer as *Reading Leviticus,* many of which I have used in this volume.

I received another such gift when my husband and I spent a month in Jerusalem in 1996 as the guests of the Van Leer Foundation. Jacob Milgrom, Harvey Goldberg, and Moshe Greenberg, with the help of Israel Knohl, organized four seminars on Leviticus. The formidable lions and eagles of Bible scholarship were present, they sat down peacefully with me, did not roar or pounce, and did with great charm and politeness introduce me to important problems I had not otherwise known. Aaron Demsky was there, Judith Goldberg, Moshe Greenberg, Sara Japhet, Zev Kalifon, Baruch Schwartz. Moshe Weinfeld was there too, and others up to twenty. Between them the Jerusalem scholars created an exemplary forum in which everyone who was present contributed their grace and learning. And after the seminars they were all ready to talk, solving to my great joy my usual problem of finding anyone to talk about Leviticus. In Jerusalem Shemaryahu Talmon has been a special friend since he lectured in Northwestern many years ago and we found we had an interest in sectarianism in common. In Tel Aviv, where I met other old friends, Al Baumgarten organized a workshop on Sectarianism from which I benefited, as also from his subsequent book. Also in Tel Aviv Edward Greenstein gives me learned and subtle comments on particular issues to this day.

My deepest thanks have to go to Jacob Milgrom. As the doyen of Numbers and Leviticus studies he could have felt affronted at my brashness. He could easily have warned me off at the beginning, but now it is too late. Thanks to his unfailing support I have done what I wanted to do. His habit of replying by return with detailed comments on students'

xii *Acknowledgements*

drafts is well known. Even in illness, or while travelling, he has never spared his help. I fear that if his second volume of the Anchor Bible Commentary on Leviticus is late my importunity has often caused delays. His frankness is famous, and makes it possible to stay friends without always agreeing. It is at least a satisfaction to know that when he catches me out in mistakes that he has failed so far to correct, he will not hesitate to publish a list of my errors.

There are very many more who were generous to me with their time and advice, direct or by correspondence. I must thank the two who struggled to teach me enough Hebrew to read the JPT version and the dictionary, David Meyer and Frank Rosenwasser, and finally, also John Sawyer who accepted to watch over the Hebrew terms that appear here. The brief review shows that I have not lacked support at any stage, and that the shortcomings are entirely my own. I thank everyone who has helped me to come close enough to Leviticus to love it.

CONTENTS

Contents

FIGURES

TABLES

ABBREVIATIONS

AAR American Academy of Religion

BDB F. Brown, S. R. Driver, and C. A. Briggs, *Hebrew and English Lexicon of the Old Testament* (Clarendon Press, 1951)

CBQ *Catholic Biblical Quarterly*

JAAR *Journal of the American Academy of Religion*

JANES *Journal of Ancient Near Eastern Studies*

JBL *Journal of Biblical Literature*

JCS *Journal of Classical Studies*

JPS Jewish Publication Society

JPT *Jewish People's Torah*

JSOTS *Journal for the Study of the Old Testament Supplement Series*

JTS Jewish Theological Seminary

OED *Oxford English Dictionary*

(1)

The Ancient Religion

I am the Lord who practise steadfast love, justice, and
righteousness in the earth; for in these things I delight;
says the Lord. (Jeremiah 9: 23)

The Lord is gracious and merciful, slow to anger and
abounding in steadfast love. The Lord is good to all, and
his compassion is over all that he has made. (Psalm 145:
8–9)

Happy is he whose help is the God of Jacob, whose hope
is in the Lord his God, who made heaven and earth, the
sea and all that is in them; who keeps faith for ever; who
executes justice for the oppressed. (Psalm 146: 5–7)

Leviticus is usually put into a kind of glass cabinet: it can be
looked at, respected, and wondered at, but the real heart of
the religion is presumed to be found in other parts of the
Bible, especially Genesis, Exodus, and Deuteronomy, and
the writings of the psalmists and prophets. The tradition
does Leviticus wrong. This study's aim is to reintegrate the
book with the rest of the Bible. Read in the perspective of
anthropology the food laws of Moses are not expressions of
squeamishness about dirty animals and invasive insects. The
purity rules for sex and leprosy are not examples of priestly
prurience. The religion of Leviticus turns out to be not very
different from that of the prophets which demanded humble
and contrite hearts, or from the psalmists' love of the house
of God. The main new feature of this interpretation is the
attitude to animal life. In this new perspective, Leviticus has
to be read in line with Psalm 145: 8–9: the God of Israel has
compassion for all that he made. His love for his animal creation lies behind his laws against eating and touching their
corpses. The flocks and herds of the people of Israel are

brought under the covenant that God made with their owners, and the other animals benefit from the promises he made
in Genesis after the flood, that he would guarantee the regu-
larity of the seasons and the fertility of the ground. The more
closely the text is studied, the more clearly Leviticus reveals
itself as a modern religion, legislating for justice between
persons and persons, between God and his people, and
between people and animals. One of the central problems
then becomes the question of why it has been read so differently hitherto.

An anthropologist has one first, necessary, step to make
when setting out to study an ancient religion. That step is to
locate the religion in some community of worshippers in
some known historical time and space. Anthropologists are
not trained to interpret utopias. We always try to place the
religion to be studied alongside the other religions of its
period and in its region. Morton Smith said that it would be
misleading to regard 'the religion of Israel as a unique entity'.
Surely everyone agrees to that. He went on to recommend
thinking of 'the religion of the Israelites as one form of the
common religion of the ancient Near East'.[1] Though it
sounds such sensible advice, it turns out to be impossible to
follow. There is no lack of information about the religions of
Canaan, Phoenicia, Mesopotamia, or Egypt. But the Bible
itself made a clean sweep of its regional connections. Both
Deuteronomy and Leviticus fulminate against foreign cults,
especially those of Canaan and Egypt. The religion of the
Pentateuch claims to have nothing in common with the
neighbouring religions. Commentaries on the Pentateuch
have been trying for two millennia to reconstitute what the
religion of biblical Israel would have been like if those practices had not been abjured.

Look at the catalogue of differences to realize how radically the Pentateuch separated this religion from what had
gone before. All the other religions were polytheistic in one
sense or another, only Israel's religion was severely monotheistic. There were no subsidiary or rival deities at all, only one
true God who forbade any cult to be paid to any others. This

---

[1] Smith, M., 1971: 21; 1952: 135 ff.

does not mean that the existence of other spirits was denied.[2] In fact the Bible has a role for angels as messengers of God or as manifestations of God; Satan figures as an independent agent in Zechariah, the angel of God appears in the Book of Numbers to rebuke Balaam. The wicked thing was to pay cult to the spiritual beings around.[3] Only the one God has any power, and it is pointless to apply to lesser spiritual beings, as well as an unpardonable insult to the majesty of the one God. Everything else flows from this. It is hard to realize how completely their strict monolatry separated the religion of Israel from the others in the region.

The first major difference is monarchy. The role of king is completely missing in biblical rituals. The peoples in the surrounding regions were all kingdoms, some large, some small; sacral kingship[4] with cosmological theories about the king's body figured in various forms, with rites for royal inaugurations and funerals. This is not to be brushed aside as unimportant. The books of Samuel, Kings, and Chronicles are histories of the kings of Israel and Judah; but the kingship has left no trace in the religion. It is true that Deuteronomy gives some superficial advice to kings (not to maintain extravagant harems and stables, and to keep the faith, Deut 17: 14–20); but there is nothing in the cult about the role of the king, alive or dead, and not a word about kings in Leviticus.

The silence on this subject is sometimes explained by saying that the last editors of the Pentateuch wanted no more of kings and so went straight back to the primal religion of the time of Moses. Genesis is about the beginning of the world, Exodus, Leviticus, Numbers, and Deuteronomy are about a time long before kings, so why should anyone expect there to be anything about kings in a document which antedated them? This answer is not so obvious as it seems, no religion stands still. In just a few years a lived religion syncretizes and elaborates different themes, so that it is generally difficult to say what came first and what came last. The scholarly

---

[2] 'Worship of several deities is compatible with monotheism, one has only to believe, for example, that the supreme ("true") deity has created beings inferior to itself but superior to men and has ordained that men should worship them.' Smith, M., 1952: 165 n. 111.

[3] Sawyer 1984. [4] Frankfort 1948.

opinion is that the Pentateuch was edited soon after the fall of the last king, which makes it exceedingly strange that kings left no mark on it. A literary *tour de force* eliminated monarchy from ancient texts about rites in which the role of king had been central for at least 600 years.

Ancestors were also eliminated. Ancestors are humans who have been decorporalized, in other religions they have become spiritual beings, intelligent agents with some powers to act. Consistently, Israel's religion ruled out cults of ancestors and propitiation of ghosts. There are plenty of signs of cults of the spirits of the dead in the Bible, but the religion recorded by Leviticus and Deuteronomy abhors interaction with the dead, there is no official cult of ancestors. They also rule out belief in demons. When access to both demons and spirits of the dead is forbidden, divination, as a technique for consulting the dead or other spiritual beings, becomes impossible. Except the oracle of the high priest, all forms of divination were banned. If this were the only change it would have left a devastating gap in the religion, affecting ritual, doctrine, and practice. Magic, as a set of cultic techniques for recruiting the powers of minor spiritual beings to the purposes of the magician or his client, was ruled out too. This does not mean to say that at a popular level magicians and oracles were not consulted, there is plenty of evidence that they were, but officially in Leviticus they were banned. There were to be no more horoscopes or auguries, no auspicious times for engaging in work or war and inauspicious times for staying at home, only the one holy sabbath day of God. Add to all this that images were banned because of their association with idolatry, and the gulf between the religion of the Bible and those of the surrounding peoples can hardly be exaggerated.

Even more significant would be the gulf between the writers and their own past. A complex oracle provides a complete system of the world in which the diviner locates the particular information that his client brings, and from it draws a wealth of distant implications enriched by assiduously gathered local understandings. Abolishing divination would have eroded a mnemonic system and obliterated a store of knowledge, and more, it would have dealt a lethal blow against the coherence of knowledge. Without the practical use in consultation the grand system of balanced analogies would atrophy into a jangling mumbo-jumbo. These gaps in information would be one source of pressure for Leviticus' new synthesis, but no one could have been able to reconstitute the religion as it had been.

To present an ancient religion as if in its original form, but actually purged of its central elements, calls for a great effort of rethinking. Cutting out polytheism, kingship, oracles, ancestors, demons, magic, diviners, healers, and images meant that very little of the superseded religion would be left intact. The Levitical resynthesis has been so skilful that the reader is easily lulled into accepting the antique pastoral scene. Only very alert scrutiny discovers where the seams have been stitched over and the gaps closed, sometimes real gaps in knowledge. The basis for the synthesis has three planks, three principles which govern what the religion of Leviticus took and what it rejected from the religions in the region. The first is the justice of God. The central teaching of Leviticus is God's righteousness. The second is the covenant which laid down his relations with his people. This means not one covenant, to be sure, but the whole series, the covenant with Noah, the covenants with Abraham, Isaac, and Jacob, culminating with the covenant on Sinai.

The third principle is circumcision, the sign of the covenant. For the people of Israel and for no one else, there are two modes of affiliation: one is natural descent from father to son, the other is cultural, alliance through the covenant.[5] Leviticus is an elaborate teaching of the difference between sexual and ritual reproduction. It opposes natural fertility to the ritual for making heirs to God's promise. Descent by the seed of the loins on the one hand, and the cut and blood of the circumcised penis on the other, its laws keep the two bodily fluids, semen and blood, meticulously apart. It is not likely that these three principles were new. The justice of God, the covenant, and the two dispensations, nature and law, were the basis of his people's religious belief. Whatever else had been rejected, these central principles were stable.

[5] Goldberg 1996.

CHRONOLOGY AND THE WRITING

In spite of this, the strong impression remains that the Pentateuch must have been the book of a totally reformed religion. Royal rites eliminated, no kings, no spirits of the dead, no local fertility spirits, no shape-shifting demons, no oracles, no magicians or diviners. The Pentateuch is written in an attempt to rebuild faith and trust, not on new but rather on old foundations. Leviticus goes back to a primordial revelation, it is fundamentalist in the sense that its teachings are founded on the word of God given to Moses and recorded by him. Why does a people make a clean sweep of its old religion and adopt overnight a radical, puritanical, egalitarian bias? Such an overthrow of old institutions would be undertaken after a major catastrophe. When would that have been? Robertson Smith opined that Bible studies had reached 'a point where nothing of vital importance for the historical study of the Old Testament religion still remains uncertain'.[6]

He said that a hundred years ago, but in the passage of time the chronology of writing the texts remains uncertain. As to the history itself, the period between the ninth and fifth centuries BCE gave plenty of cause for religious revival: a continuing record of foreign war, invasion, destruction, deportation, and political disaster. Both Israel and Judah drawn violently into western Asiatic political affairs were quite unable to direct their own. In the eighth century the northern kingdom of Israel was defeated in war, laid waste, and made tributary to Assyria. In the sixth century the southern kingdom of Judah was defeated in war, Jerusalem captured, the king, nobles, and learned men deported, and the temple destroyed. Between the two catastrophes, is it necessary to choose the one to which the Pentateuch responds? The choice of a precise date could perhaps be evaded and yet a context be found for the writing of the Bible in the extended period of tribulation. Moshe Weinfeld (writing of Deuteronomy 30: 4 and 4: 27) said: 'Most scholars tend to assign these passages to the post-exilic period. But this is

[6] Smith, W. R., (1889) 1972.

unnecessary. In the background to these passages there is clearly the fact of a captivity and of an extensive dispersion, . . . but not necessarily the captivity of Judah, since it could be the captivity of Samaria.'[7]

It helps the reading of Leviticus and Deuteronomy to recall that the books were composed and edited during a long period of continuing political upheaval. Though they are different, at least that much common context can be proposed for them: the anguish of living with the disasters of war and the need to rebuild solidarity, this would be the context and the impetus for producing the Pentateuch. But, alas, the bad experience of invasion and defeat is too general to provide a guide to interpretation. To this day it is the lot of too many peoples; some react to it one way, by resort to rejection of the world and a call to fundamentalist renewal, others by trying to establish legislative control, others by gestures of reconciliation. The responsibility of deciding whether Leviticus relates to the eighth or fifth century or earlier, or later, cannot be completely evaded. Just for the sake of writing about the book, some standpoint in time has to be adopted. For lack of historical skills in the region the anthropologist can only accept the largest scholarly consensus, and this at present points to the post-exilic period, the Second Temple community in the fifth century.

The new version may have been first worked out intellectually by the writer of Leviticus, using very old fragments of laws, and subsequently applied to the reform of the cult. Alternatively, the laws could have emerged unsystematically in the course of organizing ceremonies and teaching, the practice first, and the ratiocination and the doctrinal synthesis afterwards. Another possibility again is suggested by the studied elegance and powerfully contrived structure. A literary composition that is so impressive could suggest that writing a theological treatise was the full achievement. The sceptical likelihood that the book is a beautiful fantasy, a vision of a life that never was, hangs heavily over the interpretation. But in this study the question will be kept open so as to leave room for an anthropological reading.

[7] Weinfeld 1976: 35.

RECONSTRUCTING THE PRIMORDIAL RELIGION

The priestly editors intended no doubt to reinstate the pure Mosaic legacy, shorn of accretions. Ironically, it would have been much the same exercise as William Robertson Smith's when he tried to discover the most primitive elements of the religion of the Semitic peoples. The priests tried to reach back, beyond their kings, to the original form of the religion that God had given to Moses. Likewise, Robertson Smith tried to reach back beyond the Bible that they edited. His method was to study the surviving forms of what he called pagan religions in Arabia, religions which he believed to have been unaffected by the Bible teaching.

The method was inherently flawed: there is no reason to suppose that religions in the region would have remained static over the millennia; there is no justification for the moral evolutionism by which he hoped to track certain changes. Robertson Smith tried to relate the Bible religion to set phases in the development of humankind, from most primitive hunters, to less primitive pastoralists, to settled communities of agriculturalists. A text that referred to sedentary farmers was taken to be later than one that referred to nomadic cowherds. He thought that the rest of Arabia would have escaped Bible influence, so if he could study religions of pastoralists, whether pagan or Islamic, he would have a line on what had preceded the Bible religion. In spite of these obvious weaknesses, his results suggest what would have been involved in introducing an anti-monarchical, monotheistic religion in that region.

First he found the relations of the worshippers to their gods to be governed by a close tie between the people, their territory, and their god. In a region of small, sparse, and scattered communities each would have had its own god as their final resource, maintaining their local moral order; in their endemic feuds with each other the gods would have been hostile to the enemies of their worshippers. A king who wanted to consolidate a larger political unit would inevitably be forced into the position of defending the weak against the strong, and so the ideal of kingship would have been seen as the source of 'even-handed justice through the nation, without respect of persons'.[8] He quotes the Hebrew prophets on the one true God as the king of absolute justice. As patron–client relations linked persons to persons, so the worshipper was seen as the client of his Baal, the name for the local god. It follows that when only one God was to be worshipped, that one God would take on a patron's role, and his congregation became his client: he would be invoked as the fount of absolute justice.

The concern for fertility in Baal worship is equally important for Leviticus. A republican-minded congregation can accept a religion without kings, so long as the idea of justice is transferred to the one God. But no congregation that has been in the habit of expecting its god to watch over its conceiving, birthing, and rearing of infants and of livestock will be ready to do without its fertility cult. If the one true God were to supersede the local Baal deities, he would have to take on their responsibilities. Fertility is not something that is just wanted in a general way, it is the aggregated longing of particular women to conceive, the wish of particular men to have descendants, the anxiety of particular mothers for the life of their own babies, of particular farmers for their own livestock and crops. Mere talk is not going to be enough to assuage these ardent personal desires. It is all very well for the God of Genesis to tell his creatures to go forth with his blessing on their breeding, or to declare that he will give numerous descendants to Abraham and Isaac. There has to be something that these anxious worshippers can do in the here-and-now to bring their particular cases to his mind. There have to be offerings that they can make to direct his life-giving power to their own lives and to the vegetation and animals on which they depend. In the Canaanite religions first fruits were offered to the Baal.[9] The Pentateuch redirects all sacrifices and the first-fruit ceremonies to the honour of the one God.

Redirecting the positive cults that honoured Baal to the worship of the God of Israel is an easy accommodation to monotheism. But what to do about cults to avert the harm

---

[8] Smith, W. R., (1889) 1972: 73.

[9] 'As the Kirta epic and other Ugaritic texts indicate, El, the supreme god at Ugarit, was concerned with healing, specially infertility' (Avalos 1997: 454).

caused by demons? The priests can hardly take over the ther-
apies designed to subdue or chase demons away without
acknowledging their dangerous power. Nothing is said about
any demons in Leviticus, unless Azazel mentioned in the
scapegoat ceremony (Lev 16: 8, 10, 26) is one. Demons were
important in Canaan, Mesopotamia, Egypt, and all around.
They had the ability to transform themselves into animals, so
they were partly corporeal, they had a putrid smell, they
could suffer death and when they died a corpse was to be
found, usually the corpse of an animal. They inhabited wild
places, desert, mountains, and woodland; from their usual
haunts they could come out and catch a person and strike him
or her with illness. They attacked pregnant women, caused
miscarriages, made women and cattle barren, and killed off
babies. Demons, in the Canaanite beliefs, were regarded as
impure, antithetical to the cult of Baal. In so far as the Baal
was a source of fertility, demonic agencies would be a stan-
dardized explanation of barrenness and failure.[10]

To take demons out of the religion would leave a huge gap.
It is not just that the worshippers are wishing for fertility, but
also that they are wanting to understand the innumerable
losses and diseases which they are in the habit of ascribing to
demons. If they are told not to fear demons any more, how are
they to explain their misfortunes? Leviticus finds one solution
for the two problems, replacing the demons and satisfying the
need for explanations. Briefly, Leviticus separated the theory
of impurity from belief in demons, and classified impurity as
a form of *lèse majesté*, an attack on God's honour as the
covenanted lord of the people of Israel. The simple move,
expressed in rules for controlling ritual contagion, teaches the
people not to blame non-existent demons for misfortunes.
The rules prescribe action to remove impurity, washing in the
case of minor impurities, sacrifice in the case of bloodshed,
genital discharges, and the set of skin afflictions called leprosy. Leviticus prescribes a sacrifice for atonement once a
year for the sanctuary and altar to be purified. In the new synthesis the congregation which would have been very worried
about attacks from demons now finds that demons cannot

[10] Stuart 1991.

harm them. But they still suffer from all the things that used to be attributed to demons. They are taught that they are safe so long as they keep the rules and control impurity. In the ongoing history of the religion Leviticus' doctrinal effort to transcend fear of demons is a modernizing move which stands parallel to the effort of Christian doctrine to transcend fear of incurring physical impurities, focusing the congregation's attention on fidelity to the love of God.

The adaptation of the folk religion to the new doctrine creates another problem. When impurity was associated with demons any animal might become impure as the result of an attack: the impure animal was a victim. There would have been no conflict between the doctrine of a merciful, just, and loving God who made the animals, and the theory that an animal might become a source of impurity. But now that demonic agency is excluded, the idea emerges that the impure animals might be noxious in themselves, abominable. This is the established reading of animal impurity. But here we ask why the good kind God would create abominable animals? In Genesis chapter 1 God made teeming, fecund animals, in the waters and in the skies, saw that they were good, blessed them and told them to multiply and fill the earth. Having made these living creatures the God of Genesis does not suddenly turn round in Leviticus and revile them. God is not capricious and inconsistent. Concentrated in God is the life-giving power of the local Baals, God is the protector of animal and vegetable life. Of course he would not let his human clients abuse his other creatures. The God of Leviticus requires an account of blood of animals shed.

Ritual purity is a kind of two-way protection, a holy thing is protected from profanation, the profane thing is protected from holiness. The idea that hands that were clean become unclean after touching a holy thing is paradoxical for us, but seems to have been acceptable to the early exegetes. When asked why anyone who touched the scriptures had to wash their hands, Rabbi Yochanan ben Zakkai explained the 'uncleanness' of scriptures by saying, 'as is their preciousness so is their uncleanness'.[11] By declaring that the holy scriptures

---

[11] The *Mishnah*, 6th Division, Tohoroth (Cleanness), 4–6.

'make the hands unclean' the rabbis were accepting the double-edged paradox of holiness, inherently dangerous, liable to break out and needing to be protected from profane intrusion. This is very hard for a secular culture to understand.

In this chapter and in pages to follow the term 'theology' is used. In a non-denominational sense, theology means a theory of God, his attributes, and his actions. Among some Jewish and Christian Bible scholars there is a half-joking convention that 'theology' is Christian and that the word does not apply to the Jewish religious thinkers. Theologians are specialized practitioners, but theology, like philosophy, may be homespun, popular, and implicit. It can never, by the nature of the subject, be exhaustive, it is not necessarily coherent or even very well articulated. Leviticus reveals itself as a theological treatise in the full sense of the word, and fully in the biblical tradition. Its teachings about God's grandeur, his unswerving justice and unfailing compassion, are best read in the light of the prophets and psalms. So far from being disorganized, it systematizes a theory of divine justice which underlies Genesis and Exodus.

However, real difficulties beset the reading of Leviticus. Judah was conquered by Rome; Judaic and Christian thought, along with Greek and Roman, are the foundation of Western civilization. In the long powerful push to modernity the reading of the Bible was successively transformed. Every succeeding age marvels at how well the Bible speaks to its own understanding. No doubt it has suffered reinterpretations, but it seems to stand as a beacon of clarity and light in spite of radical changes of emphasis. After all the centuries of rereading two books in the Pentateuch remain obdurately opaque, the priestly books of Leviticus and Numbers. This is partly due to a rhetorical style which defies straightforward reading. Numbers is redeemed by its narrative; it takes the history of the people of Israel from the time they escaped from Egypt to their arrival at the River Jordan. But Leviticus is not a historical work. It is an archaic book of laws and it has tended to be read alongside other Near-Eastern law books of its period. Modern Western readers have to make a deliberate effort to read it otherwise. The next two chapters lay the groundwork for a fresh reading.

(2)

Two Styles of Thought

Living with Equations

As I emerged from my hip-bath it suddenly dawned
The facts might be remarshalled and shown to rhyme.
Now the era need never end: its coefficients learn
To crack their knuckles, or reach for a handful of silver.
I watch the entangled sums unspool, as if the weight
Of earth pressed fitfully upon their mad proposals.
Stray hints lead across perilous forecourts, around
Noisy corners, then out into featureless, sandy scrub.
The devolved particulars—a shoe, a mole—reappear
In compounds that seem so explicit one forgets to gasp.
The remainder can only imperceptibly dwindle, retreating
Backwards until their long lost premises turn inside out.

Mark Ford[1]

Leviticus is not the same as Deuteronomy, it has a different style, and often the teaching differs. Nonetheless, through two millennia Leviticus has been read through Deuteronomy, with divergences reconciled by imposing the Deuteronomic version on the Levitical one.[2] The commentators have tried piously to conflate the two sources, papering over the differences that might impugn the authority of the law. Given the highly specialized form of education they were developing, the rabbis would be likely to favour the

---

[1] Ford 1997.

[2] The following is evidence that the school which produced the commentary on Deuteronomy also produced the commentary on Leviticus: 'The Sifra is a commentary on the whole book of Leviticus, and is the production of the School of Akiba, which is also responsible for the Deuteronomic part of the Sifre. The rival school of R. Ishmael produced the Midrashim known as the Mechilta on part of Exodus, and the Sifre on Numbers. Thus these halachic Midrashim are more or less equally divided between the Schools of Ishmael and Akiba' (*Sifra* 1994: xlvii).

Deuteronomic version with its rousing fervour and direct
nationalist appeal. But even the most basic concepts take on
different meanings in the two books.

When Deuteronomy uses a conception of the body it is the
body politic,[3] in Leviticus the body is a cosmic symbol. The
two books were very likely to have been composed by writers
living in different social circles, and they could have been
contemporaries. What seems very clear as the study proceeds
is that there was some break in the continuity of interpretation of Leviticus. Either the priestly writers went away leaving no school or tradition behind them, or they were silenced
by factional attacks on the priesthood. Or maybe the general
state of upheaval in the region was so disruptive that all the
traditions were blurred, if not actually lost. In any of these
cases the rabbinical schools that started several hundred
years later to expound the Torah would have had to make a
fresh start. It is truly said that the Leviticus writer is theo-
cratic and his institutions are sacred, while the Deuteronomy
writer is governmental and his institutions secular.[4] Deuteronomy is more interested in human affairs and generally
more sympathetic. This contrast between two books and two
ways of thinking about religion will underlie all that follows.
Both are deeply venerated.

Following on the Book of Exodus, Leviticus records
instructions that God gave to Moses on Mount Sinai about
how to perform his cult and how to live together as a holy
people. Sacrifice means killing and cutting up large animals
and disposing of their blood. The book gives gory instructions for how to sprinkle the blood seven times, dash it
against the side of the altar, pour it out at the base, smear it
on the altar and on the priests. Its descriptions of skin diseases are fit to turn the appetite, its sins lusty and punishments violent. Although the formal style softens the macabre
effect by making it all seem unreal, it is not a book for the
squeamish. Yet, Leviticus is the Bible book to which many
little Jewish children are first introduced. There does not
seem to be much here to attract the young mind. A child is
not likely to enjoy the literary finesse, the subtle cross-

referencing and elaborate balancing of themes. Friends have confided that this early confrontation has put them off the book for life. Others revere it as one would a family heirloom. If they do not expect to like or understand it, they are justified. It belongs to a now obsolete and completely foreign order of thought which the rest of this chapter and the next will describe.

ANALOGICAL VERSUS RATIONAL-INSTRUMENTAL THINKING

In studying ancient Chinese texts some sinologists have found it necessary to distinguish an aesthetic or analogical mode of thought. It stands in contrast to our own habits of thinking. The concern of Graham, and of Hall and Ames, is to introduce Confucius' social and political theory.[5] Their object is to emphasize the difference between the aesthetic ordering of the Han cosmology and the rational ordering which we have inherited from Aristotelian logic. Their thesis is so important for reading Leviticus that it is worth saying more about it. Our logic is based on part–whole relations, the theory of types, causal implications and logical entailments. It organizes experience in theoretical terms. Rational construction based upon it always goes in a direction away from the concrete particular towards the universal: 'Persons in society are construed rationally to the extent that their idiosyncracies are abstracted and their general or universal characteristics are made relevant'.[6] For example, rational construction creates contexts in which 'human nature', or 'human rights', or 'equality under the law', can be invoked. Most important of all, the rational ordering which we employ presupposes a unique structure or pattern, complete, comprehensive, and closed. These authors indicate how much the rational ordering has come under philosophical attack in the twentieth century from the critics of the Enlightenment, naming Ryle, Kuhn, Feyeraband, Derrida.

---

[5] Graham 1989; Hall and Ames 1987; 1995.   [6] Hall and Ames 1987: 137.

For the other type of thinking they introduce the term 'correlative', or 'aesthetic' or analogical ordering. It is not based on dialectical principles, its arguments do not run on a linear, hierarchical model. It is based on analogical association, 'it is "horizontal" in the sense that it involves the association of concrete experienceable items'.[7] For examples, consider the humour theory of medicine, or astrological charts whose elements are selected and correlated from the perspective of the correlator.

From the perspective of correlative thinking, to explain an item or event is, first, to place it within a scheme organized in terms of analogical relations among the items selected for the scheme, and then to reflect, and act in terms of the suggestiveness of the relations. Correlative thinking involves the association of image—or concept—clusters by meaningful disposition rather than physical causation.[8]

They give totemic classification for an example. The Han dynasty cosmologists used the five directions, North, East, South, West, and Centre, five phases (water, fire, wood, metal, earth), five smells, five sounds, five tastes, etc. to build up a correlative cosmos. Correlative thinking came first, and remains the basis of the common-sense thinking of daily life, but it gives way when there is a need to criticize the accepted correlations. This is not a salute to an evolutionary theory of thought; the authors do not imagine causal and logical thinking being highly developed long before the Enlightenment, but that is because their matter does not suggest the possibility.

Bible interpretation is still dominated by the evolutionary approach to language, myth, and morals developed in the 1870s and 1880s by Max Müller. It was pursued and confidently affirmed by the philosopher, Ernst Cassirer, who died only in 1945, which almost brings us to mid-century. With readings from Codrington about mankind's earliest religions, from Lévy Bruhl about the pre-logical mentality of primitives, and from Malinowski on the origins of myth,[9]

---

[7] Hall and Ames 1995: 124. [8] Ibid.: 124–5.
[9] The influence of these anthropologists is generously acknowledged in Cassirer 1946.

Cassirer authoritatively identified two kinds of thought and their order of appearance in human history. Thus he brought mythology into the scope of philosophy. We have some cause now to regret the strong antiquarian bent that biblical studies received from Cassirer. Historical priority became the most important question. That mythology undoubtedly came first was a commonplace not worthy of intellectual excitement, hardly interesting in itself. For Müller the one issue that made comparative religion worth while was to marvel at how far humanity had come on its way from its early beginnings. 'Human culture taken as a whole may be described as the process of man's progressive self-liberation.'[10] The mythology project also carried a hidden baggage (well, not so hidden) of prejudice. Mythology and religion were shown to be primitive and therefore inferior to rationalist agnosticism and science. The celebratory note remained strong in Cassirer: he assumed, reasonably, that the rational-instrumental mode of thought as we know it was the result of slowly evolved cognitive experience, and that mythical thought was primitive. This was fair enough since in his time thought dominated by religion had been superseded by thought dominated by science. He would probably not have denied that rational-instrumental thought must have been present wherever people negotiated with each other or passed judgement, but the fashionable analogy with geology suggested that mythical thought was a relic, a kind of intellectual fossil. He praised mythical thinking, it was creative and imaginative, beautiful, the basis of poetry, but at the same time he saw it as condemned by its conservatism.

Mythical thought is, by its origin and by its principles, traditional thought. For myth has no means of understanding, explaining and interpreting the present form of human life than to reduce it to a remote past. What has its roots in the mythical past . . . is firm and unquestionable. To call it into question would be a sacrilege . . . Any breach of continuity would destroy the very substance of mythical and religious life . . . Primitive religion can therefore leave no room for any freedom of individual thought . . . Religious life has reached its maturity and its freedom; it has broken the spell of a rigid traditionalism.[11]

[10] Cassirer 1944: 224.   [11] Ibid.: 225.

His frank preference for openness, where nothing is reserved from questioning, partly explains why his ideas were so uncritically received. When it is put like that, who would not prefer progress and change to stagnation and constraint?

But preference, like prejudice, is a poor basis for interpretation. The past does not speak for itself, the myth-makers speak for it, transforming history at all times. The assumption of primitive rigidity was soon to be questioned by social anthropologists. So far from being a rock-solid shrine for the past, myth-makers are always busily at work transforming their myth. Cassirer's insight was true, there are times and places where myth is part of a stable way of life, but the myth is not so much the cause of the stability as the result. What was wrong was to pit the past against the present, and mythology against reason. As Hall and Ames have shown, the mytho-poetic mode in China has its own logic behind it and it has forms that can arise at any time. The rest of this chapter will justify the claim that writing in a mytho-poetic style does not give internal evidence of a thought that is hidebound by ancient tradition, for myths change all the time. Moreover, it does not give clues to dating.

Leviticus' literary style is correlative, it works through analogies. Instead of explaining why an instruction has been given, or even what it means, it adds another similar instruction, and another and another, thus producing its highly schematized effect. The series of analogies locate a particular instance in a context. They expand the meaning. Sometimes the analogies are hierarchized, one within another making inclusive sets, or sometimes they stand in opposed pairs or contrast sets. They serve in place of causal explanations. If one asks, Why this rule? the answer is that it conforms to that other rule. If, Why both those rules? the answer is a larger category of rules in which they are embedded as subsets or from some of which they are distinguished as exceptions. Many law books proceed in this concentric, hierarchical way. In Leviticus the patterning of oppositions and inclusions is generally all the explaining that we are going to get. Instead of argument there is analogy.

Suzanne Langer, pupil, friend, and translator of Cassirer, called the two kinds of thought 'presentational' and 'discursive'.[12] 'Discursive' is our idea of rational discourse, it develops propositions by the logic of non-contradiction. 'Presentational' discourse presents analogies which are abstract projections lifted from one context to another. Her first examples are from painting. A few strokes of the pen or brush turn the flat canvas or paper into a space on which objects are depicted. The picture space is not the infinite space of the world, or the limited space of a field or a house in which we can move. She called it a 'virtual space' in which objects are recognized by their relation to one another: 'The space iself is a projected image, and everything pictured serves to define and organize it.'[13] She went on from painting in the plane to sculpture, an organized set of volume relations which produce virtual volume, and to music, whose organization creates virtual time, and to architecture which creates a virtual domain. For all of this she drew on the work of the German musicologists who took human movement in space and time, dance particularly, as the necessary point of reference in art appreciation. This synaesthetic approach originally owed much to the Pythagorean school, which expected harmony between mathematics, the planetary bodies, music, and the other arts.

When Langer wrote about perception as not a passive seeing but an organizing activity, following Immanuel Kant, she intended to offer a contribution to the philosophy of art rather than to the conversation going on in the West about two kinds of thinking, one primitive and one modern. In effect what she wrote should have been received as a blow against the prevailing current of evolutionism. There is nothing primitive about art; it is not less logical than discursive reasoning, it is the logic of analogy, used all the time in the highest civilizations. She accepted or took for granted the evolutionary model which, in effect, she dismantled.[14] Whereas philosophers assumed analogic discourse to be anti-logical, Suzanne Langer took a step towards removing that reproach. She succeeded in analysing the two genuinely

[12] Langer 1942.   [13] Langer 1953: 77.

[14] 'Language, the symbolisation of thought, exhibits two entirely different modes of thought . . . discursive logic and creative imagination . . . Logic springs from language when that greatest of symbolic forms is mature . . . language takes us away from the mythmaking phase of human mentality to the phase of logical thought and the conception of facts.' (In Cassirer 1945: viii.)

distinctive modes of thought, showing both the discursive and the presentational to be equally legitimate forms of logic. Furthermore, she did not push any historic or psychological explanations. Neither mode is more primitive or more evolved than the other, each serves different purposes, the former isolates elements, it deconstructs, while the latter projects whole patterns.

Should we see Leviticus as an example of mytho-poetic reasoning?

Definitely, Yes.

Is it written in the style of discursive logical reasoning?

Definitely, No.

Can a work that reasons in the one way be read as if it had been written in the other way?

Again, No, or it will certainly be misread.

As we read any part of Leviticus we see that the rules build up verbal analogies: the consecration of a priest has a pattern of points in common with the consecration of the altar. We should read them as projections[15] of one another and learn from each something more about what consecration means. The same applies to analogies drawn by the ritual of consecrating a priest (Lev 8: 23–4) and the ritual cleansing of a cured leper when he is to be brought back into the community (Lev 14: 14). The anointing says something, but is it something about the meaning of cleansing? Or about the meaning of leprosy? Or about the meaning of priesthood? Only the whole system of analogies in which it nests will show how it is to be read. By discrediting universal evolutionary stages of thought, Langer can teach Bible scholars to stop searching in the style for historical clues about Leviticus and Deuteronomy.

FROM ANALOGIC TO DIALOGIC

The lesson is not fully learnt. Even if not earlier and primitive, analogy has continued to be seen as the inferior and

---

[15] For the most radical and consistent view of analogies and models as projections not images, see Goodman 1968, and for a commentary on how it applies to ethnography, Douglas 1993b.

opposite of Aristotelian discursive logic. If this were so, those people who habitually use it would be intellectually disadvantaged. But analogic thought is not a handicap. An example of the disparagement of analogy: Adolph Meyer in his 1900 survey of microcosm theories of the world dismissed them one and all as 'lacking scientific confirmation and depending too much on reasoning from analogy'.[16] However, he had a very limited idea of 'scientific'.

The English philosopher, Mary Hesse, has pointed out that an 'analogy' is the same as a 'model', and that models are central in the thinking of mathematicians and scientists.[17] She made what should have been a definitive stroke in its favour when she described how heavily the process of scientific inference rests on analogy. Among many examples, she cited the billiard-ball model as playing an essential part in the development of the kinetic theory of gases.[18] Analogy is entrenched in scientific thought, and in all thinking in so far as it relies on projection and exemplification.[19] Aristotelian logic can start when the categories present themselves ready made, but there is a preliminary process by which the categories are constructed and compared.[20] Reliance on analogy is not in itself the main difference between our modern thought and theirs, archaic or primitive. The real differences are where the initial categories come from, in their case from their social experience, in our case from a specialized professional process. Rational thought operates most powerfully where the thinking can be cut off from social experience and work inside the module of its own creation. It depends, in other words, on the institutionalization and professionalization of many different kinds of thought.

Hesse further helps our problems with Leviticus by insisting that a model never fits perfectly all of its exemplars. In science a model has some positive areas where fit with

---

[16] Meyer 1900. This reference is taken from Conger 1922: xv.

[17] Hesse 1963. See also Cohen and Hesse 1980: 'basic classifications are not wholly dependent on cultural background. That they could be wholly independent is surely unbelievable . . . Which classification is adopted at any given time may well be a matter of cultural tradition and convention, but it is the *empirical resistance* of the world, not cultural convention, that determines whether they are or are not convenient and successful instruments for scientific prediction' (241).

[18] Hesse 1963.   [19] Goodman 1968.   [20] Douglas and Hull 1993.

experience is quite clear; it usually also has negative areas which have to be ignored in the building of theory, and it has neutral areas where fit to the next example may be dubious. The ambiguity of these grey areas stimulates the mind to find new extensions of theory. According to Mary Hesse the non-fit plays an essential part in extending scientific theory.[21] Not only in science, the models of everyday thought also have areas of poor fit with their examples. Learned habit and the support of the speech community protect the analogy that does not fit very well by restricting the range of interpretation.[22] The thought is embedded in a speech community and if the latter shifts significantly it will be easy to change the interpretation of the analogies, foregrounding grey or neutral areas that were formerly disregarded. This supports the idea of Hall and Ames that correlative thinking is flexible. It follows that the way to analyse a system of thought is to relate it to the world it organizes. Fortunately structuralism, which was developed first in linguistics, was going to demonstrate how to do that, and so to bring great advances in the theory of analogy.

Before Lévi-Strauss applied structural analysis to the study of myth and totemism[23] it seemed plausible to look for the meaning of a rule, for example, against eating pork or mixing milk and blood, either in a historical event, or in foreign cults, or in something that the pig, or the mixture, or blood, might stand for.[24] After the 1950s such itemized explanations became impossibly old-fashioned. The meaning of one element would now always have to be sought in whole systems of meanings. No longer can the meaning of one thing be sought in the way that it represents or copies or corresponds to one other thing. No more is it useful to consider what separate items such as bread or blood symbolize. It is not just a change in our methods of work, but a change in our understanding of human thinking.

---

[21] Hesse 1974: 28.   [22] Kuhn 1974.

[23] Lévi-Strauss 1963; 1966a; 1964; 1966b; 1968.

[24] Beyond anthropology the structuralist revolution was primarily used in literary criticism, and from this angle it has had a major impact on biblical interpretation. However, the implications go deep into the theory of representation and support more recent philosophers' attacks on the exaggerated importance of representing in our traditional epistemology. See Hacking 1983.

Lévi-Strauss opened this approach by a study of totemism.[25] Like the words for 'family', 'sacrifice', 'religion', which resist theory by fragmenting into uncontrollable varieties, totemism turns out to be best understood not as a thing in itself but as part of a process, in this case the process of classifying nature. The short definition of totemism is that it postulates a logical equivalence between a society of natural species and a world of social groups. Each totemic group of humans is connected logically with a totemic species, but what is important is not the one-to-one relations of group to species but the overall confrontation of human society and nature.

It is a relational theory. Each thing has its meaning only in the relations it has within a set of other things. For example, later we will discuss why suet fat is forbidden in Leviticus. This will cause us to ask how suet is classified among other items of anatomy, and on what sort of model the set of items which includes suet has been constructed. We would also have to know whether there is another model from which this was derived and how the principles of the classification are projected on to the constructed sets.

Lévi-Strauss's starting-point in totemism obliged him to study food prohibitions, since the totemic group is forbidden to eat its totemic species. Humans and nature are always confronting each other face to face, but never more so than at the division of the meat. Totemism led him beyond animal species to plants, stars and planets, colours, and within animal species to the anatomy of the animal. He showed that not only are relations between animal species constructed as an analogy of external relations between human groups, but also and by the same token how animal anatomy is constructed to match internal divisions, the anatomy, if you like, of the human group. Consider the complicated prohibitions on eating observed by the Bushmen of South Africa.

All game killed by means of bows and arrows is forbidden, *soxa*, until the chief has eaten a piece of it. This prohibition does not apply to the liver which the hunters eat on the spot, but which remains *soxa* to women in all circumstances. In addition to these

[25] Lévi-Strauss 1963.

general rules, there are permanent *soxa* for certain functional or social categories. For example, the wife of the man who killed the animal can only eat the superficial covering of meat and fat of the hindquarters, the entrails and the trotters. These pieces constitute the portion reserved for women and children. The adolescent boys have a right to the flesh of the abdominal wall, kidneys, genital organs and udders and the person who killed the animal to the ribs and shoulder blade from one side of it. The chief's part consists of a thick steak from each quarter and each side of the back and a cutlet taken from each side.[26]

Lévi-Strauss's concern in quoting this was to show how a non-totemic society is classifying the inside of the animal according to totemic principles. The origins of these details are incidental to his objective. Why the women can never eat liver is irrelevant. The origin of the rule may be that they are not on the spot when it is killed and that in a hot climate it goes bad before it can be carried back to camp, and from there it may have gained implications as a specifically male food. It does not matter how it started, the point is that the classification of anatomical parts provides a notation scheme[27] for the system of social categories. By the performance the pattern of ideas is reinforced and each part, whatever other meanings may accrue, has its main explanation by its relation to the rest. It is a relational theory of meaning. Lévi-Strauss inaugurated the idea that every thought style is implanted in a way of life.

Once in place, the Bushmen's daily division of meat generates other particular meanings. Gender classification is emphasized by the allocation of certain meats to the women and children, regardless of what the meats are, and once the trotters and entrails have been allocated to women they would not be seen as fit for men. Giving the genitals to the adolescent boys has an obvious reference to puberty. Does singling out the wife of the hunter make her the chief guest at the feast? Or does it put her in a hostess role toward the other women and children? What ideas about chiefship are implied in the care to cut for the chief a piece from each of the four quarters and from each side of the animal: something about

[26] Quoted by Lévi-Strauss 1966a: 103, from Fourie 1926.
[27] Goodman 1968; Douglas and Hull 1993.

fairness and impartiality perhaps, and perhaps something about the cardinal points, orientations in space, and the meanings attached to the right and left side of the body.

Here are Mary Hesse's scientific models transported to everyday behaviour. Here is Suzanne Langer's presentational thought exemplified. The carcass of the animal is a virtual space on which social distinctions are projected, and more than that, they are validated by giving the right portions of meat to the right people. Before the structuralist explanations of the distribution are finished the carcass of the animal will have presented a microcosm of the whole universe. Extending totemism to the partitions within an animal postulates a logical equivalence projected upon the parts of the organism and the parts of the social world. This is just what a microcosm is. Microcosmic thinking uses analogies as a logical basis for a total metaphysical framework. A distinctive way of thinking, it is the essentially other thought style, foreign to our own. The idea of projection and the idea of microcosm give a closer grip on the question of thought styles.

Suzanne Langer's ideas must be brought out of the studio into everyday life and Mary Hesse must be taken seriously in valuing analogic thought as inherent in the scientific enterprise. An item of behaviour can never more be interpreted as if its meaning were enclosed in itself, and hereafter only social life will be the place to look for the meanings in the microcosm. The question in the history of ideas has been moved from which idea came first or last to how one mode of thought replaces another. Does analogic thought always come first? Analogic thought systems are so well protected by custom, it seems unlikely that they ever break down? But this is not true. Can the two systems mutually understand one another? How do thought systems change? These have been important questions in Greek classics. We can add another question: Was Leviticus bound to be misread by rabbis coming fresh from commenting on Deuteronomy? The answer is, Yes. How can we discount this obscuring bias in our reading of Leviticus?

SOCIAL BASIS OF THE GREEK BREAKTHROUGH

Thirty years ago Marcel Detienne addressed this question[28] when he compared two kinds of ancient Greek society according to their speech/thought styles. The first, which he called 'mythical thought' or 'magico-religious speech', and which corresponds to our idea of microcosm, was based on Cassirer's work. This speech was 'efficacious, atemporal, and indissociable from symbolic behaviour and meaning'. By efficacious, he meant that certain words pronounced in certain ways by certain people had a binding irreversible effect, such as oaths and promises. Such speech coming from the mouths of inspired speakers was embedded in a timeless network of religious values.[29] In contrast the other case, 'dialogue speech', was secular. It was open, enquiring, a complement to action, set in a temporal context. This was the speech of the warrior group. No need to belabour how dialogue speech indicates the beginning of the rational-instrumental mode and magico-religious corresponds to mytho-poetic.

The innovation in Detienne's argument was to pay attention to the status and institutions of the warriors. They did not coincide with family or territorial groups, they were divided into age groups and fraternities, and were linked by contractual relations. They had separate distinctive institutions, they had their own initiations, they recognized their warrior vocation for death, they honoured their dead in funerary games, they honoured justice in the distribution of booty. Detienne makes a subtle and strong analysis of these secular institutions and the dialogic structures they fostered. Above all, he is interested in the deliberative assemblies that demarcated a distinctive field, the public domain in which every member had an equal right to be heard. The hoplites, the warriors, had their own military community within which they were practising dialogue speech, while outside its boundaries magico-religious speech still held sway. Their conventions made their speech egalitarian and secular. They met to deliberate on action, their speech was concerned with

[28] Detienne (1967) 1996.   [29] Ibid.: 88.

affairs of immediate concern to each of them, often matters of life and death. The argument is that the shift to widespread dialogue speech followed on the 'hoplite reform', the opening of the warrior class to include the influential institution of the city.

Detienne was continuing a tradition of classicists who had been describing the shift from myth to reason as the secularization of speech. A world that formerly had been revealed by oracles was now to be revealed by argument and persuasion, and dialogue would be the instrument of persuasion. The process he described starts in Greece in the eighth century BCE, a rift in the mind of the city:

with this rift came a different kind of speech, a different framework, a different kind of thought, marked by temporal divisions (the eighth century for Homer; the midseventh century for the qualitative leap represented by the 'hoplite reform'; between the two, the first circular agora laid out on the ground by the founder of the Magna Graecia cities from about 730 on).

Excellent though it is to have demonstrated how a social process makes a mental process possible, two points must be qualified. First, Detienne describes the movement as a journey from mythical to 'positive and abstract thought'. However, it is a mistake to allot positive, abstract thought to only one side of the rift; both kinds use abstractions and both are positive about what the physical world is like. Second, the idea of secularization is distracting. Both kinds use persuasion and have the vocabulary for arguing about other persons' intentions. Herodotus' *History* is a good example of a literature oriented to religious explanations of the outcomes of events, and with well-developed psychological awareness of how individuals adopt particular objectives and use thought to achieve them, with a very positivist view of how the behaviour of rivers, seasons, space, time, and materials affect their success. The difference lies elsewhere, not in deference to religion or in degree of abstraction, but in the kind of truth that is sought. The analogic system of thought has a more comprehensive idea of truth; what is true is so by virtue of its compliance with a microcosm of the world and of society; to be convincing, what is true must chime with justice; it looks to match microcosm with microcosm in ever-expanding series. The other, the dialogic system, sets its sights more closely, the truth it looks for is more pragmatic; truth is vindicated not by its match with ancient history or with the demands of morality, but in a strict framing of time and space. The questions avoid the moral complications of, 'Why did this happen to me?', they ask, 'What did actually happen?', and 'How did it happen?' In the first type the search for truth is driven up to seek remote chains of ultimate responsibility, in the second it is driven down to the immediate event, material factors, and immediate responsibility.[30]

Furthermore, it is a mistake to go on thinking that the change from analogic to dialogic requires a watershed in time. Two communities can coexist and display very clearly the difference between analogic and dialogic thinking. His incipient evolutionism has given rise to some questioning of Detienne's scheme. He takes Parmenides in the fifth century BCE as a watershed. Before Parmenides, truth was the prerogative of persons occupying certain truth-controlling roles: poets, diviners, and 'kings of justice', were automatically masters of truth, and the truth in question was the religious truth of prophecy or justice, backed by oracle. Then, at some particular point in time, different in different countries, the secular philosophers took over and claimed to reveal a truth that was not religious but depended on argument and proof. The chronological break is unnecessary and too sharp. All that is needed is the account that Detienne gives of the social life of the warriors, its differences from the social life of other citizens, and the historical extension of their customs to the larger community. The events take place in history but the theory is sociological, not historical. In the same vein but another context, Hugh Lloyd-Jones has questioned whether a sharp historical divide attended the origins of Greek science and suggests a more gradual change.[31] He argues that 'the notions of argument and proof owed their prevalence to the legal and political development of the Greek communities . . . as law and government became more and more the subject of open debate and depended more and more on popular

---

[30] Evans-Pritchard 1937.   [31] Lloyd-Jones 1983: 179–83.

consent, the notion of a higher personal sanction for the laws came to be undermined'.[32]

It would be very satisfactory if this contrast of before and after a social revolution were able to give some guidelines for reading Leviticus. Detienne has described for one historic example the social conditions for breaking out of the grip of a microcosmic thought style. In practice the movement is from thinking in concentric analogies to thinking in lines of abstract reasoning. The main precondition of this movement is the liberation of enquiry, a world made open to question and doubt, and the resulting high value set on persuasion. This precondition does not necessarily appear in turbulent times as the result of the overthrow of established authority; it depends on a shared determination to live as independent citizens. Once the new kind of thinking goes into general practice everything that was written in the previously ana-logic speech now becomes opaque. This may be relevant to the question of how Leviticus has generally been read. Scholars reared in the Deuteronomic tradition would have difficulty following the simplest meaning of Leviticus, to say nothing of deciphering its convoluted subtleties.

It must be emphasized again that the description of two kinds of thought, analogic and dialogic, helps to distinguish the peculiar style of Leviticus, but it cannot help directly with the chronology. Alas for the hope that style would provide a conclusive solution to the historical questions. The two kinds of thought and speech and writing are perfectly capable of coexisting so long as the social institutions are sufficiently seg-regated. If anything happened to make the priestly writer live in a separate, closed world and the Deuteronomy writer in a strongly challenged, wide open world, they could have had distinctive thought styles at the same period.

GREEK AND CHINESE SCIENCE

It is a great help to this argument that Detienne's old study has been recently supplemented by Geoffrey Lloyd's

[32] Ibid.: 181.

research on the same question, using a synchronic framework. His *Adversaries and Authorities* compares Greek science in fifth and fourth centuries BCE with China.[33] The first would count as modern on the criteria we are using, dialogue speech seeking a truth independent of context and religion; the second as archaic, correlative, analogical, mytho-poetic. Two things are interesting in the comparison; one is that Greece and China coexisted, and the second is that the overarching framework of the magico-religious thought in China did not prevent the growth of mathematics and science. Lloyd's comparison has the same concern to uncover the principles which generate both the social life and the thought systems. Detienne's case history compared two periods of the same community, and since the thought style that was superseded was the magico-religious one, his example conforms to the traditional evolutionary sequence, first the primitive, then the modern example. Lloyd's Greek/Chinese comparison encourages no such presumption. While the Greek culture was questioning, always ready to overthrow the system of classification in favour of a new one, always resistant to domination of any one scheme, the Chinese produced a more comprehensive, coherent, and stable model of the universe than had ever before been described and a medical theory and practice that are still a marvel to this day.

In the Chinese all-embracing cosmic theory all analogies and classifications fitted into a hierarchical organization of the universe dominated by the idea of the emperor's body as the model for all bodies, also for all systems. The system of the sun and the planets, the seasons, hot and cold, colours, music, tastes, textures, the architectural design of a house or a palace, every thing that happened at any time at any level could be classified in the same way.[34] This remarkably homogeneous thought system is challenging to the philosopher of science. First, how was it conducive to any kind of independent thinking? So, how did it produce a science? It certainly supported the advance of mathematics. Their enthusiasm for the triumph of a far-away fellow geometer is

---

[33] Lloyd 1996.   [34] Granet 1975.

enshrined in the legend that when Pythagoras established the theory of the right-angled triangle, the Chinese celebrated the achievement by slaughtering a hundred head of cattle.[35] Second, how did it resist intellectual challenge and the normal pressures for disintegration? Or again, how did it resist the corrosive effects of linear, discursive logic?

To answer the first question, we have to shake our minds free of the bonds of our own commitment to the processes of modern science, and to follow Mary Hesse in giving due credit to the power of analogy. For example, Chinese mathematical thought traditionally uses analogy to construct parallel instances, and then to scrutinize them systematically, character by character, to check exactly where the correspondences lie. With us the literary field of parallelism is restricted and vague. Chinese mathematics makes it into a tool of enquiry. A mathematical equation is not to be taken for granted as the next step in a calculation. When two items are placed in parallel they do not have all points in common, the parallelism has been founded on a complex abstraction. Recognizing that the equation is not ready-made but has itself been constructed, the mathematician examines the analogy at close quarters, takes a grip on its individual terms, checks for each component its match to the corresponding components in the other half of the comparison, develops the analysis, makes new analogies out of the first and goes on until the principles of transformation are fully grasped. Finally, the results are used to pose new problems.[36]

In this account the historian of mathematics has managed to bring literary and mathematical processes of understanding under the same rubric. The result is to overturn our Western judgements. We have been assuming that the analogic style of thinking would be a barrier to the development

---

[35] Yan and Shivan 1987. The 'gougu' theorem (that in the right-angled triangle the sum of the squares of the two sides adjacent to the right angle is equal to the square of the hypotenuse) had long been used in surveying in ancient China. The cattle were slaughtered in praise of the intellectual achievement which established it.

[36] Based on Chemla, K, 'La Pertinence du concept de classification pour l'analyse de textes mathématiques chinois', *Extrême-Orient-Extrême-Occident*, 10 (1988), 61–87.

of science. We forgot that construction of analogies is at the basis of mathematical thought and, against all our expectations, we find that analogy can be made into a precise and powerful tool of scientific enquiry. The comparison between literary and scientific modes of thought suggests a further idea. The adversarial and competitive style of the Greek dialogic culture would have ousted any archaic cosmic classification of the world; the Chinese magico-religious culture would have been favourable to the microcosm idea because it was conciliatory, incorporative, adaptive. That would have been a part of it. Geoffrey Lloyd relates the more dynamic and disorderly Greek thought system to the refusal by the Greeks to accept a political overlord. He partly attributes the survival of the Chinese microcosm to the sheer political and military strength of the emperor and his comprehensive machinery of government, and partly to the agreed ideal of a wise and benevolent emperor.[37]

The Chinese impulse towards a total microcosmic theory of existence was due to an interesting political combination: in a time of great insecurity and violence the learned men feared for their traditions and professions, they saw their interest in acquiring courtly patronage, and their desire for protection coincided with the desire of the court for the legitimation which the learned men could give. The resulting coalition of learning and government endowed the system of ideas with stability. Thus, though it was possible to challenge and to innovate within it, the system was too strong to be overthrown. The outcome was an unsurpassedly rich culture founded on the idea of the emperor as microcosm of the universe.

It is possible that by emphasizing political control Lloyd may not give enough credit to the microcosm's own generative powers. Time and space markers do mythic work, plotting the foundation story on a geographical and a calendrical base, but this takes time. A stable population can sit back passively and let the cognitive markings grow on their shared space, but a diaspora has to appropriate mythic time more actively. If the members of a community are shifting

[37] Lloyd 1992: 41–56.

their residence every few years, if the immigrants are more numerous than the settled population, it is more difficult to keep a microcosm plotted on to space. But in default of spatial boundaries, time's partitions also serve cognitive and social functions well. A series of anniversaries makes a string of dates stand out, the date of a truce, of a death, of an accession. Once it gets a footing, a microcosm has self-reinforcing, self-renewing energies which make it difficult to dislodge. We ought to appreciate this when we realize how hard it is for our own social thought to work successfully outside the influence of our own microcosm of 'Economic Man'; the people who live and think from inside a microcosm are not necessarily conscious of its contraints.[38] At first it seems that the uniformity of the Chinese system of thought was due to the power of the government to stay in control, but it must be admitted that the success of the microcosm contributes its own bit to the power to control. The microcosm will survive if it is widely used. The one thing that unravels a microcosm is the disintegration of the community in which it was used.

Finally, for the comparison between Leviticus and Deuteronomy the implication of this is not that Leviticus came before Deuteronomy because it is heavily microcosmic in its thought and more mytho-poetical, nor that it must have come later because it was so bureaucratic and impersonal. The relation is not sequential.

IMPERATIVES IN LEVITICUS

A negative bias runs throughout source criticism, a prejudice against the priestly editors. The distinctive priestly style of chapters 1–16 is deemed unattractive, loftily abstract, impersonal, dry. The God of the priestly writer is distant. A new source-critical claim has arisen distinguishing two writers within the book of Leviticus. The claim is that chapters 1–16 (that is, the first half of Leviticus) are written in a very distinctive style, and that after chapter 16 another writer with

---

[38] Douglas and Ney 1998.

another style takes over. The first writer of Leviticus, known in source criticism as P (for priestly), takes on all the less attractive qualities, he makes God speak in the third person, his God is more remote, he does not address the people directly as 'You', but indirectly, 'If a man were to . . .; if any-one wants . . .' He does not make threats. These stylistic fea-tures are supposed to be reversed in the second part where the new writer (known as H for holiness) allows God to speak in the first person, which makes him more personal, and to utter threats of violent reprisals, which makes him more pas-sionate. The distinction between the two alleged writers sounds suspiciously like a denominational preference, liter-ary interpretation driven by theology. The 'holiness writer' is like a modern Baptist, and like a good liberal, he insists on the equality of stranger and citizen. And, excitingly for those who are looking for clues to dating, P is thought to be early, and H is late. This historical claim from internal stylistic evi-dence boldly reverses Wellhausen's idea that the unattractive P was an exilic or post-exilic source. However, according to the anthropological analysis, the differences between the two halves of Leviticus do not quite follow these lines. Both halves of the book use analogies in the same way, and neither demonstrates 'causal', 'logical', 'discursive', or 'dia-logic' reasoning.

The matter is too technically philological for this essay to take sides, but there is a lot to be said in favour of a single author, adept in the mytho-poetic style. He would be using, no doubt, a variety of sources from different times. He would develop an overall compositional structure which would vary the style between the beginning and the end. Leviticus gets closer to deep, divine matters as it goes along, and so the heinousness of wrongdoing can be expected to pile up in the later part, provoking God's anger in the second part. As it approaches the throne of God's awful majesty, the idea of holiness becomes more prominent. But it is not the emascu-lated idea of holiness as kindness to the afflicted, but more like Exodus' terrifying concept of unbearable beauty and power, God known in the thunderstorm on Mount Sinai, God who warns Aaron not to come into the holy of holies improperly dressed lest he die.

In both halves direct commands are relatively few. This might come as a surprise for the book is self-described as a collection of commandments or laws. However, most law books rely on case histories for establishing precedent, and discursive explanations are rare. John Sawyer reports an intriguing linguistic analysis to the point: 'Leviticus is characterised by the extreme infrequency of imperatives (42/35: that is, a total of 42 occurrences, corresponding to 35 per ten thousand words . . . Most books of the Bible have three or four times as many imperatives per ten thousand words as Leviticus.'[39] Instead of straight imperatives we read expressions which can be variously translated as: 'He shall bring his offering . . .' or 'Let him bring his offering'. John Sawyer goes on to refer to an imaginary community receiving this oblique information about its obligations:

the language in which God addresses the people and the priests through his prophetic spokesman Moses, seems almost to avoid the normal direct means of phrasing obligations. The author seems instead to want us to imagine a state or a society in which some elaborate procedures are to be carried out, some things are to be done, and some not to be done. Sanctions are there, including the death penalty . . .

Sawyer finds that this distribution of imperatives holds for both of the two halves of Leviticus (which undermines the thesis of two authors). The death penalty occurs in both halves, unless the execution of the sons of Aaron in chapter 10 is not counted as such.

Direct commands are not necessary when authority is clear and if everyone knows what is to be done. Even field notes sent in the heat of battle are not necessarily couched as imperatives. In the nineteenth-century British army the commander in chief might 'direct' that such and such be done, or 'request and direct'; in the navy where the officers knew each other on longer standing and more intimate terms, it was more likely to be 'request',[40] or 'expected' as in the following Memorandum.

---

[39] Sawyer 1996: 15–20.
[40] Conrad Cairns, personal communication from researches in military history.

TO THE RESPECTIVE CAPTAINS.
Victory, off Cadiz, 10th October, 1805
Mem.
It is expected in fine weather that the Ships in Order of Sailing do
not keep more than two cables' length from each other.
NELSON AND BRONTE[41]

When crossed, the Duke of Wellington used the subjunc-
tive: 'Let my order be obeyed!'[42] Some would take this style
to be the expression of a very formal society, aristocratic and
enclosed, the kind of company that the Duke of Wellington
would keep, and according to Wellhausen the kind of company the priestly writer would have kept. But it would be a
mistake always to take formality of style for a sign of belonging to a superior social class.

Compare a contemporary speech style which is authoritative, does not give direct commands, does not discuss emotions, does not explain, avoids discursive speech, and uses
vivid analogies. In the case to be cited these characteristics of
the analogic style belong to the speech of the lower not the
upper class. According to the educational sociologist, Basil
Bernstein, speech styles vary according to the modes of control. The theory was developed in socio-linguistic research
among working-class and middle-class families in London
in the 1960–70s. Two types of family were distinguished
according to the preferred mode of control, positional or personal. The children in the first, the working-class 'positional'
families, were reared in a logical structure of analogies. There
was no incentive for them to question the rules that were
being applied, for no one was going to enter into a dialogue
with them. If they asked 'Why?' they were given a positional
reason, 'Because you are the oldest . . . or . . . the youngest'.
Or they would see a show of authority : 'Because I said so!' or
'You better, or else!' Explanations did not go beyond the reference to a pattern of positions, gender, age, generation, and
so on. This is the 'restricted code' which closely resembles
the analogic style of thought.

The most general condition for the emergence of this code is a
social relationship based upon a common, extensive set of closely

[41] Nicholas 1846: 105.   [42] Glover 1988.

shared identifications and expectations self-consciously held by the members. It follows that the social relationship will be one of an inclusive kind. The speech is here refracted through a common cultural identity which reduces the need to verbalise intent so that it becomes explicit, with the consequence that the structure of the speech is simplified, and the lexicon will be drawn from a narrow range. . . . The speech will tend to be impersonal . . . the intent of the listener is likely to be taken for granted. The meanings are likely to be concrete, descriptive, or narrative rather than analytical or abstract.[43]

The relative absence of direct commands in Leviticus may be attributed to a society of this kind. As to the relative absence of explanations, some laws are too obvious to need explanation; for example, why the people of Israel should not turn to mediums or worship Molech, all they get is the heavy-handed warning (Lev 18: 31; 20: 3–4) that God will set his face against the sinner ('Because I said so'), or 'That man will be cut off' ('You better, or else!'). When God says that it is to be a perpetual statute for ever that they do not eat fat (Lev 3: 17) the explanation is, 'All fat is the Lord's' (3: 16), a positional statement about ownership.

Causal relations are absent in Leviticus, unless it counts as a causal relation that the land when defiled spews out its inhabitants (Lev 18: 24–30). The laws against incest in Leviticus 18 are supported by positional statements. They start with the general principle: 'None of you shall approach anyone near of kin to him to uncover nakedness: I am the Lord' (Lev 18: 6). Then follows relentlessly an extended list of all the relationships which are either members of the class of 'near of kin' or classified with it (Lev 18: 7–18). The classifications constitute the explanation, except the law against taking a woman as rival to her sister which suggests jealousy as a motive (Lev 18: 18).

But we look in vain for an explanation of what it is about the hoofs of camels and pigs that puts them in the prohibited class of animals, or what it is about water animals without fins and scales, or those that crawl on land or in the water, that they must not be eaten, or why honey may not be burnt in sacrifice, or why the hard suet fat of herd animals must be

[43] Bernstein 1971: 118–39.

burnt on the altar and not be eaten. The reader is presumed to share a common cultural identity which makes explicit verbalization unnecessary.

The two contrasting types of family were called by Bernstein 'positional' and 'personal'. In the latter the mode of control rests on appeals to personal relations and personal feelings; since everything has to be verbalized, speech is 'elaborated'. This is the family which may expect to be upwardly mobile, or it could be a family of expatriates or exiles whose members have to meet people they have never seen before, with whom they have no shared understandings about space, time, or objects. They must teach their children to find words for everything, and specially for feelings, since words and feelings are the common denominators for communication with outsiders. They must also teach their children to enquire, and to demand information, so as to fit them for an adult world where established classifications are open to challenge, a rapidly changing world constructed by dialogue.

Inducement to obey based on gratitude counts as an appeal to emotion and at the same time a kind of explanation, a reason for why something should be done. When Leviticus says: 'I am the Lord your God who brought you out of the land of Egypt' it is a peremptory statement about a relationship, about a covenantal obligation, a debt incurred. When Deuteronomy refers to the same relationship it appeals to emotions of wonder, awe, and gratitude: 'He is your God, who has done for you these great and terrible things which your eyes have seen' (Deut 10: 21).

In so far as the priestly writing is strongly schematized and not given to explaining or to direct commands, it is tempting to suppose that its analogic style is an antique example of a restricted speech code. But one would be wrong to conclude that such a community would necessarily be an elite or aristocratic class. In this socio-linguistic research the impersonal restricted code was characteristic of the English working classes, and the feelings-ethics-oriented elaborated code characterized the middle classes. The theory is that the former would be found wherever social conditions were held stable: it would be a response to fixed ceilings on endeavour,

or to a closed social situation. The people in question expect
to stay where they are, and only to talk to, eat with, drink
with, and marry with, people who share their background.
This is precisely how they have built up their store of shared
assumptions. Sometimes silence is more powerful than
speech. In one of Wellington's campaigns two officers disobeyed orders, took a road that turned out to be blocked, and
were stuck there for two hours until Wellington himself
found them. Asked afterwards what he said to them, he
replied: 'Oh, by God, it was too serious to say anything!'[44]

Putting the antique Leviticus' writing style and the modern restricted speech code under the head of analogic thought
is not too far-fetched. The actions which Leviticus describes
for sacrifice unfold in spatial and temporal sequences, lessons
are given by analogies between one physical object and
another. Nothing can be justified in this universe except in
terms of the proper position in the spatial/temporal order
whose rightness is the only justification for anything. This
being so, it will be necessary to enter as far as possible the
world of concrete logic constructed by Leviticus. It was
framed from a structure of classifications, often overlapping,
usually congruent, sometimes independent of one another.
The identities that are learnt by doing what is expected at
each stage of the day, and the week and the year, need not be
verbalized. Like the carving of the meat at a Bushman feast,
meaning depends on shared knowledge about the logical
relations of objects in time and space. Meanings are not carried primarily along verbal channels, but conveyed obliquely
by reference to established analogies.

Leviticus presents its philosophical doctrines in the form
of rules of behaviour. Its paradigm lesson about God and
existence is enacted on the body of a sacrificial animal, or on
the altar, or on the body of a human person. There is no need
to make the simple moral principles of reciprocity and fairness more explicit, since they are known already. As well as
the gain in vividness and power, the practical lessons on sacrifice afford rich intertextual referencing to the rest of the
Torah. To sum up, the difference between correlative and

---

[44] Glover, M., 1968: 211.

causal thinking described by Hall and Ames for ancient Chinese thought, and the difference between analogic and dialogue speech described by Marcel Detienne for two stages of organization in ancient Greece, are both strikingly similar to each other and also to the difference between two kinds of modern communities and their respective speech codes, as described in socio-linguistics. In the first kind of community the main uses of speech are to hook a given moment into an articulated time-space which is known, and whose value is self-validating and authoritative. Words in such a culture decorate rather than convey the meanings, which depend on strictly local contexts; both speech and writing are able to elaborate upon unchallenged classifications. In the second type speech is directly used for persuasion, challenge, and argument.

Differences in writing styles can be expected to follow suit. In ancient Greece the earlier writing was traditional, narrative or based on establishing formal analogies, for instance Hesiod;[45] the later style, from the fourth century BCE onwards, after a major social revolution introduced moral persuasion and open enquiry (for instance Aristotle's zoological taxonomy). Though fashions in writing styles will change more slowly, the rhetorical conventions for both speaking and writing will eventually be influenced by the form of community. Leviticus is unequivocally in an archaic literary form corresponding to the thought style described as magico-religious or mytho-poetic. No wonder we find it obscure.

[45] Vernant 1983.

(3)

Two Styles of Writing

The Lord created me at the beginning of his work . . .
When he established the heavens, I was there, when he
drew a circle on the face of the deep, when he made firm
the skies above, when he established the fountains of the
deep, when he assigned to the sea its limit, so that the
waters might not transgress his command, when he
marked out the foundations of the earth, then I was
beside him, like a master workman. (Proverbs 8: 22,
27–30)

THE LANGUAGE OF FEELING

Cosmic analogies are unnecessary to Deuteronomy's purpose, and metaphysics barely relevant. It teaches in a different style, by a writer with a different kind of experience from
Leviticus. The Deuteronomy writer is political, brilliant at
rousing congregations to enthusiasm, not so happy in the
library or class-room, frankly not very interested in the ritual
service of God. As Moshe Weinfeld has said,[1] he comes from
a completely different social circle, although, as we saw in the
last chapter, that does not necessarily mean a different time.
For his overall structure he chooses a poignant narrative
moment, Moses' valedictory sermon to the people of Israel.
Moses' death is the foreseen conclusion. He writes in the
heroic manner, 'Hear, O Israel!' (Deut 6: 4). He admonishes,
'Take heed' (Deut 24: 8). He exhorts, evoking fear, dread,
anguish, and trembling (Deut 2: 15). The contrast with the
laconic priestly style, reticent, highly patterned and controlled by the literary form, suggests how difficult it would be

[1] Weinfeld 1972: 179.

to try to meld the two sources into a single teaching. The one uses the language of feeling and cause and effect, the other the language of position and analogy. One looks out to the readers, the other, involuted, looks in towards itself, to the text to be embellished.

Our own experience warns that it is difficult for the person reared in the dialogue or rational style to make sense of, and even more difficult to use, the analogical style, and the other way round. Bernstein's work on the two ways of thinking was inspired by observing the difficulties of working-class children who have achieved entry to middle-class schools. The child is looking for his own place in a pattern of positions and is disconcerted when he is given feelings and abstractions. Not having been trained in a habit of introspection or given a language of subjective feeling he keeps missing the point of the pedagogic exercise.[2] In the closed community talk about feelings is not the way to persuasion. When everyone is agreed upon preventing ego's private feelings from upsetting the general design it is neither necessary nor useful to draw attention to ego's emotional demands. For the same reasons the equivalent archaic style of thinking would have few words to describe emotions and subjective attitudes. As Hall and Ames explain so well, the analogical or correlative style does not focus on an individual person. As Bernstein explains, a restricted code is not given to expatiating on moral values in the abstract, its style is more to do with a concrete logic of positions and objects.

In a famous passage Leviticus requires that a person should love his neighbour as himself (Lev 19: 18, 34). And in the same chapter there is a command not to hate your brother in your heart (Lev 19: 17). Abraham Malamat gives a lucid explanation of what is meant by these commands, showing that on linguistic grounds the words should be translated in a much more concrete way, more as an injunction to be useful, be helpful to the neighbour, take care of them, rather than to develop a particular kind of warm feeling.[3] In English a closer translation than 'love', which has now got to be a word for an emotion, would be 'cherish', which implies tak-

---

[2] Bernstein 1959.   [3] Malamat 1990.

ing care, providing for a beloved object. 'Love the stranger' would be something like 'Cherish the stranger'. The same view is developed by Yochanan Muffs' essay on ancient Near Eastern legal documents.[4] Muffs found that expressions such as love and joy when used in legal contexts have nothing to do with emotion, but convey the specific legal idea of free and uncoerced willingness. Volitional metaphors are found in a wide range of legal situations, and Muffs found them also in a much wider range of contexts in Deuteronomy and Chronicles, and he cites Ben Sirach and Philo, the sermons of Paul, and so on. He asks how

the ancients living in the ambience of Near Eastern cultures, express (a) the free and gracious will which underpins a divine grace to kings or priests; (b) the spontaneity with which a man accepts divine grace or the free resignation with which he accepts divine chastisement, and (c) the willing and joyful alacrity with which man reciprocates the divine gifts and blessings with his sacrifices, tithes and offerings?[5]

These are straight religious contexts. He also asks why the volitional expressions are necessary in secular legal contexts. Briefly they are necessary at law for conveying rights to any property, to show that the transmission is uncoerced; if the donor was not free and willing, the transfer would be illegal. When the king or the owner of land is recorded as having conceded it as a free gift, he does so 'with love and joy'. What sound like subjective expressions of emotion are in fact necessary legal requirements of contracts. The Christian marriage service makes a similar provision by asking the bride and groom each to testify to their love; if they were either of them coerced it would not technically be a valid marriage. Muffs has brilliantly illuminated the concept of contract and covenant, and he has cast doubt on, even removed, the subjective emotion from the legal documents. The retranslation should be simply that the king or the landowner consented to the contract, freely and willingly, neither has been coerced into the contract. On Muffs' legalist approach to certain biblical expressions of feeling, 'love' means 'give loyal support',

[4] Muffs 1992.   [5] Ibid.: 122.

and 'Do not hate your brother in your heart' means 'You should not avoid your brother.'

Can Muffs' exercise on the legalistic sense of the verb 'to love' be applied to the verbs 'to abhor' and 'to detest'? The JPS translation of Deuteronomy 14: 3 is: 'You shall not eat anything abhorrent', the same word used for the wrongness of idolatry (Deut 7: 25–6). Abhorrence and detestation are emotions. They belong to another tradition, where argument depends on appeal to feeling. In the Hellenistic period the dominant reading could easily have been on these lines. The possibility that Leviticus has been written in one style and read in another will account for many of the difficulties encountered in its interpretation.

This makes room for an argument against the idea that the Leviticus writer was not imbued with ethical concerns. In an analogical style, the more comprehensively nested the categories of thought and the more richly developed the series of analogies, the more completely would they have included moral as well as material principles. As we examine what is implied in an analogical thought system, it becomes frivolous to suppose that it excludes something we call 'ethics'. The nearest equivalent to morality in such a system is the idea of 'correctness' or 'righteousness'.[6] Any person raised in a closed and strongly positional society would know what is moral and what is immoral. Injunctions to be compassionate would not be necessary because kindness would be predicated in the rules of behaviour as well as exemplified in the narratives. The idea of goodness in Leviticus is encompassed in the idea of right ordering. Being moral would mean being in alignment with the universe, working with the laws of creation, which manifest the mind of God. In this case the laws were given by God to Moses.

> Thou hast made the moon to mark the seasons;
> the sun knows its time for setting.
>
> Psalm 104: 14–29

In this psalm right judgement, correct time and place, and correct behaviour would incorporate all that is needful for knowing the moral law. Simple exemplars, small and great,

[6] Murray 1992.

expound the regular distinctions in space and time. Verbal abstractions are unnecessary, but the abstract idea about fixed times, places, and gradations is implicit.

Shakespeare gave Ulysses a famous homily about 'degree' as the basis of all morality. It might have been an excellent speech to quote here about a certain style of life in which order predominates. However, it will not do for an example since Ulysses does not use the literary style that belongs to that form of life, nor has Ulysses, the bold and cunning adventurer, lived according to these principles. He says:

> The heavens themselves, the planets and this centre,
> Observe degree, priority and place,
> Insisture, course, proportion, season, form,
> Office and custom, in all line of order
> . . .
> Take but degree away, untune that string,
> And hark, what discord follows!
> *Troilus and Cressida*, Act I, scene 3

In his mouth it is an artifical genre, loaded with heavy abstractions, degree, priority and place, course, proportion, season, form. If it were a genuine example of mytho-poetic speech it would be replete with strings of concrete examples. The only example he gives is 'untune that string' and 'discord follows'. This is a good example of how unlikely it is to find a language style which has not been acquired in a style of life and thought. Not just Ulysses, but few intellectuals of our day, could manage to speak convincingly in a mytho-poetic style.

The priestly writer has several rhetorical techniques to serve his own preoccupation with due times and spaces. Though his style is quite different from the lyrical simplicity of the psalmist he also, and typically, strings one analogy after another. The analogies are complicated, because his idea is complicated. He is teaching the people of Israel to honour in their lives the order of creation, and by doing so to share in its work. The living body is his paradigm. In the space of the animal's body he finds analogies with the tabernacle and the history of God's revelation to Israel. When he talks about virtue, honesty, and justice, he uses simple measuring examples: 'You shall do no wrong in judgement, in measures of length or weight or quantity. You shall have just balances, just weights' (Lev 19: 35). The body is also treated as a measure of justice. Only the perfect body is fit to be consecrated, no animal with a blemish may be sacrificed, no priest with a blemished body shall approach the altar, 'a man blind or lame, or one who has a mutilated face or a limb too long, or a man who has an injured foot or an injured hand, or a hunchback, or a dwarf . . .' (Lev 21: 16–20). Leviticus makes physical blemish correspond to blemished judgement, the scales that judge weight, length, or quantity in the market invoke the scales of divine judgement. The smallest case miniaturizes the cosmos, but it is always the same cosmos, constructed on the same principles.

Once Leviticus' delight in craftsmanship and design is recognized, the interpretation is transformed. The priestly writing would have used the rhetorical forms that were most highly esteemed in the region. The region is the eastern Mediterranean and Aegean hinterland, but, unfortunately, the time is not known. However, the literary forms that Leviticus uses are in an old style that fell out of fashion in the region around the fifth century,[7] superseded by metric forms. If the date of final editing was as late as the fifth century, the style of Leviticus would already have been archaic. But style does not necessarily betray the history. An author may have reasons for choosing a nearly obsolete style. In this case the archaic literary form hallows the teachings and supports the claim to be a text handed down from the time of Moses.

As in the rest of the Bible, Leviticus' favourite literary form is parallelism. Bishop Lowth, who first discovered this rhetorical device in the eighteenth century, took it to be typical of the Bible, and to this day scholars associate it with Semitic languages. It consists of a statement that gains emphasis by being repeated in the same order, that is, in parallel structure. An example from Leviticus is the following verse in which the first line makes a law for outsiders, then the second line explains the term 'outsider'.

An outsider shall not eat of a holy thing.
A sojourner of the priest's or a hired servant shall not eat of a holy thing. (Lev 22: 10)

---

[7] Kugel 1981.

James Kugel writing on biblical poetry considers that the word 'parallelism' has been overworked and the device over-formalized by commentators. The good bishop did not make a discovery that had been missed for two millennia, he invented a word. In Kugel's formula, parallelism consists of nothing more than A, a pause, and A's continuation, B (or B + C). He renders biblical parallelism as a simple sequence: 'A, and what is more, B.'[8]

The Pentateuch also uses more complex forms of the sequenced parallel, called 'chiasmus' because of the thematic cross-over that takes place in the middle. It is an inverted parallel, for the ending repeats the beginning. The lines that follow those just quoted above are an example, for having started with who may *not eat* the consecrated food in the priest's house, they go on to say who *may eat* it, mentioning the slaves and children born in the house; then it mentions the case of the priest's daughter who has probably been born in the house. That would correspond to Kugel's pause: if she is married to an outsider she *may not eat* it, but if she is divorced or widowed and returns to her father's house she *may eat* it. Then the lines repeat the beginning: no outsider shall eat it. Such a chiastic structure is sometimes called 'introverted parallelism' when instead of running two units in parallel the turn at the middle reverses the direction so that the ending reaches the beginning again. It is usually presented in this wedge shape:

A– An outsider shall not eat of a holy thing. A sojourner of the priest's or a hired servant shall not eat of a holy thing;

    B– but if a priest buys a slave as his property for money, the slave may eat of it; and those that are born in his house may eat of his food.

        C– If a priest's daughter is married to an outsider she shall not eat of the offering of the holy things.

    B'– But if a priest's daughter is a widow or divorced, and has no child, and returns to her father's house, as in her youth, she may eat of her father's food;

A'– yet no outsider shall eat of it. (Lev 22: 10–13).

---

[8] Ibid.: 58.

In this rather pedestrian example, the prohibition on the outsider features at the beginning and at the end; the second and the penultimate verses are about how the rule affects those who are the priest's own family and also those who were born or who live in his house, and who count as family; the middle verse distinguishes the status of a daughter married to an outsider and presumably not living with her father. Though they look very contrived, spread out like this, James Kugel is right to regard these forms as quite common. So far from being a local Semitic style, parallelism also governs the form of millennia-old Chinese poetry[9] and is found in oral literature throughout the world.[10]

The great linguist Roman Jakobson, in his analysis of Russian poetry, has shown how parallelism is based on grammatical and syntactic structures and argues that it is essentially involved in the organization of thought.[11] In literary function it stands somewhere between metre, a joke, a rhyme, and a pun. Metrical form gives a structure to the work. It enhances the mood by making a match between the pace patterns of the metre and the content, like the match between the words of a song and the melody, or like the match between the words of the song, the rhythms of the music, and the bodily movements of the dance. The joy of a verbal rhyme is more than the match it makes with words, they have additional work to perform apart from what they do in the syntax: the words are there to ring consonances and make rhymed line endings that call attention

---

[9] Zong-qi 1989.

[10] Fox 1977.

[11] On the differences between poetry and prose, Jakobson says: '. . . there is a notable hierarchical difference between the parallelism of verse and that of prose. In Poetry, it is the verse itself that dictates the structure of parallelism. The prosodic structure of the verse as a whole, the melodic unity and the repetition of its metrical constituent determine the parallel distribution of elements of grammatical and lexical semantics, and inevitably the sound organises the meaning. Inversely, in prose semantic units differing in extent play the primary role in organizing parallel structures. In this case, the parallelism of units connected by similarity, contrast, or contiguity actively influence the composition of the plot, the characterization of the subjects and objects of the action, and the sequence of themes in the narrative.' Jakobson and Pomorska (1980) 1983.

to each other, complete each other, and give warning when the ending is near. The ear is attuned to expect from them a containing structure for the contents. A well-turned parallelism does all of this. There is pleasure in seeing complex meanings separated, spread out, twisted, folded over, and presented again, more shining and beautiful than ever.

Freud has explained within his psychoanalytic theory the satisfaction given by jokes.[12] The ego exerts constant control over meaning and action, and the perception of a double meaning gives delight because it eludes control. His idea of the nature of the joke is in itself a model of his general theory. His best examples are unexpected scatological puns. Discovering that one word means two things, suddenly juxtaposing situations normally kept apart, the psyche rejoices at release from control. In addition to the half-stolen licence to let the two remote senses of a word play together, there is also the interest in how the meanings develop in their unwonted company. Parallelism skilfully used is a contrived and sustained form of punning. The phonetic match of words itself is a miniature parallelism. Drawing analogies between sounds and words is a stylistic effect that tends to accompany analogies of meaning.

The Bible is sprinkled with famous puns, and Leviticus is no exception. For example, two distinct verbs are used in the Bible to refer to God's bringing the Israelites out of Egypt: the commonest is literally 'to bring out', the rarer one, only used in Leviticus 11: 45, is literally '*to bring up*'. In Hebrew the same word means 'to regurgitate'. In this one rare case the verb for the Lord's saving action is the same as that used for '*bringing up the cud*', one of the criteria of a clean animal. By this literary device the whole of chaper 11 is bracketed between the opening law that says the only animals to be used as food are ruminants which *bring up* the cud and the concluding passage, 'I am the Lord your God who *brought you up* [regurgitated you] from Egypt.' It is more than a verbal felicity, since only the clean animals and only the people of Israel are to be consecrated. The sly 'inclusio' at the opening and

---

[12] Freud (1905) 1960: 122.

the ending of the chapter[13] is typical of Leviticus, who loves to show the working of God's mind in body-logic language.

For sheer enjoyment of wit people like to develop a self-reflexive verbal style with esoteric cross-referencing and otherwise pointless puns. Such literary accomplishment is not a sure sign of an elitist scribal class. It only needs a group to be sufficiently closed to be able to develop shared verbal jokes (so not necessarily an elite in the sense of an upper class). An extreme example of verbal games is the cockney rhyming slang based upon a set of rhymed equivalences which substitute for the word itself. Instead of 'my wife', you say 'the bane of my life'; instead of 'hat', say 'tit for'. Why? because 'hat' rhymes with 'tit for tat'. To 'talk' is to 'rabbit' Why? there is no 'why' about it, nothing obvious, except that everybody knows the pie called 'rabbit and pork', and 'talk' rhymes with 'pork'. If someone is 'apples and pears' they are upstairs. Rhyming slang illustrates how easy and naturalistic are the different forms of parallelism.

Ring form is the basis for a consciously contrived literary form, ring composition, used in antiquity to construct longer pieces. In ring composition the conclusion matches the start and so encloses the piece as in a ring. The opening unit, thus matched by the conclusion, is repeated in the mid-term. This puts the main idea, the central thesis, at the turning-point or centre of the literary work, splitting it into two halves which frame the middle: 'all we have to do is open the book to its middle and read. This reveals the book's focal concepts.'[14]

In Leviticus and Numbers the ring form dominates the whole composition, every couple of chapters, or four or five chapters, form a clearly defined ring, and each book is a maxi-ring containing all the constituent rings.[15] Not expecting this amount of order in the text, the reader looking for a linear development gets an impression of disorder. And yet biblical scholars are adept at finding parallelisms in small prose units. Cassuto analysed the stories of the flood and garden of Eden

[13] *hosi'*, literally to bring out, and *he'elah*, literally to bring up. (Rendsburg 1993. And see n. 4.)

[14] Radday 1981.

[15] This formal structure is described in full for the Book of Numbers, in Douglas 1993.

in Genesis in ring form;[16] Magonet convincingly presented the first fifteen verses of the story of Jonah as a ring;[17] Milgrom has revealed ring structures in Numbers and Leviticus. That successive rings should be arranged together in a coherent way has often been demonstrated, as for example by John Sawyer for the Book of Job.[18] However, learned apologies for biblical incoherence still abound in the commentaries. Commenting upon the arrangement of laws in Deuteronomy Jeffrey Tigay mentions that it 'often does not follow systematic principles of the sort that modern readers expect, such as keeping to a subject and completing it before going on to another, and arranging laws about a subject logically or chronologically, or in some other systematic way'.[19] One might expect, for instance, that in Leviticus the laws about bringing all offerings to the central sanctuary would be followed immediately by the other laws relating to that topic, instead of which dietary laws, and laws about debt and priests, intervene.

There would not be such puzzling transitions as those between the dietary and the tithe laws (14. 3–21 and 22–29); between the laws about manumission of slaves and about the consecration of firstlings (15. 12–18 and 19–23); and between the laws about the judiciary (16. 18–20; 17. 2–13) and those about worship sandwiched between them (16. 22–17. 1).[20]

Martin Noth was similarly baffled by the editing of the Book of Numbers.[21]

Bible students have to choose between accepting the muddle made by imposing a Western linear reading upon an archaic text, or trying to read the book through its own literary conventions. The former course ends by frustration and strange methods attributed to the antique editors.[22] In effect, when he speaks of concatenation of ideas, free association, or smooth transition, the commentator thinks that there may have been some system, but he is blest if he knows what it is. The Book of Numbers was considered by qualified commentators to be incoherent because the stories are interrupted by collections of miscellaneous laws and the laws by stories. In

---

[16] Cassuto 1964.   [17] Magonet 1983.   [18] Sawyer 1978.
[19] Tigay 1996: 449.   [20] Ibid.: 449.   [21] Noth 1968.
[22] Tigay 1996: 450.

actual fact, when the groups of stories and intervening laws are analysed as individual ring compositions, the whole book presents itself as a macro-ring of major rings: law and narrative units set in alternating rings, and these decomposable into minor rings again. It has to be read synoptically, rings laid in parallel to each other in a strict twelve-point pattern in which the last point, number twelve, recalls number one and also echoes the mid-point. So far from being disorderly, the elaborate rhetorical style is very coherent. Furthermore, the sequence of the passages has more meaning when they are systematically juxtaposed according to the literary rules.

Leviticus has a single overall pattern. It is a ring composed of rings, but the structure is not at all the same as that of Numbers.[23] Leviticus provides very explicit prologues and perorations which guide the reader to recognize the units of structure in the composition. Recognition in itself is pleasurable. As Freud said, 'Rhymes, alliterations, refrains, and other forms of repeating similar verbal sounds which occur in verse, make use of the same source of pleasure, the rediscovery of something familiar.'[24]

One of the technical problems of any writer is how to conclude. Clear signals of closure are necessary when literary conventions require numerous digressive analogies to build up the theme. The reader or listener needs to be warned that the end is imminent and eventually there must be a recognizable signal that it has come. Ring composition has an unequivocal ending in the return to the beginning. Awareness of structure throughout gives the antique composer many other techniques for signalling that the end of a ring or the end of the whole narrative or treatise is imminent. This may explain why modern readers of classics often expect a 'terminating motif',[25] and register frustration at 'false endings': the modern writer using linear exposition needs to say goodbye to the reader in so many words. By contrast, antique literature foresees its own ending, or you could say that the struc-

---

[23] Many scholars are nervous of this aspect of literary criticism as they have had bad experience of subjective interpretations of structure. But in the case of Numbers the dangers of subjectivity are under control. Whether the alternating sections are narrative or legal is easy to determine. (Douglas 1995.)

[24] Freud (1905) 1960: 122.

[25] Roberts *et al.* 1997.

ture has written the conclusion into the beginning. In modern terms we would be comparing prose writing with cinema montage techniques which freely anticipate or flashback to build up to a prepared conclusion.[26]

A narrative has its plot to indicate progression towards the anticipated ending. A series of narratives can be incorporated in another structure, as the Genesis stories are incorporated in a structure of generations from Adam. The whole composition can consist of episodes strung together on the progression of an event, such as a journey, a pilgrimage, a quest. It can be pegged out on a well-known circular process, such as the seasons of the year. The journey has its own start, a place or moment, and its own ending by arrival at the destination. The year's seasonal cycle comes to an end when it returns to the beginning. The structure provides a meta-theme, or an underlying analogy which the constituent stories embellish, and which points up their meaning.

So Exodus' story of escape and rescue concludes fittingly on Mount Sinai with the giving of the law and the building of the tabernacle. Arrivals after perilous journeys are a regular form of closure, as for Exodus arriving at Sinai, for Numbers arriving at the Jordan. Battles won serve the same function, as Joshua taking Jericho. The lives of leading protagonists provide internal structure and their deaths provide endings, as the death of Jacob closes Genesis, and the death of Moses closes Deuteronomy. Narrative is full of opportunities of this kind. A book composed of strings of parallels risks losing its central thread completely under the weight of case after case piled on to the initial statement of a law. Leviticus has very little narrative, so without the benefit of a plot structuring the book the skilful writer has to deal differently with the problems of closure.

CONTAINING AND COVERING

An old technique for creating focus is to set up a series of concentric circles. Leviticus frequently places parallel cases in an

---

[26] Miriam Hansen, Director of the Chicago University Film programme demonstrated this to me in personal discussion.

ascending order, so that the last includes the second and the second includes the first. They can be run backwards or forwards with the closure at either end. It is a very ancient formula. In Mesopotamia in the classical period, 2000 to 1500 BCE, the following magic incantation was recommended to wash a mote out of the eye:

> Earth, they say, earth bore mud,
> mud bore stalk,
> stalk bore ear,
> ear bore mote, . . .
> the mote entered the young man's eye.[27]

A modern Hebrew example of concentric incorporation is the old doggerel recited by the children at the Passover ceremony:

Only one kid, only one kid, which my father bought for two zuzim
. . .
And a cat came and ate the kid, which my father bought for two zuzim; only one kid, only one kid.
And a dog came and bit the cat which ate the kid, etc.
And a stick came and beat the dog which bit the cat which ate the kid, etc.

The English parallel is 'The House that Jack Built', which ends with a grand inclusive finale:

This is the stick that beat the dog, that bit the cat, that killed the rat, which ate the grain which lay in the house that Jack built.

Leviticus applies something very like this literary trope in a slow and measured fashion to the layers inside the body of a living being, and also to the body's outer coverings. It uses the simple idea of covering to build up a series of analogies for atonement (Lev 12–16): from the skin covering the body, to the garment covering the skin, to the house covering the garment, and finally to the tabernacle: in each case when something has happened to spoil the covering, atonement has to be done.

Many religions use a house (usually a temple, but often any and every house) and project upon it the structure of the cosmos and intervening organisms. The projection can start

---

[27] Black and Green 1992: 119.

with the roof as a cover, or with the alignment of the front
and back of the body with the entrance and rear of the building; in the vertical plane foot to head corresponds in an obvious way with floor and roof, in the horizontal plane the right
and left of the body can be projected on to the internal space
by taking the entry as a fixed point of reference. When this
fixed point is the front, if the entry corresponds to the sunrise
the whole space is aligned with the cardinal points, and so
made capable of bearing cosmological structure.

In Africanist accounts of religion the idea of the spatial
microcosm is prominent. Perhaps the most illuminating of
many fine accounts of body image in African spatial understanding is that of the Fang, a people of Gabon described by
James Fernandez.[28] They recognize three directions, the first
is the up–down, or sky–earth vertical direction; the second is
the upstream–downstream direction, which correspond to
east and west, sun and moon, male and female; the third is
front–back, or head and foot. Given this background of
structured space, when the Fang develop a new cult its
rituals draw upon the microcosm of the body to affirm their
macrocosm of the world. Some of their rituals make an equation between the clothing of the body and the roof as the
cover of the hut. For a difficult childbirth, the healing rite is
'roof medicine', in which the father climbs on top of the hut
and pours a medicine through a hole in the roof on to the
belly of the woman in labour.[29] In this cult God is a female
principle, accordingly the cult's chapels are associated with
the womb.[30]

It would generally be arbitrary to separate the morphology
of the body from the system of cardinal directions. The
abstractions that are being made from the body and from the
geography can be so closely assimilated to each other it makes
little sense to say which generated which, or which is projected upon the other. The biblical system of reference to
cardinal points is as diverse and rich as any others.[31] The language tends to economize by using the same word for the
conventional alignments, as in Hebrew where the words for

---

[28] Fernandez 1977; 1982.   [29] Fernandez 1982: 114.
[30] Fernandez 1977: 35.   [31] O'Connor 1991.

south and north are the words for right and left respectively, with the tacit assumption that the body is fronting east in alignment with the tabernacle. In English there is a concern to make the distinction between the rear part of a car or a building and the rear part of a person. 'Behind' as a noun is a decidedly familiar way of referring to a person's rear, 'behind' as an adverb is normally unproblematic. At a rehearsal of one of the early Gilbert and Sullivan performances, W. S. Gilbert asked a stage hand: 'Where is my wife?' On being told, 'She's round behind', the Edwardian wit said, 'I know that. I asked you WHERE she is.' It may be that the propositional style of writing tries to eliminate linguistic ambiguities of this kind, while typological writing cherishes the overlap of meaning with its scope for analogy and punning. So in Leviticus the Hebrew word for thigh,[32] referring to the femur of the body, is displaced to refer euphemistically to the genital organs, and by further extension to a building, to the innermost part, the rear, or 'hinder part'. This is argued more fully in the next chapter. Exodus uses the same word for the inner parts of the tabernacle (Exod 26: 22, 23, 27; 36: 27, 28, 32).

In many cultures one of the cardinal directions is given by the up-river–down-river direction.[33] Hindu temples are explicitly built on the model of the human body.[34] The projection of the shape of a living body on a shrine lends itself easily to divination. A Hausa group in Nigeria regards the cardinal points as three-dimensional powers, each with four sides, front, back, right, and left. The object of much of their ritual is to bring the powers and their sides into propitious alignment. A person and a person's body are also oriented and divided between four quarters depending on the cardinal points. The fundamental direction for anyone is the east, the word for which is derived from the word for chest and front. The east and the most masculine and virile aspects of the

---

[32] *vareca* (BDB, 438).

[33] For example, the Fang in Gabon use the upstream–downstream as if it were a cardinal direction (Fernandez 1982). Douglas 1963: the Lele of the Kasai also use the upstream–downstream direction of flow not only for directions in geographical space, but for the flow of food through the body or for liquid poured from a calabash into a beaker (Douglas 1990).

[34] Michell 1977.

body are contrasted with the two weaker, feminine, directions, the back and the left.[35]

In a similar mode the Malagasy have projected upon the house a dynamic model of destiny. The rectangular building is always oriented with the long sides running north and south, with many cosmic and social significances attached to both. The major aspects of destiny are assigned to the four corners of the house and its minor aspects to the walls. With the temporal succession of lives and seasons spatialized, 'one can follow the aspects of destiny as they revolve round the earth or around a house'.[36]

In Exodus the details that are lavished on the building of the desert tabernacle carry a doctrinal principle in the gradations of quality. Menahem Haran points out that the gradations of holiness are expressed in the quality of the sacred furniture. The finest quality of wood and metal and textiles is for the inner sanctum, and the elaboration and rarity of the pillars and screens diminish progressively towards the outer court. As he says, the layout and its decor make three concentric circles, with the cherubim beside the ark of the covenant at the focal point.[37]

In an aniconic religion, in default of pictures, the play of analogy would be likely to favour architecture and even make it a privileged medium of instruction. Leviticus is in a literary tradition that regarded the alphabet not as a conventional medium of communication but as a divine gift. Letters and word stems were respected as independent existences. Writing is not for making depictions of something that the words stand for, letters are things in themselves on which meanings can be projected. It follows that the projection of a building on a book, or a mountain on a building, does not contravene the law against images. At the same time these people made puns and enjoyed acrostics, so they appreciated the element of convention in writing. The law against images and the iconizing of letters balanced out. When the Bible forbade graven or molten images the words were carefully chosen. It did not forbid mental nor verbal images. Spatial projections over bodies and objects do not raise the spectre of

---

[35] Nicolas 1975: 228–9.   [36] Verin and Rajaonarima 1991.
[37] Haran 1978: 165.

idolatry. They do not seduce the eye or compete with the thought of God for the worshipper's attention.[38]

In the chapters that follow we shall show that Leviticus is a sacred text designed on the proportions of a temple. The entrance and compartments provide a journey-type structure and the closed architecture prepares the ending. Such a turn is thoroughly in keeping with the Jewish culture, where the word has always had a privileged claim to reality. Lest the idea seem too bizarre, recall some other things about the literary uses of architectural space. Narrative, whether literary or dramatic, must unfold in space of some kind. If the theme is complex, systematic reference to a known structure supplies a framework.[39] Temple architecture tends to carry heavy cosmological symbolism.

In antiquity there was a tradition that plotted a literary composition on a picture or on sculpture or on the parts of a building. Explaining its use by Herodotus, John L. Myres describes 'pedimental' composition as very widespread. A pediment in classical architecture is the triangular-shaped portion of the wall above the cornice which formed the termination of the roof behind it; it corresponded to the gable in Gothic architecture; in Roman architecture it decorated the tops of doors or windows. Whereas, in a romance or a drama, event follows event, in an order of time, to a final climax or catastrophe, in 'pedimental' composition,

whether in narrative or sculpture and painting, the climax is central and episodes are ranged on either hand—or in narrative, before and after—to prepare for it or to reveal its consequences. The pediments of the temple in Aegina, a war-memorial from the years after Salamis, display the Greek victory by setting triumphant Athena in the midst of a convergent melee of Greeks and Persians.[40]

He finds pedimental composition in heraldic groupings on engraved seal-stones, and on the 'Lion Gate' relief at Mycenae; in early bronze reliefs and vase-paintings, on the 'Shield of Achilles' in Iliad xviii, and the Hesiodic 'Shield of Heracles'. In all these and other examples this pattern is the

---

[38] Kochan 1997.
[39] Cohn 1981 records convergence of prominent geographical and anatomical features in sacred texts, for example, mountains in the Song of Songs.
[40] Myres 1953: 62–4.

antithesis of the progressive order of the frieze, in which one episode follows serially on the next. The pedimental style puts the climax in the middle. Sometimes the frieze is combined with the pediment, a serial presentation of successive episodes climaxing in the central image, and then repeated with variations in the other direction.

MOUNT SINAI

The central idea of this book is that Leviticus exploits to the full an ancient tradition which makes a parallel between Mount Sinai and the tabernacle. Various antique transpositions between houses, bodies, and temples prepare us for believing that Ramban, the mystic philosopher and revered medieval interpreter, was drawing on very ancient traditions when he read Exodus so as to draw a parallel between the desert tabernacle and Mount Sinai. The tradition goes back to Exodus. Remember that the same priestly hand that wrote Leviticus is credited in source criticism with the chapters in Exodus in which God gave Moses the plan of the tabernacle, and fenced off Mount Sinai. God forbade the people to go up into it or even to touch it until permission was given by the sounding of a horn (Exod 19: 12–25). In his commentary on chapter 24 of Exodus Nahum Sarna expounds Ramban's parallel between mountain and tabernacle. Each was divided into three zones, each zone represented a further step in approaching God, the graduated holiness coming to a double climax at the top of the mountain and in the inner recesses of the tabernacle.

Both Sinai and the Tabernacle evidence a tripartite division. The summit corresponds to the inner sanctum, or Holy of Holies. The second zone, partway up the mountain, is the equivalent of the Tabernacle's outer sanctum, or Holy Place. The third zone, at the foot of the mountain, is analogous to the outer court. As with the Tabernacle, the three distinct zones of Sinai feature three gradations of holiness in descending order. Just as Moses alone may ascend to the peak of the mountain, so all but one are barred from the Holy of Holies in the Tabernacle. Just as the Holy Place is the exclusive reserve of the priesthood, so only priests and elders

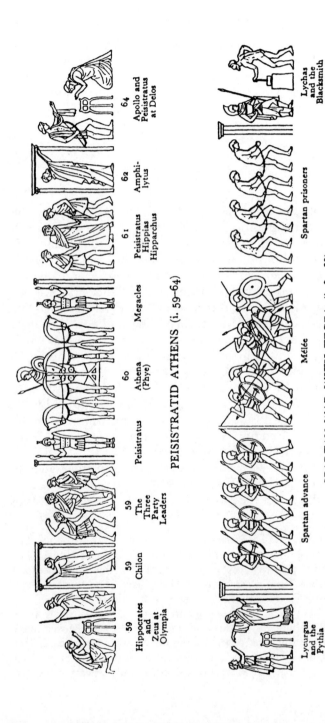

Figure 3.1. Myres' drawings for pedimental composition in *Herodotus*
Source: Myres 1953: 85.

are allowed to ascend to a specific point on the mountain. The confinement of the laity to the outer court of the Tabernacle, where the altar of the burnt offering was located, evokes the parallel with Sinai in the restriction of the laity to the foot of the mountain, where the altar was built.[41]

The parallel is made even more strongly when two more items in the Exodus account are considered. At God's express invitation Moses and Aaron, two of Aaron's sons, and seventy of the elders of Israel go up to the Lord to worship from afar off, the people shall not come up at all, but Moses is to leave Aaron and the elders and go on further up still (Exod 24: 1–2). This threefold movement in the narrative reinforces the threefold division of the slope. So the elders actually saw the God of Israel: 'there was under his feet as it were a pavement of sapphire stone, like the very heaven for clearness. And he did not lay his hand on the chief men of the people of Israel; they beheld God, and ate and drank' (Exod 24: 10–11). Commentaries have discussed the fact that the elders beheld God and were not endangered in approaching so close, and speculated on whether the blue floor of heaven was made of sapphires or lapis lazuli. Assuming that the mountain is a projection of the tabernacle, we can see that if the tabernacle were up-ended to be in the same vertical position as the mountain, the floor of the top compartment becomes the ceiling of the middle compartment, and the elders are looking up at the floor of God's abode, through the clear glassy blue paving. Thus they can behold him, without being endangered by his laying hands on them, safely separated by the transparent ceiling/floor.

And why did they eat and drink in the middle zone of the mountain? Sarna suggests that the feast corresponded to the solemn covenant meal that was the formal part of treaty making, and that they ate the sacrifices mentioned in verse 5.[42] If so, why did they eat it just there? Leviticus unequivocally says many times over that the law for priests requires them to eat the sacrificial meat that has been reserved to them in a 'holy place', that is near the altar in the court of sacrifice. In which case, following the paradigm of the tabernacle, the

---

[41] Sarna 1991: 105.   [42] Ibid.: 153.

elders and priests in Exodus would be 'dining' in the wrong place: they should be feasting on the lower slopes of the mountain where the people have been let through after the blast of the trumpet, and which corresponds to the outer court. Too bad, it would have been nice to have found that the elders' banquet under heaven corresponded spatially to the priest's 'dining room', but it does not quite fit. What is meant by a 'holy place' in this context has given rise to long discussion: it seems inappropriate that the priests should dine in the area accessible to the laity; there may have been two priestly traditions, the outer court may have been divided into a forecourt in front of the altar and a more private rear court behind the altar, and in practice the priests had the habit of eating in the latter.[43] However, all this speculation supposes that God was not offering his visitors a banquet from his own resources. In that case, when the elders (who are not said to be priests anyway) ate what God provided they did not have to conform to the later proprieties of the priestly dining room.

It might well be objected that this is a medieval fantasy of no relevance for Leviticus. Ramban is the name of Rabbi

Table 3.1.　Two paradigms of the tabernacle aligned

Mt Sinai	*Tabernacle*
Summit or head of the mountain, smoke, like cloud (Exod 19: 18); God came down to top, access for Moses only (Exod 19: 20–2).	Holy of holies, cherubim, ark and testimony of covenant, clouds of incense.
Perimeter of dense cloud, access restricted to Moses, Aaron, two sons and seventy elders (Exod 24: 1–9).	*Sanctuary*: table of show bread, lampstand; incense altar and smoke of incense; restricted to priests.
Lower slopes, open access.	Outer court, open access.
Mt Sinai consecrated (Exod 19: 23).	Tabernacle consecrated (Lev 16).

[43] Milgrom 1991: 392–4.

Nachmanides (1194–*c.*1270) and his conjectures might have had nothing to do with Leviticus but come straight out of thirteenth-century mysticism. Milgrom, who is well aware of this question, considers that Ramban was drawing on an ancient tradition. He bases the interpretation on the text of Exodus itself, and particularly on the name of the tabernacle as the Tent of Meeting. After considering and dismissing several speculations on the origin of the term, he says: 'Nevertheless, the immediate archetype for P's Tent of Meeting is not some mythic Canaanite model or hypothetical Hittite example, but the ancient Israelite tradition of the theophany at Mount Sinai. P (Exod 24: 15b; 25: 1) concurs with and indeed incorporates the epic tradition (Exod 19. 20; 20: 1) that God descended upon Sinai . . .'[44] This was where the initial meeting between God and Moses took place. At the end of Exodus, God transferred his earthly presence to the tabernacle in the form of fire and cloud. The tabernacle thereafter became the site of all subsequent meetings. God's direct presence is too terrible to be endured, so it is veiled in cloud, and the holy of holies in smoke of incense. The cloud is the sign of God's presence as he journeyed with his people in their wanderings. At Sinai when all the work of the tabernacle was finished, 'Moses was not able to enter the tent of meeting because the cloud settled upon it and the glory of the Lord filled the tabernacle' (Exod 40: 35). In Genesis smoke of sacrifice attracted God's attention after the flood. In Exodus the incense altar was used for the priest to send up clouds of fragrant smoke (Exod 30: 7–8, 34–8; 40: 26). Smoke impedes visibility, like a cloud.

Thus, Milgrom argues, the name 'Tent of Meeting' gives grounds for thinking that the correspondence between tabernacle and Sinai are at least as old as Exodus. The same argument is made by Alfred Marx when he shows that God's presence at Sinai and his presence at the altar at the time of sacrifice are to be read as strictly parallel. The mountain and the altar are figures of one another.[45] It could even be older, derived from the ancient symbolism of the cosmic mountain used in Canaanite religions. The idea of a cosmic centre of

---

[44] Ibid.: 142.   [45] Grappe and Marx 1998: 24.

the world, on a raised place, on which a shrine has been built, is common around the Mesopotamian region.

From the point of view of the Bible there is a snag about Mount Sinai being such a mountain because the wilderness of Sinai is relatively flat. So is Egypt; so is Mesopotamia for that matter. Canaan is a more likely area for the locus of the belief and the location of the sacred mountain of Israel, since the Syro-Palestinian littoral mountains are prominent features of the landscape. In the Ugaritic texts a different mountain was associated with each divinity. This is the argument made by Richard Clifford in his study of cosmic-mountain doctrines.[46] It accords well with Frank Moore Cross's theory that the origin of the tent of meeting in the Bible is the royal temple of El.[47] If it were actually a relic of the monarchical social structure of Baal, that might be why it was transferred to Sinai, and why a twofold microcosm of mountain and god's house should have been shunned. However, we have been warned against flogging the anti-Canaanite principle too much. Perhaps it is more relevant to remember that microcosmic thinking is not at all Deuteronomy's style, and that Leviticus read through Deuteronomic eyes would be another reason for the analogy being missed.

There is evidence that the analogy was widespread and revered in late antiquity. It was used to good effect, for example, by Ephraim the Syrian, famous preacher, poet, and defender of Christian orthodoxy who lived in Mesopotamia in the first three quarters of the fourth century.[48] As a Christian he was hardly going to use Mount Sinai as a model of the desert tabernacle, but he shifts the basis of the first analogy to paradise. His *Hymns to Paradise* draw three-zoned theological models combining paradise, Mount Sinai, and Noah's ark.

[46] Clifford 1972.   [47] Cross 1973: 185–8.   [48] Séd 1968.

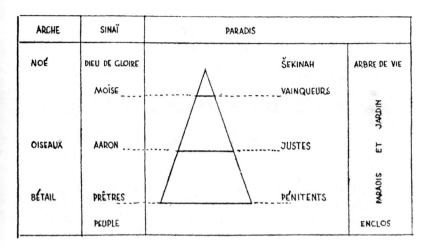

Figure 3.2. Paradise, Mount Sinai, and Noah's ark, from Ephrem's *Hymns on Paradise*

Source: Séd 1981: 463, fig. 8.

(4)

Mountain, Tabernacle, Body
in Leviticus 1–7

Rabbi Levi said: 'The upper waters are male and the
lower waters are female, and these say to those: Receive
us, you are the creation of the Holy One, blessed be He,
and we are his envoys. Immediately they receive them,
like the female that opens before the male' . . . Rabbi
Abahu called the upper waters 'bridegroom' and the
lower waters 'bride' . . . other sages speak of the earth as
the wife of the rain, which is the husband.[1]

When Deuteronomy speaks of sacrifice, sacrifice is all that it
means. In its more political agenda sacrifice is less important,
but Leviticus has taken sacrifice in the same spirit as the
wisdom literature uses seafaring, trade, or horticulture, and
made it the framework for a philosophy of life. Sacrifice is
one of the main figural motifs with which it presents the principles of God's creation, and the divine order of existence.

Many consider animal sacrifice strongly repulsive, a bar-
baric custom, only one step away from human sacrifice. The
critic says that it may please the butcher to disguise the violence with rites and pretend that the animal consented to its
death, but why it is killed makes no difference to the victim.
Whether religiously consecrated or unceremoniously dis-
patched, the deed of killing and the pain of death are the
same. Sacrifice is a collusive fraud practised by the priest and
congregation for the benefit of their own delicate consciences. Far more honest and dignified is to seek to cause the
least suffering to the victim, admitting frankly that the killing
is for food.

[1] Patai 1947: 67.

Starting from here no one is going to understand sacrifice. The assessment of human motives is too immediate, material, and fundamentally secular. Yet the criticism has point: whether humans should eat meat at all is a live moral question. One way to answer it honestly is to adopt total vegetarianism. Jean-Louis Durand, a french classicist, turns the tables on modern protest against sacrifice by asking how anyone can defend the unspeakable horrors of the modern abattoir.[2] The moral issue forces a practical choice between total abstention from meat-eating, or consecrated death. If people want to have sacrificial rites there is no strict necessity to kill real animals. Christians, without being vegetarian, have vegetable sacrifice. In some Hindu cults vegetable sacrifice is the rule. The instructions and words for the rite of sacrifice to the Hindu god of fire, Agni, speak of a goat being led in, but the sacrificial goat is represented by a packet of grain or rice.[3] Durand waxes angry against Christianity for depriving animals of the privilege of dying with meaning and dignity, and against Christianity for abolishing in the same stroke an archaic tradition of reflection on the death of the body. He indicts us for practices which betray our contempt of animals: we have disqualified ourselves from moralizing on ancient animal sacrifice, and even from interpreting it.

LOGIC OF THE BODY

Normally through the world wherever sacrifice is practised an elaborate symbolism governs the selection of animal victims, each gesture for the sacrifice is minutely prescribed, the animal parts cut and coded, and every detail loaded with meaning. Sacrifice invokes the whole cosmos, life and death. Not every congregation wants to be confronted with ultimate things, but some do, and it so happens that Leviticus focuses its metaphysical resources on that very point between life and death. With sacrifice Leviticus expresses its doctrine of blood, of atonement, of covenant between God and his people. If we read the instructions for sacrifice and try to

---

[2] Durand 1979: 134.   [3] Staal 1983.

imagine them being carried out, we can see it as a form of philosophy by enactment. Leviticus exemplifies a way of being and doing based on analogies which prescribe the same actions in multiple contexts.

In many parts of the world philosophizing by sacrificing can be quite paradoxical and abstruse.[4] Many religions are forced into casuistry to avoid contradiction between their affirmation of life and their act of taking life in sacrifice. Leviticus' solution is to allow no profane slaughter, the only shedding of animal blood it permits is in the consecrated killing of sacrifice. This view is contrary to that held by many established Leviticus scholars, but is central to the argument of the present volume. The extreme sensitivity to bloodshed and loss of life, human or animal, shown throughout the book, is consistent with the prohibition of profane slaughter. Contrast this restraint on killing with the more idealized and symbolical way that the Gurma on the Upper Volta deal with the potential contradiction. They are also very concerned with the morality of taking animal life, but they say that sacrificial slaughter is not death-dealing at all. It is a restoring to life, not a killing but the opposite. In their doctrines, sacrifice is equivalent to childbirth, the gesture of the knife that actually kills the animal is the very gesture of the midwife's knife as she cuts the umbilical cord. In childbirth the placenta represents the body of the sacrificial victim, in sacrifice the victim's body is the placenta and the gesture of cutting the cord releases the animal life to birth at a new level of existence. Concrete logic makes sacrifice the point of contrast between true killing and true giving life: the Gurma do not deny death, and their ceremony does include a real killing, the smashing of an egg.[5]

Such a play with inverted symbols of life and death is matched in Leviticus in the JPS translation which says that the priest 'turns all the offering into smoke' (Lev 1: 9, 13, 17; 2: 16; and repeated 3: 5, 11, 16; 4: 10, 26, 31, 35). The formula repeated eleven times warns that this is no casual remark. Milgrom notes that in Hebrew the verb[6] 'to turn into smoke'

---

[4] See Cartry and de Heusch 1976; 1978; 1979; 1981; 1983.
[5] Cartry and de Heusch 1976: 154–6.
[6] *hiqtir*, cf. *getoret*, incense. Milgrom 1991: 160.

is not the same as the verb 'to burn', used for non-sacrificial incineration: it means turning something into something else, smoke. In the Iliad (1: 317) the savoury odours of sacrifice mixed with curling smoke went up to the gods in the sky (Hicks 1953); in Leviticus the 'offering is not destroyed but transformed into smoke, sublimated, etherealised'. If the verb in this much-repeated sentence means turning everything into smoke, Milgrom is saying that the act of sacrifice is less a killing than a transformation from one kind of existence to another.

We know how prominently the idea of smoke figures in the Pentateuch. But the analogy between incense smoke and cloud cannot be lightly imposed upon a text. The problem is how to make a bridge between our own and the writer's experience. Durand, the classical scholar quoted above, when faced with interpreting sacrifice in Greece advises seeking a third ground that is common to the interpreter and the writer of the text. In the case of sacrifice he argues that the knowledge of the body is common ground to ancients and moderns, and so he turns to close examination of pictures of bodies on Greek vases. By this means Jean-Louis Durand reveals what he calls a logic of the body, that is, a 'topology of meanings' displayed in layout, gestures, and movements in space and time.[7]

We cannot follow his example, we have no contemporary pictures of Bible sacrifice: images are forbidden. But the first chapters of Leviticus are largely about how to make a sacrifice, how to select the right animal victim, how to cut it, what to do with the blood, how to lay out the sections on the altar. To find the underlying logic we have to look carefully at what it says about bodies and parts of bodies, especially what is inner and outer, on top and underneath, and pay special attention when it emphasizes by frequent repetition and strong prohibitions.

After the animal has been killed, flayed, and its blood drained, the burnt offering is cut up into sections.

And the sons of Aaron the priest shall put fire on the altar, and lay wood in order upon the fire; and Aaron's sons the priests shall lay

---

[7] Durand 1979: 134–5.

the pieces, the head and the fat, in order upon the wood that is on the fire upon the altar; but its entrails and its legs he shall wash with water. And the priest shall burn the whole on the altar, as a burnt offering, an offering by fire, a pleasing odour to the Lord. (Lev 1: 7–9).

This densely packed statement right at the beginning is the first time we hear the refrain about the meat being quartered, then the priest laying the quarters out, with the head, and the suet fat, on the wood, on the fire, on the altar. It soon comes again,

cut it into pieces, with its head and its fat, and the priest shall lay them in order upon the wood that is on the fire upon the altar (Lev 1: 12)

and the last part once more, concerning the offering of birds, the order varied:

on the altar, upon the wood that is on the fire (1: 17)

and the same several times repeated in chapter 3.

This is the 'House that Jack Built' style: 'the cat that ate the rat that ate the malt, that was in the sack, that lay in the house that Jack built.' Repeated so deliberately in the pro-logue part of the book it warns us to expect more of one thing laid successively upon another, and that they will be organ-ised in inclusive sets. It also says that Leviticus insists on due order in the disposition of the sectioned body. The verb to set up, to arrange, to lay out in order, is applied to arranging the fire, the sticks, and the sections of meat. Setting up the sticks for a cooking fire is a skilled task as every boy scout knows. The sticks have to be cleverly laid so that they can support a lot of meat in a space that must be restricted because if the fire is allowed to spread around too much it will go out. But information about the right order of the meat is sparse.

The rule for the daily burnt offering only says that the head is on the altar first, and the fat, the sections are added to these, and last of all the 'entrails and legs' after they have been washed (Lev 1: 7–9, 12). In chapter 3 the rules about suet fat going first on the altar are expanded. The priest is told exactly what to do. He must present, as an offering by fire to the Lord, the fat that covers the entrails, and all the fat that is on them, that is at the loins, and the protuberance on the liver which he shall remove with the kidneys (Lev 3: 4, 15; 4: 9). This is the suet fat. This rule is repeated three times: for the case of a sheep (Lev 3: 10), and for a goat (Lev 3: 14–15) and for the bull of a sin offering (Lev 4: 8), and the suet on the tail of the sheep is also banned. The rule against eating suet is paired with that for blood: the people of Israel are prohibited from eating suet in the same strong terms as they are forbidden to eat blood (Lev 3: 16–17; 7: 22–6).

FORBIDDEN ITEMS

Here we are reading the rules of the sacrificial sysem for disposing of the parts of the body. So, first of all, what is suet, exactly?

Both Milgrom[8] and Levine[9] in their recent commentaries agree that the forbidden 'fat' is not to be confused with ordinary animal fat. Indeed, the words specifically refer to the hard suet that is found around the kidneys and intestines. When Leviticus uses the word that is translated as 'entrails'[10] it refers to the bowels and intestines, the inward parts. The dictionary translations of these words, viscera, entrails, innards, internal organs, vital organs and so on, are vague and overlapping. Even a demonstration from a kosher butcher, though it would represent a long tradition, would not necessarily gloss this old text correctly because it is impossible to allow for the accretions of centuries.

Two other items are also prohibited in the same sentence: one is a protuberance on the liver, a long lobe sticking up like a thumb or a tail, called the caudate lobe, and the other is the pair of kidneys, both destined to the same dignity of being burnt on the altar with the suet (Lev 3: 15 and *passim*). Of these, more will be said when the suet fat prohibition has been discussed. At this point the enquiry needs more

---

[8] *peder* or *helev*; Milgrom 1991: 159, gives some Mishnaic readings for the word *peder*, which used to be translated as fat. Targum PS-J says that peder is 'the suet that covers the internal organs', also Ibn Janah, Saadia; Ramban explains it as 'the suet of the diaphragm'; the Akkadian cognate term, *pitru*, is the suet on the liver. The hard fat is suitable for tallow for candles.

[9] Levine 1989: 16 n. 3.   [10] *qirbo*, its entrails, or *gereb*, entrails.

instruction in the anatomy of ruminants.[11] What would the priests know about the inside of the animals they sacrificed? What would the animal's body look like when opened up?

The first textbooks consulted showed diagrams of the digestive system with the liver carefully disengaged from surrounding tissue, and of the urinary system with the two kidneys also systematically disengaged from any surrounding suet. This is not how any butcher would ever see the organs in real life. Reasonably enough Durand considers the butcher's viewpoint to be the normal one for describing the inside of an animal, whereas the scientist's view is highly artificial and specialized. We are in good company with Aristotle, who seems to have based his anatomical classification of animals on the priest/butcher's eye view.[12] The wish to see the organs and the suet in one picture is frustrated for a good reason: the fat covers the organs so completely that none of them is visible at all. The inside of the animal would have appeared to the sacrificer with the important organs wreathed in their yellowish-white protective covering, difficult to see and very difficult to extract. From this angle (as it says in the text) the suet is over and around the kidneys and over the loins. It divides the top of the carcase, ribs containing the lungs and heart, from the innards, which it encases.

Returning to the words of the text and looking up 'entrails' in the Hebrew dictionary, this hard casing of suet covers the soft, innermost parts of the animal. The suet lies over and around the seat of life, the seat of thought and emotion.[13] The House-that-Jack-built model implies that the suet is a protective covering for the innermost parts as the skin is the covering for the whole body.[14] Be that as it may, it does not justify the prohibition.

Leviticus explains the rule against eating blood by saying that the life (or soul) is in the blood (Lev 17: 11) and sets it in a chapter in which God warns that he will demand account-

---

[11] The discussion of bovine morphology is indebted to Dr David Williams of the Animal Health Trust.

[12] Durand 1979: 149.　　　　　　　　　　　　　　　　　　　[13] BDB: 899.

[14] Note that the equivalent fat over the liver and kidneys of pig is not hard but soft and creamy, lard not suet. Possibly this is another reason for not sacrificing or eating the pig. Suet is a hard protective covering, which may be relevant to theological exposition.

ability for every animal life. By comparison there is nothing to explain the second very solemn rule that forbids the people of Israel to eat hard suet fat, even though the two rules are given together: 'All [suet] fat is the Lord's, it shall be a perpetual statute throughout your generations that you eat neither fat nor blood' (Lev 3: 16–17). There are two contending explanations, but they contradict each other: some hold that the suet is forbidden to worshippers to eat because it is the best part, reserved to God, a theological principle, and others hold that it is forbidden because it is inedible, a hygienic principle. Some texts support the first: having the best is 'living off the fat of the land' and so it makes sense always to give God the best, but that expression which we ourselves read first in Genesis 45: 18 could simply be based on the Levitical rule: Leviticus says that the suet fat is divinely selected for God, so it must be the best part. As to the other idea, that suet is inedible, try telling it to inhabitants of the polar regions who practically live on blubber, or tell it to the traditional English cook for whom beef suet was an esteemed ingredient in Christmas pudding, mince pies, dumplings, to say nothing of the crust of the prestigious steak and kidney pie.

Suet is definitely edible, though like most good things it is possible to have too much of it. The idea among Jewish Bible scholars that it is inedible may explain why they regard this as a less important dietary law. They believe that divine decree saves them from eating something that is bad for them: nineteenth-century medical materialism rears its head again. Baruch Levine offers the unlikely double explanation that the suet fat, *helev*, 'was desired by God', and at the same time that suet fat is not 'regarded as choice food for humans'.[15] Jacob Milgrom, after a thorough survey of the literature, withdraws defeated: 'The reasons for reserving the suet for the deity are shrouded in mystery.'[16]

We know better now than to look for a causal reason for why suet is solemnly prohibited. Leviticus proceeds by establishing its context, saying where suet is found on the animal: that is, in a middle zone, over and around the kidneys, and over the entrails. This information must be

---

[15] Levine 1989: 16.   [16] Milgrom 1991: 207.

important for it is given many times over. The obvious way
of resolving a puzzle in concrete logic would be to study relative positions. Outside the body is the skin, a container for
the blood which is the life or soul. Under the skin is the bony
structure of the skeleton, within which the rib cage protects
the heart and lungs and upper abdomen. Below the rib cage
the hard suet forms a middle area, separating the upper layer
from the lower abdomen.

The vital pieces of anatomy (kidneys and liver lobe) which
have been selected for a special consecration on the altar are
found in the body engulfed in the suet which lies around the
diaphragm. The suet separates the entrails, which comprise
the seat of thought and emotion, and the semen which is the
seed, the principle of fertility, from the upper part which in
the live animal is accessed through throat and mouth. The
account in chapters 1–7 of two protective containing layers,
skin and suet, will be balanced by the account in chapters
12–15 of damaged skin and leaking vital fluids. The law of
sacrifice is about to unfold a pattern of the cosmos under
cover of God's protection.

In most sacrificial systems the way the animal is cut up and
the allocation of the different parts are prescribed. The
Greeks, as also Leviticus, allowed only domesticated animals
for sacrifice. After the animal is flayed the first strokes of the
knife separate the meat of the trunk from the internal organs
or offal (that is the liver, lungs, spleen, kidneys, heart). Then
all are divided again by the rules for cooking: the meat is
boiled, the offal is roasted on a spit and eaten on the spot by
an inner circle of persons, the contents of the lower abdominal cavity, stomach, intestines, bowels, are made into
sausages. The carving of the meat depends on the system of
distribution. Some Greek sacrifices are centred on privilege,
the haunch, shoulder, and tongue being reserved for the
priest, or king, or first city magistrates; others are to be dis-
tributed by lottery, in which case the butcher must carve the
natural joints into equal parts. And so on.[17]

The details of distribution for the Greeks is more minutely
prescribed than for biblical sacrifice. The Levitical disposi-

[17] Detienne 1979: 17–23.

tion of sacrificial meat ensures that the priests get their share, the altar gets the Lord's portion, and the sacrificers and their friends and family usually get their part of the feast. The rules for the sacrificial meat ought to be weighty with metaphysical and social analogies. But at first reading the analogies seem to be missing. Where are they?

In this research on Leviticus it is interesting to note how very few items of anatomy receive any mention at all. Conspicuously missing in these chapters is any express mention of neck, heart, tongue, lungs, stomach, genital organs, which are usually prominent in various other sacrificial systems. Leviticus allocates meat, haunch, chest, and shoulders to different parties, head is mentioned once for the burnt offering and once for the sin offfering, but of the innards only the long liver lobe, two kidneys, and suet receive special instructions, they are always to be burnt on the altar. Nothing is said about the liver itself or about other internal organs. The account is highly selective and thin. At the same time, it is very simple, only the blood, suet, and three items forbidden. The blood is ancillary to the sacrifice, it is not eaten or burnt on the altar, but smeared on it and poured out around it; the named items are always burnt on the altar.

A strong prohibition on eating warns that the order of sacrifice is being used to demonstrate the boundaries of God's pattern of the world. Some archetype or paradigm is undoubtedly being developed, and it will not do to reduce the problem by looking for item-by-item meanings. We can be sure that the right explanation will be in accord with other teaching paradigms used in the text, and probably with other dominant paradigms in the literary stock of the Bible. Any satisfactory interpretation of Leviticus must also be convincing about the meaning of the rules against eating fat or blood. Imagine a game of building blocks in which God is the player and the object is to rearrange the dismembered body so as to model some divine construction of the universe and a teaching about life and death. In this architectural game rules about positioning, such as 'over' or 'under', are necessary for interpreting not only sacrifice, but the whole book. In a diagram, position is everything; in a sacred text, the prohibitions that set things apart are crucial.

Two kinds of ordering are in play, one the arrangement of the internal parts of the living being, that is, the normal order of the animal's anatomy, and the other, their order on the altar. For the altar in every case the middle zone, the suet or fatty area, is taken out first and burnt on the altar. There are no exceptions to this. For a burnt offering, even though every part of the animal is burnt on the altar, the fat is mentioned as being there already, with the head, when the sections of meat are laid on it (Lev 1: 6–9). In the offering of well-being described in chapter 3, the suet fat, the long liver lobe and the kidneys are specified for burning on the altar, the rest of the carcass left to be eaten in a feast of the congregation and the priests (Lev 3: 4–5, 9–10, 14–16). The rule is meticulously repeated for the bull, the sheep, and the goat, always naming the fat covering the entrails, the two kidneys embedded in the fat, and the lobe of the liver, all to be burnt on the altar. The same for the sin offering, and see the rule in Exodus for the sin offering for Aaron's ordination (Exod 29: 13).

The priests could eat the meat of the sin offering and the guilt offering when the ceremony was the inauguration of Aaron (Lev 16: 24–30; 7: 1–10). But if the sin offering is made for the sin of a priest, no person can eat the meat, the reserved parts are burnt on the altar as usual, and the rest of the carcass is carried out of the camp to be burnt (Lev 4: 11–12). The ordinary member of the congregation can join the feast provided from his herd in the case of a well-being offering, but if the offering is to expiate for his sin, it can only be eaten by the priests (Lev 6: 19–23), and likewise in stronger measure, if the priest is the sinner (Lev 4: 8–11), or the whole congregation (Lev 4: 21), no one can eat it, presumably to honour the principle that a person may not profit from his ill-doing.

ENTRAILS AND LEGS

The rule for the arrangement of meat for the burnt offering is that the head, the suet, and the three items it covers always go on the altar first, then the rest of the meat, then the items called 'entrails and legs' always go on last. The phrase uniting entrails *(kerev)* and legs *(kera'ayim)* occurs in Exodus' instructions for the cooking the Passover lamb (Exod 12: 9), and its instructions for the anointing of Aaron and his sons: 'You shall cut the ram into pieces, and wash its entrails and its legs, and put them with its pieces and its head, and burn the whole ram upon the altar' (Exod 29: 17). It is usual to treat them as separate items, and the latter term[18] has usually been translated 'legs', 'shanks', or 'thighs'. But the thing that is odd and needing to be explained is their regular appearance as a pair in so many verses (Lev 1: 9, 13; 4: 11; 8: 21; 9: 14), and (except for Exod 12: 9) they always have to be washed. The need to wash them gave rise to the idea that they were the 'hind legs', dirty from adhering semen, urine, and dung. Since the priests have a reputation for acute anxiety about cleanliness and sex, it would seem right to them that God should direct these parts to be washed, but Milgrom has argued that the word for legs means 'shins',[19] which would apply to forelegs as well. We saw that in the burnt offering, where nothing is reserved from the fire, the four legs or shins would be the last item in the series of animal parts to be burnt on the altar. Why should legs be the last? And if the expression is always 'entrails and legs', would it not be better practice to treat them as if they constituted a regular pair? If they are taken thus as a set, it is unlikely that the literal sense is right.

The Hebrew words for parts of the anatomy often have diverse meanings. The word for head can mean summit of a mountain, leader, chief, as well as the head of a body. Similarly, feet *(regel)*, is a common biblical euphemism for human sexual organs. In Jacob's blessing on Judah's progeny, 'The sceptre shall not depart from Judah, nor the ruler's staff from between his feet' (Gen 49: 10), the ruler's staff and the feet are taken to be an oblique reference to the male genitals. The dictionary, after dismissing the idea that 'staff' refers to the mace that might conceivably be lying between Judah's feet, says: 'However, a widely held view sees here a euphemism for the sexual parts and prefers the meaning "offspring".'[20]

---

[18] *kera'ayim*   [19] Milgrom 1991: 159.   [20] BDB: 920.

The word translated 'loins' (*kesilim*) is another circumlocution for male reproductive organs. If for humans 'feet' is a euphemism for genital organs, when it comes to animals, 'legs', accompanied by the word for 'entrails' suggests reference to the male animal's genital organs. Taken as a set it makes much more sense for the words to be translated as 'entrails and genitals'. At least that rendering explains why they are always together, and why they come last in the pattern of the reconstructed trunk and contents, and it makes sense with the association of the tabernacle with fertility.

The orderly pattern made on the altar from a dismembered animal present the innermost soft parts of the body under an inclusive series of outer casings. The suet-covered area divides the top of the carcass from the bottom, making it into three parts, the thick layer of suet around the diaphragm which contains liver and kidneys making a middle zone, while in the last zone are the other entrails. The procedures for sacrifice have broken up the order of the living body, separating each segment and drawing attention to the middle part, which would not otherwise have been distinguished from the rest. Ramban's model of the holy mountain has been transposed on a tri-zoned anatomy of the sacrificial animal. In the interior of the body is the pattern made by the suet covering the liver and the two kidneys, in the interior of the tabernacle is the pattern of its furnishings and activities, and both can be assimilated to the pattern of the holy mountain.

At the entry to the carcass the enveloping skin has to be opened, which would correspond to entering the large courtyard which encloses the whole sacred area. At the entry to the tabernacle is the outer court, the place of sacrifice, where the animal body is pierced. It is an area much bigger than the sanctuary; on the animal the corresponding front part is the enormous barrel-like rib-cage containing the heart and lungs. Note the animal shape tapering up and off towards the withers, and note that the suet around the diaphragm makes an occluded zone. Beyond the suet and its contents, another small separate area of the lower abdomen containing the entrails and loins would correspond to the inner sanctuary.

Table 4.1. Three paradigms of the tabernacle aligned

Mt Sinai	Animal offering	Tabernacle
Summit or head, cloud like smoke (Exod 19: 18); God came down to top, access for Moses (Exod 19: 20–2).	Entrails, intestines, genital organs (washed) at the summit of the pile.	Holy of holies, cherubim, ark, and testimony of covenant.
Perimeter of dense cloud, access restricted to Aaron, two sons, and seventy elders (Exod 24: 1–9).	Midriff area, dense fat covering, kidneys, liver lobe, burnt on altar.	Sanctuary, dense clouds of incense, symmetrical table and lampstand, restricted to priests.
Lower slopes, open access.	Head and meat sections, access to body, food for people and priest.	Outer court, main altar, access for people.
Mountain consecrated (Exod 19: 23).	Animal consecrated (Lev 1–7).	Tabernacle consecrated (Lev 16).

THE INMOST BEING

On this reading the meanings of cloud and its association with fire for the people of Israel are enough to explain the suet being forbidden. The suet that divides the body at the diaphragm below the lower ribs is not just a covering. It corresponds in the body to the boundary of a forbidden sacred space on the mountain. The solemn terms forbidding them to eat the suet fat support the parallel between body and Sinai.

The torso as a funnel going to the most intimate sacred area has a lot of meaning for Leviticus. The tabernacle runs horizontally with a slight tilt upwards, the holy mountain goes up vertically to the summit, and the sacrificial pile starts with the head underneath and goes up to the entrails. Each interpreted by reference to the others is a figure of the same world. Mountain goes up vertically, tabernacle and living body go along horizontally. The three exemplars come close to the inexpressible paradoxes of Jewish mysticism which allow going up to the Throne of God to mean the same as going down to the Chariot. If the tabernacle as a figure of Mount Sinai raises for the literal-minded enquirer further questions about the location of God at the summit of the one and at the same time in the deep interior of the other, remember that in mystical thought the whole scheme of spatial orientations can be reversed, 'upper' and 'inner' can be equivalent. Look at his creation where you will, the pattern is always there, with God in the depths or on the heights of it all.

If the tabernacle is also a body, the polite scholar from another tradition may be beset with hesitation, perhaps supposing the obvious reading to be vulgarly unworthy of the great themes. Bashfulness apart, it is important to ask why the innards should be at the point of highest esteem, the position that corresponds to the holy of holies, instead of the face or head or heart to which we accord more honour. The question calls for difficult comparative psychography, but at least recall that there has always been in the Jewish culture a strong association between body and tabernacle in respect of fertility.

The Bible locates the emotions and thought in the innermost parts of the body; the loins are wrung with remorse or grief; the innermost part is scrutinized by God; compassion resides in the bowels. The psalmist said: 'Truth is in the inward being' (Psalm 74: 8). The same interiorizing movement is seen in the space of the body as in the space of the tabernacle building. The temple was associated with the creation, and the creation with fertility, which implies that the innermost part of the tabernacle was a divine nuptial chamber. Even from complete ignorance of mysticism, the analogy of the inner sanctuary with the centre of creation is intelligible. It was fitting that the sanctuary was interpreted as depicting 'in a most tangible form the union between God and Israel'.[21]

---

[21] Patai 1947: 91; Zohar Hadash 1947: 183.

The erotic interpretation is in accord with early Jewish as well as with medieval mysticism. An ecstatic, swooning union is described as taking place in the sanctuary, referred to as 'the couch'. Scholars who have been interested in tracing nuptial imagery across the region have tried to locate the Jewish erotic parallels in the Feast of Tabernacles. But Ralph Patai finds it in the holy of holies of the temple. He says that it is only in a late period that 'we find the express statement that the couple, whose nuptial chamber it was, were God and the Holy Matrona, personifying the Community of Israel'.[22] The medieval Zohar is much too late to be relevant to Leviticus, nevertheless the idea is worth noting. In Patai's felicitous words, creation was thought of as a 'time of abounding fruitfulness, a sort of cosmic rutting season'.[23] That the tabernacle was associated with creation and connected with 'abounding fruitfulness' should be carried forward for interpreting the rest of Leviticus.

THE DOCTRINE OF REMAINDERS

So much for the trunk of the animal, and the prohibition of suet fat. What about the kidneys and the liver lobe? There has been a lot of learned speculation on why the long lobe should have been forbidden. In Aramaic, Hebrew, and Ugaritic it was the seat of the emotions. This part of the liver has been used in sacred ceremonies and in divination from very ancient times. In Greek divination a liver without a lobe was a presage of disaster.[24] Ezekiel mentions it being used for consultation by diviners (Ezek 21: 26), but, as Milgrom says, that cannot have been the reason for its being forbidden, for in that case the whole liver would have to be prohibited. If there was a law forbidding the eating of things used in rites of foreign gods, those things would not be consecrated on the altar. He concludes cautiously: 'Why the caudate lobe was reserved for the deity is unknown.'[25]

---

[22] Patai 1947: 89.
[23] Ibid.: 69.
[24] Halliday 1913: 193; Van de Meer 1987.
[25] Milgrom 1991: 208.

The Hebrew word for this protruding lobe, translated as liver appendage,[26] suggests something left over, a remainder, also excess, superiority, profit, or advantage. It would be a pity if this lobe, named superior, turns out to be underneath, for the House-that-Jack-Built conceit is realized in the model of the animal by the head being on top of the body and the suet on top of the entrails, and everything is on top of the fire, on top of the sticks, on top of the altar. From the name, 'superior' or on top, we could expect that the long lobe is on top of the liver. Maimonides, perhaps checking on whether the literal meaning of the word would explain the prohibition, actually looked to see if it is on top of the liver, but he reported that it is from 'the lower end of the liver'.[27]

On being consulted, the butcher in Swain's Lane[28] produces a huge slab of offal meat, smooth and shining, with no protuberance on top at all. When the problem is explained, he first agrees with Maimonides and with the encyclopedias and dictionaries; if the animal is alive and standing, indubitably the long lobe lies underneath, on the under side. But he turns the liver over and points out that if the animal has been butchered for sacrifice, after being slaughtered it would be laid on its back, first cut in half horizontally, and then the rib cage opened for emptying the contents. At this point the liver would have to be cut free of the arteries: from that aspect the long lobe would be on top, no doubt about it. On top and underneath depend on how you are looking at the thing. Leviticus actually says it is *upon* the liver and the name certainly suggests on top, and if the viewpoint is that of the slaughterer who has opened up the carcass to get out the innards, it would show on top.

A parallel with the cereal offering suggests a common paradigm for vegetable and animal sacrifice. The priest takes a pinch of flour with salt, oil, and frankincense (Lev 2: 2) out of the rest of the meal, and burns it on the altar 'as an offering by fire to the Lord' (Lev 2: 16). It is called the token or

[26] *yoteret*, cf. *yeter*, excess; *notare*, to be saved.

[27] Levine 1989: 16.

[28] Grateful acknowledgements to Martin Leahy, butcher of Elite Meats, Swains Lane, for the demonstration and advice.

memorial portion,[29] a reminder, something not to be forgotten. If the model for the animal sacrificed in the peace offering is also projected for the cereal offering,[30] the threesome, long lobe, and two kidneys, with the suet, would correspond to the token portion of flour with its three components, salt, oil, and frankincense: they are also picked out to be burnt on the altar while the rest of the sacrifice will be eaten. It is never said in so many words that these organs are token or memorial, or 'the Lord's portion'. But the parallel with the cereal offering is there and it is important to remember also that the suet is the Lord's (Lev 3: 16–17). A seemingly weak correspondence lurks here which becomes stronger when it is remembered that this book is centrally concerned with the things that are the Lord's.

Position within the threefold pattern gives no explanation for why the liver lobe should be singled out. Look again at the meaning of the Hebrew word[31] and see how the Leviticus writer uses it. The verb from the same root, 'to be left over', is actually quite common in the Pentateuch, especially in Leviticus. Turning back to the cereal offering, after the priest has taken a memorial portion for burning on the altar, '*what is left of the cereal offering* shall be for Aaron and his sons; it is a most holy part of the offerings by fire to the Lord' (Lev 2: 3); 'Aaron and his sons shall eat of it, and *what remains of the flesh* you shall burn with fire' (Lev 8: 32); 'and *the rest of the oil* that is in the priest's hand he shall put on the head of him who is to be cleansed' (Lev 14: 18); 'Take the cereal offering *that remains of the offerings by fire to the Lord* and eat it unleavened beside the altar, for it is most holy' (Lev 10: 12). The term is so constantly used for describing the sequence of movements in preparing the sacrifice that it seems to be banal and unremarkable.

Throughout Leviticus a prohibition indicates a strong meaning. Anything that is left over from a sacrifice is marked by prohibition. For example, for the sacrifice of peace offerings which is to be eaten largely by the people who have offered it the rule is:

[29] *azkarah*.
[30] The parallel is insisted upon very strongly by Marx 1994: 47 *passim*.
[31] *yoteret*.

It shall be eaten the same day you offer it, or on the morrow; and *anything left over until the third day* shall be burned with fire. If it is eaten at all on the third day it is an abomination: it will not be accepted, and everyone who eats it shall bear his iniquity, because he has profaned a holy thing of the Lord, and that person shall be cut off from his people. (Lev 19: 6–8)

Leviticus has another unexplained rule that seems to be as important as the rule to 'Eat no blood' and 'Eat no suet of animals sacrificed': 'Do not eat sacrificed meat that *remains* after three days' (Lev 7: 15–18). After the sacrifice time is allowed for the feasting and sharing out of the meat, for the first two days the feast is still the reigning mode, but after three days the meat has been left too long, it has to be classed as a leftover from the sacrifice, and sacrificial leftovers are sacred.

Most religions disallow leftovers from sacred offerings. There are usually severe rules to protect something that has been dedicated to God from being profaned. Brenda Beck in her article, 'The symbolic merger of body, space and cosmos in Hindu Tamil Nadu',[32] so well named for this topic, says that the same holds for Hinduism. It would be like taking back a gift, or rejecting bonds of affection, or kinship, or fealty, a grave insult to the one to whom the offering was first made. Leviticus' teaching on remainders and on the wickedness of profaning any sacred leftovers is not eccentric, and not for nothing.

Such weighty rules for leftovers should not hang in the air unconnected with the rest of the symbolism of sacrifice in Leviticus. In particular they should throw light on the rules for the liver lobe. The complex symbolism that parallels the sacrificial body with Mount Sinai and the tabernacle call all the more for a reason why Leviticus draws attention repeatedly to the liver lobe. But Leviticus does not give causal explanations. The reasons are in the pattern of due order and often in the literal meanings of the words. The concentric 'house-that-Jack-built' rhetoric emphasizes the 'on top of' position of the liver lobe very strongly, on top of the meat, on top of the fire, on the altar, which indicates another meaning. The word suggests surplus, excess, what is not required. So

---

[32] Beck 1976.

the liver lobe is to be classed as a remainder of the liver. Taken literally, the rules against profaning remainders evoke God's promises on behalf of those who would return from exile. Usually different words[33] are used for the holy remnant that will be saved from the exile or other disaster. The following references to the holy remnant of Israel use a word closely related to the Hebrew for the long liver lobe:

The *remnant of my people*. (Zephaniah 2: 9)
But *the rest* of the people shall not be cut off. (Zechariah 14: 2)
The *remnant of Jacob* shall be in the midst of many peoples. (Micah 5: 7, 8)

The same word is used as a verb in 'Yet I will *leave some of you* alive' (Ezekiel 6: 8). In an ingenious word play the long liver lobe would stand for the remainder of the people after the disasters that befell them. The leftover liver lobe could relate to a remnant after the invasion of the northern kingdom in the seventh century, or it could refer to the remnant after the destruction of the temple of Solomon in Jerusalem in the sixth. It would express the Leviticus writer's concern about the fate of Israel and Jerusalem. In such a context, consecrating the liver lobe on the altar is like praying for a remnant to be saved, a reminder to God that he promised to bring his scattered people back again.

The trouble with this solution is that it sounds too ingenious. The long lobe as the holy remnant—is it not too inventive? But whose ingenuity, the priestly writer's or the modern anthropologist's? If it seems too bold, recall that there are no contending explanations. Did the priests invent the projection of carcass on tabernacle? At the time of writing they were recasting an old religion from old materials. Formerly the religion would have been unified around the sacral kingship, the basis of the state. The new version was to be the religion of a commonwealth, kings would not be central or even necessary to the ritual. The old reading may have been too iconic for later times; or too connected with something else that had to be forgotten, the cosmic mountains of Canaanite religions, for example, or funeral sacrifices for the former kings? Could the projection of an animal's body on Sinai and the

---

[33] *she'ar, she'erit.*

tabernacle have replaced a ceremony that related the king's body to the shrine and to the cosmos?

In the search for understanding the same choice keeps recurring for the reader in almost every chapter of Leviticus. The solemn prohibition of suet fat and the burning on the altar of the liver lobe can remain uninterpreted. Should we be content to leave it shrouded in mystery? If not, the reader can follow the path of the three paradigms. The rules for suet construct a coherent tripartite model of tabernacle/carcass/mountain.

The summit of the mountain is the abode of God: below is the cloudy region which only Moses was allowed to enter; and lastly the vast, lower slopes where the priests and congregation waited. The order of placing the parts of the animal on the altar marks out three zones on the carcass, the suet set around and below the diaphragm corresponding to the cloud girdling the middle of the mountain. In presentational reasoning the analogy speaks for itself, this is mythopaeic in Cassirer's sense, a perfect example of analogical writing. It is not at all the way that Deuteronomy thinks. Concrete logic is fragile and easily dissolved by the attacks of rational instrumental reasoning. Certainly this particular reading seems to have been lost along with the sense of the law on suet. It is one of several signs of a break in the continuity of interpretation. Leviticus has been read in an itemized way, items of law corresponding to elements of morality, or to elements of narrative, or to elements of hygiene, but not to their place in an integral composition.

(5)

The Totally Reformed Religion

O house of Jacob, come, let us walk in the light of the
Lord. For thou hast rejected thy people, the house of
Jacob, because they are full of diviners from the east and
of soothsayers like the Philistines, and they strike hands
with foreigners . . . Their land is filled with idols; they
bow down to the work of their hands, to what their own
fingers have made. (Isaiah 2: 5–8)

This chapter carries on the comparison between Deuteronomy and Leviticus in two specific domains. One is the
question of whether the Levitical laws supported the idea of
one central shrine at Jerusalem. Here it is argued that the two
books are at odds. The other is the question of cults of the
dead, on which they are at one.

Deuteronomy and Leviticus have in common the idea of
the covenant. According to Weinfeld Deuteronomy modelled the relations between God and his people on the treaty
formula holding between a political overlord or conqueror
and the subject people, a treaty which contained the covenant
between the lord and his vassals.[1] He found the same
covenantal principle in Exodus and Joshua. Leviticus is not
normally associated with the covenant. But now that it is eas-
ier to read the antique writing of Leviticus a feeling for the
covenant of God comes strongly to the surface. It is not the
treaty form (though chapter 26 has the blessings and curses
that go with the treaty form) so much as the general principle
of a feudal relation. The vassals express it by offerings of food
to their Lord, hence the law of sacrifice, and by respect for
the lives of his other followers and his belongings.

---

[1] Weinfeld 1972: 66, 156.

DEUTERONOMY AND LEVITICUS

Inside the concentric circles and between the parallelisms
Leviticus writes its lessons. It is always the same, about the
mightiness of God, the vulnerability of living beings, their
weakness, their evil tendency to oppress each other, human
predatoriness, the covenant with God, his protection in
return for obedience. The teachings refer continually to
Genesis and Exodus, showing their grounding in the two first
books of the Pentateuch. The first covenant that God made
with humankind was with Noah, a promise of regular
seasons, and of waters kept within their limits. It is also a
promise to the ground and to the animal creation that lives on
it. After he smelt the pleasing odour of the sacrifice, God
relented, and gave his blessing to Noah, telling the people to
be fruitful and multiply and fill the earth. The repeated formula of the smoke of sacrifice rising to God as a sweet savour
is a reminder in Leviticus (chs. 1–3, 23) of the first covenant,
with Noah. The second covenant is with Abraham, a
covenant of fertility:

> I will make your descendants as the dust of the earth;
> so that if one can count the dust of the earth, your
> descendants also can be counted.
>
> Gen 13: 16

The third is the covenant of Sinai, the construction of the
tabernacle and the giving of the decalogue.

The thought of Sinai is ever-present in Leviticus. The feudal relation of a lord with his vassals accounts for the requirement of human obedience and of responsibility for animal
life. The people are God's dependants because he rescued
them from Egypt. If they break their side of the covenant by
failing to deliver loyalty and obedience, he will be released
from his side: his violence and anger against them will be
unrestrained. The underlying relation is reciprocity modified
by relative rank. Reciprocity does not mean symmetry. The
higher the lord's rank, the more heinous any offence against
the lord, and the higher the rank, the greater the generosity
from the lord. Furthermore, the reciprocity principle is soft-
ened by God's compassion and mercy

For he delivers the needy when he calls, the poor and him who has no helper. He has pity on the weak and the needy, and saves the lives of the needy. From oppression and violence he redeems their life . . . (Psalm 72: 12–14)

In listing a number of differences between the books Moshe Weinfeld says Leviticus is ritualist, sacrificial, formal; Deuteronomy is rationalist, humanist, anti-ritualist. It is surprising to see the word rationalist applied to the text of an ancient religion, but it is justified, and one of the necessary tasks of biblical interpretation is to assess carefully the differences between the two texts, instead of trying to elide them.

Specifically, the one difference of which most has been made concerns the presence of God in the tabernacle. Deuteronomy distances God, he does not abide in the tabernacle, only his Name and the glory of it are present, whereas Leviticus and Numbers believe God to be present, close to his people at all times, and meeting them in the tent of meeting. Deuteronomy does not speak of sin and guilt offerings, there is no 'pleasing odour' from the smoke of burnt offerings. Instead, in Deuteronomy sin is expiated by prayer and good deeds; so strictly speaking, in this book there is no need for an elite hereditary set of priests among the sons of Levi whose duty is to make atonement. In Deuteronomy the eleemosynary aspect is prominent, the sacrifices are consumed by the sacrificer in the sanctuary, and shared with the poor, the alien, the Levite, orphans, and widows. Whereas in Leviticus the division of meat, as shown above, is a continuation of the sacrificial action, under strict priestly control. In Leviticus the blood of all herd animals calls for vengeance unless slaughtered in the rite of sacrifice; the bodies of their wild counterparts if killed in hunting should be covered respectfully by dust. Deuteronomy repudiates this teaching, and allows secular slaughter. Deuteronomy says that all the first-born of the flocks and herds must be consecrated to the Lord (Deut 12: 6; 15: 19), but this infringes one of Leviticus' most salient laws: certain things belong to the Lord and therefore cannot be offered to him. For example, firstlings of the herds belong to the Lord anyway, they cannot be dedicated to God (Lev 27: 26), as if giving him something he has already is a nonsense.

Difference of focus and interest explain these disagreements. A man of action, an adminstrator, a political orator, cannot be expected to be well-versed in the details of doctrine and cult. The things which Deuteronomy does not know or seems to get wrong are not necessarily disagreements with Leviticus. Many would be topics entrusted to the priestly writer precisely because they lie outside the province of Deuteronomy. One difference between Leviticus and Deuteronomy that should not be minimized, a disagreement of substance and policy: Deuteronomy taught that sacrifice could be offered only at one central shrine, but several shrines are possible according to the Leviticus text.

THE CENTRAL SANCTUARY

At any period of biblical history you choose to take, rival claims of shrines would be contested. Bethel, where Jacob wrestled with the angel of God, or Shiloh, where the ark of the covenant rested, were eventually superseded by Jerusalem. Neither the invasion of Israel by Assyria nor the invasion of Jerusalem by Babylon would have quelled these rivalries. On the contrary, competition between old shrines would have been inflamed by the weakening of civil authority.

Bible scholars are divided as to whether Leviticus is teaching the same as Deuteronomy about the place of sacrifice. Baruch Levine puts the weight of the interpretation on the sense in which the word for 'to slaughter' is to be taken. It has two meanings, one specialized for sacrifice, and one a general sense, to kill.

The significance of Leviticus 17: 3–4 has been debated since late antiquity. It was always apparent that verses 3–4 could be taken to contradict the laws of Deuteronomy 12.15f. The latter clearly state that the Israelites were allowed to slaughter animals for food without recourse to the sacrificial altar, so long as they took care to drain the blood from the slaughtered animal and refrained from eating blood.

Levine surveys the debate and concludes that Leviticus and Deuteronomy concur.[2] To put so much weight on one word, 'slaughter', smacks of casuistry.

[2] Levine 1989: 112.

The alternative view is also supported by scholarly opinion. It is a recondite argument, difficult for an anthropologist to enter with any confidence, but so much depends on the outcome for the reading of Leviticus that it cannot be evaded. The reading offered in this volume takes sides with Moshe Weinfeld's view that the two books are teaching different doctrines on this issue.[3] Deuteronomy requires sacrificial killings to be brought to

the place which the Lord your God will choose out of all your tribes to put his name and make his habitation there; thither you shall go, and thither you shall bring your burnt offerings and your sacrifices, your tithes . . . and the firstlings of your herd and flock [etc.] (Deut 12: 5–7, reiterated in Deut 12: 11, 13–14, 17–18)

These are the lines which ground the claim that Deuteronomy requires one central sacrificial shrine.

Now read the opening words of Leviticus:

The Lord called Moses, and spoke to him from the tent of meeting, saying, 'Speak to the people of Israel, and say to them, When any man of you brings an offering to the Lord, you shall bring your offering of cattle from the herd or from the flock. If his offering is a burnt offering from the herd, he shall offer a male without blemish; he shall offer it at the door of the tent of meeting, that he may be accepted before the Lord. (Lev 1: 1–3)

This text is the focus of the argument about Leviticus' backing for a central shrine. It is evidently an important point as it is repeated in chapter 17, not once but four times between verses 1 and 8. Leviticus tells the people emphatically not to kill a sacrificial animal anywhere except at the tent of meeting. Taken by itself it is quite plausible to read this as conforming to the rule in Deuteronomy that all slaughter for sacrifice shall take place in one central sanctuary.

Nowhere does Leviticus say anything about a central sanctuary. It is more in keeping with all that it does say in the later parts of the book against wanton shedding of animal blood and disrespect to animal corpses to interpret the opening lines as specifically prohibiting secular slaughter of livestock. The rule only applies to animals of the flocks and herds: their

[3] Weinfeld 1972: 163 ff.

life may not be taken except the animal be first formally presented and consecrated at the altar. (No other animals at all
may be consecrated and sacrificed, see chapter 11.) Secular
shedding of the blood of animals that are classed as sacrifice-
able is explicitly classed with shedding human blood:

If any man of the house of Israel kills an ox or a lamb or a goat in
the camp, . . . and does not bring it to the door of the tent of meeting, to offer it as a gift to the Lord before the tabernacle of the Lord,
bloodguilt shall be imputed to that man; he has shed blood; and
that man shall be cut off from among his people. (Lev 17: 3–4)

A quick summary may be helpful here. From analysing
chapter 11 of Leviticus we shall see that there are several
classes of animal life. First, the clean species, these are the
livestock which are destined for sacrifice. These include
unblemished, which are fit for the altar, and blemished, of
whose fate Leviticus says not a word. It is possibly an awkward subject, since if the farmers are explicitly allowed to
cook and eat their blemished stock, there might be a temp-
tation to save them from the altar by giving them a blemish.
According to Deuteronomy the class of clean (edible)
species includes the wild counterparts of the domestic animals (wild goat, wild sheep, ibex, antelope, etc., Deut 14:
4–9). Leviticus describes them indirectly as allowed to be
killed and eaten when it requires that if they are taken in
hunting their blood must be poured out and respectfully
covered with dust (17: 13). The question of secular slaughter, then, refers only to the domesticated flocks and herds.
But the wider context is the series of rules against touching
the corpses of any other animals (Lev 11). It does not mean
that they cannot be touched when alive, or killed, and fortunately so since many of them are useful animals such as
dogs and donkeys, and many are predators and pests which
need to be discouraged. The rule prevents profit being made
from their deaths, whether from curing, working, and sell-
ing their skins, or from cutting and cooking their meat,
since it is forbidden to touch their corpses. Effectively the
injunction that no one shall profit from the blood of his
neighbour (Lev 19: 16) is echoed by the command to respect
animal blood and carcasses.

Here it is maintained (contrary to some learned opinion) that Leviticus does not allow profane slaughter of domestic livestock. The position is integral to its teaching on blood and the sanctity of life. If there is to be no slaughter except it be sacralized, easy access to the tent of meeting is necessary for the herdsman. The Levitical law for exclusively sacral killing of livestock would be practical if there were a lot of recognized shrines, preferably one in every local district. The rule of Leviticus that forbids secular slaughter and the rule of Deuteronomy that requires all sacrifices to be performed in Jerusalem are incompatible. Deuteronomy makes it easy for the herdsman by permitting unconsecrated slaughter and eating of livestock: 'you may slaughter and eat flesh within any of your towns, as much as you desire, according to the blessing of the Lord your God which he has given you; the unclean and the clean may eat of it, as of the gazelle and as of the hart' (Deut 12: 15–16). This is one of the the most important differences with Leviticus. According to Deuteronomy every killing of livestock does not have to be a sacrifice. Two kinds of slaughter are permitted, one sacred and performed at the central shrine, one profane and performed anywhere, the Deuteronomic rule is reasonable, and practical for the livestock farmer. According to Leviticus every time a herdsman wants to eat meat he has to make a sacrifice. This would be unreasonable if they had to kill the animal at the central shrine (unless all breeders lived in Jerusalem), but reasonable for distant breeders if there was a central shrine in every settlement.

Differences between parts of the Pentateuch are often explained on historical grounds with the assumption that there was a development or evolution of doctrine. There is an argument that Leviticus is older as well as stricter, and which would mean that Deuteronomy has led the movement of history by slackening priestly control.[4] Conversely, if Deuteronomy is the older text, it could be held that Leviticus tightened up the rules and stopped profane slaughter that had been permitted before. Or thirdly, Deuteronomy, coming later, might have restored a pre-Levitical state of affairs,

---

[4] Milgrom 1991: 373.

loosening things up that had once been free and subsequently restricted by the priests. Either way, Deuteronomy plays the more sympathetic role, more liberal, more humanitarian, more secular and tending to reduce sacerdotal control. Whereas Leviticus is theocentric and its institutions sacred, in Deuteronomy the opposite holds, its concern is with secular institutions.[5] Moshe Weinfeld, emphasizing the dominant humanism of the Book of Deuteronomy, remarks on the paradox that 'the very book which is so centrally concerned with "the chosen place" has almost completely ignored the sacral institutions which the chosen place must necessarily imply and without which the conduct of sacral worship is unimaginable'.[6] The text of Leviticus never says that there is only one 'tent of meeting' and only one altar in all the land. In fact, the explicit contrast in 17: 3–10 is not between a central and local shrine, but between, on the one hand, God's place and, on the other, 'outside the camp' or 'the open field'. God's place can be in many localities. There is no rule that local shrines should be superseded by a central one, only a rule to supersede the open field and the goat-demons there (17: 7). Hartog suggests that the Persian habit of sacrificing anywhere at all, in the open field for example instead of in the temple, would have been scandalous to his readers.[7] In the Second Temple period when Judah was under Persian domination, if some of the people of Israel had started to copy their conquerors' habit of casual sacrifice it would derogate from the importance of the temple. Though this would explain the Leviticus objection, it is not necessary. The interpretation that it forbade secular slaughter is embedded in the larger context of Leviticus' teaching about God's responsibility for the living beings he created.

There is a sturdy tradition that castration of livestock is against the law. A castrated man would not be eligible for priestly service because of the law excluding blemished bodies from the most holy place (Lev 22: 16–24). Castration of animals is not explicitly forbidden in Leviticus, but an animal that has been castrated is blemished and therefore cannot be offered as a sacrifice. Putting all this together with the

---

[5] Weinfeld 1972: 183.   [6] Ibid.: 186.   [7] Hartog 1988.

principle that the congregation of Israel were only to eat their own livestock after consecration and sacrificial killing, there is a strong presumption that Leviticus did not favour the central sanctuary. One can ask what the learned rabbis in the first century knew about breeding livestock and how sensitive they were to the elementary economic problems of the farmer. Perhaps not at all, or at least no more than they are now. Here it is suggested that sacrifice of young animals at multiple sanctuaries was the breeder's alternative to castration for keeping the proportion of males and females under control.

Sheep are raised for wool and meat, cows and goats for milk and meat; in either case it is wasteful of grazing land to have too high a proportion of males in the herd. In sheep farming in semi-nomadic conditions the general minimum of uncastrated males to ewes is 1:60; in arid zones it is higher because undernourishment lowers the fertility of the rams; 1:10 is the usual rate for Africa, 1:20 typical of Arabia; the Basseri of South Iran have an even higher rate, one ram only having to serve five ewes. The ratio of buck/she goat reported for nomadic Kabalish arabs is 1:30. As to cattle, veterinary research suggests that one mature bull can serve around 50–60 females. Evidently livestock breeders try to do something to keep the proportion of males to females in their herds at the most efficient level.

Castration improves the quality of meat. If we read of a 'fatted calf' being brought out, it would presumably be a castrated male animal, for it is good husbandry for those which are not slaughtered young to be castrated and kept as a living store of meat for ceremonial occasions.[8] If Bible law left the herdsman no legitimate way to kill his castrated male animals, he could only adjust the proportion of males to females by sacral slaughter of bull calves. If he were following the Levitical rule and taking his young animals to the nearest shrine, by frequent sacrifices the herdsman could achieve an economically viable ratio of males to females. The argument suggests strongly that sacrifice was the regular occasion for thinning the herds. In that case it would be impossible and

[8] Dahl and Hjort 1976: 29, 88–9.

even ridiculous to require livestock farmers to do every
killing at a central place. To impose the journey would be
inefficient to say the least. The calves and lambs would be
half-dead before they arrived from remote areas. How could
the herdsman combine ritual duties with good animal husbandry in those circumstances? It is an absurdity.

This is the problem. Secular slaughter, castration, and ritual slaughter are alternative forms of demographic control.
For Leviticus sacrifice was the chosen method, central to its
religious programme. Deuteronomy recognizes that the livestock breeder cannot regularly bring in his animals from far
away, so it allows secular slaughter and also commutation
from farm produce to cash:

> And if the way is too long for you, so that you are not able to bring
> the tithe, when the Lord your God blesses you, because the place is
> too far from you, which the Lord your God chooses, to set his name
> there, then you shall turn it into money, and bind up the money in
> your hand, and go to the place which the Lord your God chooses,
> and spend the money for whatever you desire, oxen, or sheep, or
> wine or strong drink, whatever your appetite craves; and you shall
> eat there before the Lord your God and rejoice . . . (Deut 14: 24, 25,
> 26)

This passage is telling for the differences of style, first of all
the 'because' clause and its kindly pragmatism (the way too
long and the place too far), and then the positively avuncu-
lar instructions (to bind the money in your hand and to
spend it on whatever you desire and to eat whatever your
appetite craves): it sugars over a new law which would be
very inconvenient, to say the least, if secular slaughter were
not allowed.

For a quite other reason Leviticus would not be sympathetic to the idea of a central sanctuary. Leviticus' archaic
conception of holy space has been indicated above, and
there will be more to say below. The tabernacle standing as
a figure of Mount Sinai was located in what Suzanne Langer
called 'virtual space', and it existed permanently in 'virtual
time'. The important element in the construction of a sanctuary was that its proportions should correspond to those of
the desert tabernacle of Exodus, and that it should have the
right furniture in it to correspond to the smoky zone of the

mountain and to the inside of the sacrificial animal. In this mode of thought the projection works because of the proportions and there is no reason why the virtual space should not be reproduced as many times as need be. It is a different conception of space. In this sense, the tabernacle is spiritualized, like the celestial Jerusalem and the celestial Israel. Leviticus does not need to legislate for secular slaughter because it expects multiple sanctuaries throughout the land, on the one sanctified design of the desert tabernacle, Mount Sinai, and the body.

If Leviticus never did espouse the idea of the central sanctuary, the building of other temples would not be surprising,[9] though according to Deuteronomic law they should have been a scandal. We know that four were built, the Samaritan temple on Mount Gerizim, the Qasr el-Abd of Hyrcanus at Araq el-Emir in Transjordan, the Elephantine temple, the temple of Onias IV at Leontopolis, both the latter in Egypt. The building at Leontopolis was said to have been inspired by the prophecy of Isaiah: 'In that day there will be an altar to the Lord in the midst of the land of Egypt, and a pillar to the Lord at its border' (Isa 19: 19).[10]

Joseph Dan, studying early Jewish mysticism, cannot discover the origins of the idea of a celestial Jerusalem existing in parallel to the earthly one. He takes it back beyond the destruction of the city by the Romans in the first century, and suggests that it probably developed in Second Temple period.

It thus served both talmudic Judaism and early Christianity as a traditional belief, deeply inherent in the concept of Jerusalem; the destruction in 70 CE only gave it a new impetus and a new importance. Indeed it seems that the rabbinic sources emphasise that the celestial Temple was created before the creation of the world, and that the earthly Jerusalem and its Temple were built in correspondence to the celestial ideal. Philo of Alexandria, who wrote before the destruction of Jerusalem,[11] seems to have been uncomfortable with

---

[9] 'Though the cult itself may not have been heterodox the very existence of the temple is surprising. From earliest times (Josh 22; 1 Sam 26: 19; 27: 1 f.) the idea persisted (2 Kings 5: 15 ff.; Jer 16: 13; Ezek 4: 13) that foreign soil was ritually unclean precluding erection thereon of a temple' (Porten 1984: 386).

[10] Ibid.: 387.   [11] Philo, *Tanhuma*: para. 19.

the national aspect of this tradition, and reinforced it in a cosmic, universal manner.[12]

Rabbi Nachman of Bratslav distinguished the spiritual Israel from the earthly physical place saying, 'Everywhere I go, I go to Jerusalem.' Even though Dan calls this an ambiguous statement which makes geography meaningless,[13] it represents a strong strand in biblical thinking.

NO CULT OF THE DEAD

Presumably the cult of the dead is absent in the Bible because it was erased from the religion, like the monarchy. Here Leviticus is at one with Deuteronomy: neither of them say anything about cults of the dead. Joseph Blenkinsopp[14] argues that in Israel there had formerly been cults of the dead which were deliberately eradicated. For his argument he carefully distinguishes cults in which the living interact with the dead from cults connected with the disposal of the dead and the honouring of their memory. The latter are likely to be found everywhere, whereas the interactive cults are 'inspired by the belief that the dead, and specifically dead kin, live on in some way and are in a position to influence the living for good or ill'—for example, by healing, revealing hidden information about future events, or by haunting the living till some end has been gained or injustice righted. In the Bible Abraham and Isaac and Jacob are remembered as ancestors and as loyal servants beloved of God, but once dead, they are completely dead. They do not rise up and intervene in the lives of their descendants. There is an idea of an afterlife, and of going to a place called Sheol, or alternatively of being called to join the fathers, being gathered into the bosom of Abraham, but there are no transactions going on between the deceased and the living.[15] Though it remembers the dead piously, the Pentateuch gives no scope for saintly intercession; the dead can do nothing for the living, or

---

[12] Dan 1996: 64. Dan quotes A. Aptowitzer here, but with some reservations: A. Aptowitzer, 'Beit ha-mikedash shel Ma'allah al pi ha-Agadah', *Tarbiz* (1931), 2, 137–53, 257–87.

[13] Dan 1996: 71.   [14] Blenkinsopp 1995: 1–16.   [15] Spronk 1986.

the living for the dead. Leviticus utterly repudiates the very idea of a cult of the dead. On this Leviticus writes in complete harmony with the prophets: 'And when they say to you, "Consult the mediums and the wizards who chirp and mutter," should not a people consult their God? Should they consult the dead on behalf of the living?' (Isa 8: 19). Leviticus forbids the priests to attend burials except for their own close kin (Lev 21: 1–5). They were not to show violent emotions of grief, dishevel their hair, or rend their garments (Lev 10: 6), or shave their heads, or gash their flesh (Lev 19: 27–8; Deut 14: 1). The restrictions are more severe for the high priest (Lev 21). Mediumistic consultation with the dead was to be punished by stoning (Lev 19: 26, 31; 20: 6, 27). The dead could neither help nor be helped. Any form of spirit cult was rejected. Seers, sorcerers, witches, and diviners, any who cross the divide between living and dead, were denounced as evil-doers. The Pentateuch did not just ignore its ancestors. It violently hated to be in communication with them. And this too is in line with the prophet Isaiah: 'O house of Jacob, come, let us walk in the light of the Lord. For thou hast rejected thy people, the house of Jacob, because they are full of diviners from the east and of soothsayers like the Philistines . . .' (Isa 2: 5–6). The surrounding peoples in the Mediterranean and Aegean regions all had cults of the dead, Egypt,[16] Assyria and Babylonia,[17] Ugaritic kings and commoners,[18] and Canaan.[19] But in the Pentateuch there is no sign of it. If it had been deliberately removed before the books were edited, why?

A common explanation is based on psychology: their horror of dead bodies is itself the reason why the people of Israel did not pay cult to the dead. Other psychological explanations of strong feelings or ecstasy in religion often refer to deprivation. The deprived person is readily convinced that sorrows will be healed in an afterlife, and that injustice will be punished then too, and the dear departed are not dead. Apart from the patronizing attitude, the problem is that everyone is deprived, most of the population who have not joined the ecstatic religions are also deprived in one sense or

---

[16] Erman and Ranke 1963.　　　　[17] Bayliss 1973.
[18] Levine and de Tarragon 1984; Pope 1981.　　[19] Heider 1985: 383–400.

another, including the people who are against them. The same applies to crisis theories of religious revival: crises are on most of the time. Jacob Milgrom proposes a doctrinal explanation, that this is a religion which defines itself on the opposition of life and death; the false gods have no life, the God of the Bible overcomes the power of death. Blenkinsopp (cited above) seeks a sociological explanation. He draws on an old anthropological tradition that ancestor cults reinforce hereditary principles.[20] A people organized by patrilineal inheritance and succession would be expected to pay respect to the points of articulation by which they themselves enter the system and to which they refer when they want to manipulate it in their own favour. An impressive survey of Hebrew words for ghostly human spirits and their mediums is evidence that the dead used to be consulted. He concludes that the people at some time abandoned their interaction with their dead under duress.

The argument supposes that the existence of powerful autonomous lineages would be a threat to a government trying to centralize. The cults of the dead would have supported the lineages of their descendants and made them centres of political resistance; a government that succeeded in wiping out rival centres of power would repudiate diviners and the ancestors in whose name they spoke. One difficulty for the argument is that interactive cults of the dead are not necessarily ancestor cults. The dead may be a collective resource of help and counsel for the whole community, or for clients who have chosen particular patrons among the dead regardless of ancestry, or, the other way round, the individual dead may choose their own adepts. There is no evidence that the cults of the dead abhorred in Leviticus are cults of ancestors in a genealogical sense. This caveat rules out part of the argument according to which the government of Judah would have attacked cults of the dead as 'part of a broader strategy of undermining the lineage system to which the individual household belonged'.[21]

The case is further weakened by sophisticated doubts about whether societies that have been supposed to be 'patri-

---

[20] For this tradition see Radcliffe-Brown 1952: 153–77.
[21] Blenkinsopp 1995.

lineal' are indeed patrilineal in any significant sense.[22] Just the fact that they transmit names in the patrilineal line does not in itself mean that anything else follows suit. Many people who at a superficial glance seem to be patrilineal on closer inspection have to be counted as bilateral, tracing relationships in both mother's and father's line.[23] There are plenty of signs of a suppressed popular cult of the dead in the Bible. The question is not whether it existed, but whether it was important enough to need to be put down forcibly or whether it could not easily have died a natural death from lack of interest in the later period. When we start asking whether, and when, and to what degree the people of Israel were patrilineal enough to want to pay cult to their ancestors the answers are not favourable to the thesis.[24] Actually, nothing is said in the Bible against ancestors, it is the dead in general, mediums specially, and contact with dead bodies that are rejected. We probably ought to dismiss the idea that Deuteronomy sought to suppress ancestors as part of its centralizing programme to reduce the power of the over-mighty families and rebellious clans. But the initial question still stands: why no cults of the dead?

A pervasive mistake is to suppose that no people would ever voluntarily abandon a cult; if they let it drop it would have to be because they had been forced. In fact the record is full of people giving up their old cults quite spontaneously, for a variety of reasons. In real life there is a dynamic tension between people living together, dynamic in the sense that if they believe something today there is no general guarantee that they will be believing it tomorrow. The congregation are realists, open to influence and taking account of circumstances. Every pastor knows how easily a cult can die out when the worshippers lose interest in it. Allegiances respond to the flux and flow of affairs. No one will hold on stubbornly

[22] Kuper 1988: 190–209.

[23] The Tiv are a West African people who have been reported as patrilineal but of whom Adrian Edwards says that in practice there is no sharp boundary between paternal and maternal kin, or between kin and non-kin. 'The Tiv system is one in which the relation of territorial groups can be given a genealogical interpretation, rather than one in which there is a territorial adaptation of what is generally conceived of as a genealogical system.' (Edwards 1984.)

[24] Hanson 1989.

to an ancestor cult if it does not correspond to cherished purposes. The surprising thing is not religious change, but the other way round, it is surprising that a religion ever stays still enough to be recognized.

There can be compelling reasons for worshippers wanting to reform their religion so as to omit cults for the dead. Excluding the dead frees the living from institutional controls. Cults of the dead are usually conservative. In this sense, a religion that is getting rid of ancestors is generally a modernizing religion. To the extent that it rechannels wealth the end of a cult of the dead loosens the grip of old institutions. Regarding old cults as idolatry and superstition may change the flow of resources from enriching temple treasuries to satisfying individual wants. It suits the modernizing trends.

However sentimental one may feel about them, ancestors are politically disruptive. Operating on the side of their own descendants they strengthen factional divisions. Sometimes people are not content to be divided between genealogical compartments and achieve a wider unity with alternative cults that cut across the descent groups. To play down the importance of ancestors may be a well-considered move in favour of political unity.

Lastly, when the community is divided on political lines, the priests themselves can have the misfortune to align themselves and their cults with the losing side. Priests are the protectors of the people, supposed to be the help of the innocent, the guardians of sacred objects used in beneficent ritual, but they can abuse their position. In an atmosphere of factional division, if the clergy take sides, the enmity of political opponents accrues to them. Sometimes they are believed to be themselves occult evil-doers in league with anti-god,[25] and then they will be reviled in very much the terms that Leviticus reviles magicians.

It is no good trying to understand the end of a cult of the dead in Israel without relating it to other movements in the Second Temple period. It is a crucial part of the context of Leviticus to know that there was divided opinion about the role of priests, rivalry among priestly families, and serious

[25] Baeke 1996.

conflict on interpretation of the law from Essenes.[26] This is reflected in the references to priests in the Pentateuch. Leviticus says little about Levites, but mainly refers to priests, the sons of Aaron. Numbers speaks of both, but firmly subordinates the Levites to the priests. Deuteronomy refers to 'the Levitical priests, that is, all the tribe of Levi', in asserting their right to a share of the sacrifice (Deut 18: 1). Also, Jeremiah speaks about religion without either priests or Levites, the faithful with their hearts renewed do not need the cult. In the sixth and fifth centuries BCE the priests, for good or ill, were obviously somewhere near the centre of a political cauldron.

There is a respected thesis that no religious attacks on enemies are so vicious as those by a dominant religion against the practitioners of the supplanted cults. In this perspective the furies of the Inquisition in Italy were directed against old wise women, village fortune-tellers and purveyors of magic cures, the local specialists who were still giving the laity the comfort and advice which the clergy had become too remote to supply, and who were mercilessly pursued and killed as witches.[27] We do not know who the reviled magicians of Deuteronomy and Leviticus were. Is it likely that they were just reactionary old priests still practising divination, and politically on the wrong side?

Morton Smith gave a vivid description of the religious factions which strove against each other in Palestine, the contest between assimilationists and separatists, and the eventual triumph of the Yahweh Alone movement. To the picture of intellectual and theological strife we should add the background of violence and fear, and recognize the devastation following national military defeat. Such a stressful background for the editing of the Pentateuch warns us not to be deceived by its magisterial calm. Religious leaders have to be careful, they cannot avoid being aligned, but the normal effect of foreign government violently imposed and maintained by force is to create fears of conspiracy. The religious stakes go up. To practise religion conspicuously in the old way, or conspicuously in a new way, invites accusations of

---

[26] Harrington 1996.   [27] Ginsburg 1983.

treason as well as of sin. Revolt and incipient civil war are always round the corner, instigated by conspiracy and exacerbated, as Nehemiah found, by foreign spies (Neh 4: 2–8; 6: 10–14).

DEUTERONOMY'S LEGISLATION

Against this background Blenkinsopp's analysis of Deuteronomy's legislation might acquire a different interest. In his view its aim was to free individuals from the authority and control of their kinsmen. But from what we have just said, there would not have been much authority or control. He lists the establishment of a state-appointed local and central judiciary (Deut 16: 18–20; 17: 8–13) as intended to restrict the authority and jurisdiction of heads of households and tribal elders. He includes in the same interpretation the appointment of officers with broad supervisory functions; in addition state-appointed magistrates are to supervise the village elders in the investigation of a homicide (Deut 21: 1–9); these officials must be present when corporal punishment is inflicted (Deut 25: 1–3); false witnessing must be referred to the central judiciary.

If the context were not the aftermath of invasion, it would be plausible to cite these as instances of intrusive state bureaucracy. 'Intrusive' suggests intruding on institutions that are functioning effectively. Blenkinsopp cites other instances of legislation whose effect is to free individuals from the control of their family heads. The manner in which the paterfamilias can dispose of his estate is restricted (Deut 21: 14–17); he should not deal summarily with his disobedient son but refer him to the city elders (Deut 21: 18–21); blood vengeance, 'an essential and traditional component of tribal justice, is phased out in favour of a state mandated law of sanctuary'.[28] Even the traditional idea of intergenerational responsibility is cancelled: 'The fathers shall not be put to death for the children, nor shall the children be put to death for the fathers; every man shall be put to death for his own

---

[28] Blenkinsopp 1995: 4–5.

sin' (Deut 24: 16). Combing through Deuteronomy, he finds an impressive list of laws that would undermine or break up the authority of senior kinsmen—if they had any authority. But this is moot. In the post-invasion crisis, who has any authority at all? And, a very interesting case, returning runaway slaves to their masters is prohibited (Deut 23: 15–16), which Blenkinsopp regards as 'a remarkable departure from legal practice in the Near East . . . and one which . . . would tend to undermine the property and labour base of the more prosperous households'. What prosperous households?

Deuteronomy's prescriptions for official supervision could be read another way. The context of the writing means that its legislation should not be compared with the law codes issued by great empires in their prime. Could not the rules superseding blood vengeance be aimed to stop lynch law, and those against privately administered corporal punishment be intended to prevent arbitrary violence?

In the aftermath of war and religious conflict, picking up the pieces and trying to restore order, the administration of Judah would have found the old pillars of society fallen into ruin. At an earlier stage, in the eighth and seventh centuries, Jerusalem grew in size and amassed specialized central functions for the region; the settlements around decreased, unable to compete with Jerusalem rising to be the 'primate site' in the region. But by the end of the seventh century this movement went into reverse. After Israel had been overrun by Assyria, Jerusalem itself fell into dramatic decline. In the sixth century it was in a state of collapse, following the invasion of Nebuchadnezzar and the deportation of skilled and noble families to Babylon.[29] Instead of needing to destroy the big families the writers of the Pentateuch would have found the old social framework destroyed already.

Is it not more likely that Deuteronomy's intrusive bureaucratic interferences would have been made, not to release individuals from a non-existent family control, but the other way round? If the institutional framework has collapsed, as it would have done in Judah after the destruction of the temple, the task of the Persian colonial administration would not be

---

[29] Jamieson-Drake 1991.

enviable. The traditional leaders are feuding among themselves, their authority is defunct, local shrines are the focus of fierce doctrinal conflict. What are colonial administrators supposed to do then? And what should we expect from the religious party that wants peace and order restored?

Deuteronomy backed the bureaucracy by administrative rules. It downgraded the local shrines by ruling that all animal sacrifice should be performed at the central shrine at Jerusalem. It relieved the people from the conflicts of conscience which their obedience to traditionalist fathers and senior kinsmen might have entailed. It stopped arbitrary self-help and violence by extending and reinforcing the power of a central judiciary. It limited the blood feud and it put despotic fathers under the control of the town elders, and the elders under the control of the state magistrature. As for the slave who is given his freedom, there might have been a presumption that slaves do not run away from masters who are fair to them.

Morton Smith described a background of strife for the editing of the Pentateuch which gives a different slant to the need for a centralized administrative framework. In this context we can surmise that cults of the dead were too subversive, or too much associated with the monarchy, or with priests of the wrong political leaning. The same for the mediums, who were very likely to have been fomenting political trouble. The initial question is left, how to explain the horror, the apocalyptic frenzy against diviners? Why should there be so much anger against communication with the dead?

A speculation: Judah's internal upheavals in the centuries before might well have been fanned after the exile by foreign interested parties. Heresy elided with treason, and the resulting conflicts would have been so horrifying as to make the survivors long for a new solidarity. This is a way to interpret the book of Judges' highly stylized narrative of soldiers fighting each other instead of the enemy. Gideon defeated the Midianites, a mere 300 soldiers of Israel against the enemy hosts, the latter defeated because 'the Lord set every man's sword against his fellow and against all the army and the army; fled . . .' (Judg 7: 22). The dire effects of fratricide are rehearsed again in the tale of Abimelech: finally with a shameful death 'God requited the crime of Abimelech, which he committed against his father in killing his seventy brothers' (Judg 9: 56). After other tales of betrayal and collusion we finally come to the story of the war of all Israel against the Benjaminites, and how, after Benjamin had been defeated, over 50,000 men slain (Judg 20: 35, 46), their towns burnt and their cattle killed, the people wept bitterly, saying: 'Oh Lord, the God of Israel, why has this come to pass in Israel, . . . that there should be today one tribe lacking in Israel?' (Judg 21: 3), and the story continues with the inventions they employed to reintegrate Benjamin into the community and restore its wholeness after civil war.

To recall a tragic scenario of this kind would have served the overriding objective of a call to solidarity. For that to be achieved the Bible religion would have had to be radically reconstructed. From the great diversity of doctrines in dispute they would have sought to eliminate potentially divisive teachings. It would have been impossible to eliminate all points of disagreement, but this degree of conformity was achieved: kings were not to be mentioned, the dead not to be invoked, diviners and seers outlawed, no magic, which means no healing, no images, theories of impurity made politically harmless, accusations to be ended. A concerted act of disremembering is the common basis of all five books.[30]

In such a conciliatory perspective Deuteronomy would be seeking to infuse civic responsibility and hope into a despairing community. In a completely new kind of society individuals are to be responsible, each for himself. None will suffer for the sins of the fathers, but 'every man shall be put to death for his own sin' (Deut 24: 16). How right Moshe Weinfeld was to say that Deuteronomy taught a modern religion.[31] And how different it is from Leviticus. Where Deuteronomy was working to establish a holy society by administrative improvements and legal coercion, Leviticus was working to the same end by the power of the teaching itself.

---

[30] Compare the need to forget and the difficulty of forgetting after contemporary wars, and the organization of memory. Sivan 1993; Foster, R., 1997.

[31] Weinfeld 1972.

A thoroughgoing monotheism would imply changes for worship. Leviticus had to say what practices could be allowed and which excluded. It had to do this under several difficulties. It had to use what Stephen Geller calls 'a covenant of words'[32] to overcome other problems. The other religions around could engage craftsmen to delight the eye and hearten flagging belief with carvings and pictures, furthermore the priests of other religions could enjoy the backing of a king and the historic glories and present honours of a monarchy. But this religion was austerely aniconic and non-monarchical. Other religions could give their adepts comfort from talismans and charms, other religions had healing rites, but this religion was profoundly anti-magical. Even more disabling for a reforming priesthood intent on holding its congregation, this religion had turned against its old oracular resources. A religion that once had oracles and divination and tries to do without them has lost access to the concerns of the faithful. This accounts for the air of unrealism that sometimes pervades the text, as if it were a self-contained philosophical treatise.

[32] Geller, S., 1992.

(6)

Oracles Support Divine Justice

You shall not practise augury or witchcraft. (Lev 19: 26)

Do not turn to mediums or wizards. (Lev 19: 31)

If a person turns to mediums and wizards, playing the harlot after them, I will set my face against that person. (Lev 20: 6)

A man or a woman who is a medium or a wizard shall be put to death. (Lev 20: 27)

This chapter dips into anthropological studies of oracles to illustrate the scale of the gap made by the abolition of oracles. Two things about the priestly laws would make more sense if priestly use of oracles were allowed. One is the use of the oath to bring a private case into priestly jurisdiction. The other is the use of the oracle to supplement the judicial system at its weak points.

No one knows when oracles and soothsaying were first forbidden. It may have been from the time of King Josiah in the seventh century, or they may have been banned much earlier, or later, in the exilic or post-exilic periods, sixth or fifth century.[1] If the earlier dates are preferred, the last editors would hardly know the arcane meanings of the fragments they gathered together. It is one thing to be told the principles of a divinatory system, but quite another to see it working.

The difficulty is as much for the writer as for the reader. How could he present a sacrificial cult without saying a word about the working of the oracles? It would be like using a pharmacopoeia to describe a medical system, giving only the names of the ailments and the medicines and nothing about the diagnostic process. If the gap has not been remarked, it would be because the readers are not familiar

---

[1] Van Dam 1997.

with a sacrificial cult. Animal sacrifice is not practised in the modern readers' religion, and modern sin is not directly linked with specific misfortunes. The point needs more discussion.

DIVINATION AND SACRIFICE

Divination was prominent in Egypt, Babylon, Greece, and Persia, but Leviticus only mentions it halfway through the book, and then only to condemn. Frederick Cryer remarks on how heavily Bible scholars play down divination in the Bible. He says their interest in

Israelite divination stands in starkest conceivable contrast with Old Testament texts . . . which insist that Israel parcelled out her lands, removed apostates from her midst, was guided in the desert, initiated her battles, sanctified her holy places, and confirmed the election of her first king by means of one or another form of non-prophetic divination.[2]

Cryer's list says nothing about oracles connected with sacrifice. The one source to which Bible scholars would normally look for information on divination, Leviticus, is hostile or silent. The silence could be from ignorance; or if the people are still practising a proscribed form of enquiry, it could be from discretion; but whatever the cause it is difficult to exaggerate the magnitude of the hole it makes in the account of the cult. One of the effects is to turn into ungrounded speculation any source-critical assumptions about the moral attitudes of the editor, or editors.

A few examples from other religions showing how intimately sacrifice depends on divination will expose the gap in the account of the cult. Divination is the institution that usually links sin, misfortune, and sacrifice. There is some misfortune, the oracle finds the causes and prescribes the remedy, a sacrifice. There are also judicial problems which are commonly solved by oracles, for example to find the truth between contending parties, or to support appeal from an unacceptable verdict.

[2] Cryer 1994: 236.

Since Leviticus is committed to outlawing diviners and oracles, it does not need to explain how the old system used to work. It says that when a person has sinned, a sacrifice must be offered by the priest to make atonement. But what counts as a sin serious enough to call for sacrifice, and how to know what animal to bring? How is the lay person to know which sacrifice must be done? A bull or even a goat is a big outlay, and the usual pragmatic response of a private person would be to postpone the sacrifice. As to public sacrifices offered for the whole community the high priest or an expert officially designated can announce that a public sacrifice is due but it is not safe to assume that everyone concurs. Even the calendar is not an uncontroversial subject. Disagreements about calendar reckoning wracked Judaea in the post-exilic period, and anger was inflamed on the question of whether the start of the sabbath should be counted from the end of night or from the end of day.[3]

To know when the first-fruits offerings were due would be a local matter and presumably clear enough at a local level. But how did the ancient Hebrew person know that he was obliged to make a sin offering? Or a guilt offering, or, for that matter, an offering to fulfil a vow, a peace offering, or one for thanskgiving? As they are voluntary, biblical scholars have always assumed that it was a matter of private conscience. However, it is usual for the individual to learn in a seance with the diviner whether his misfortunes are due to a sin, whether to let the problem resolve itself or whether to offer sacrifice, and if so, what to offer. Herodotus' *History* is full of examples of the conflicts between conscience and self-interest solved by recourse to divination. Or put more strongly, the seance would never have taken place unless the client was in some severe trouble; the diviner would be expected to find the cause of the trouble, and to say what sacrifice would avert it. The diviner makes the connection between the individual's private anxieties and the public cult.

Bible scholars find it hard to resist biblical contempt for superstition and magic. It will be a surprise for them to hear that far from being a snare and a sin, divination actually

---

[3] Talmon 1965.

meets a demand for truth. Some people develop enough solidarity and public spirit to be able to live together in an orderly way without seeking out the truth about each other's actions, or without having to clear their own names. Some train their conscience so finely that they are ready to believe that they themselves are responsible for the misfortunes they incur. In those cases questioning is stilled, the religion can afford to allot a minor role to divination, and if it is sacrificial, it does not require the sacrifices to be assorted to specific types of sins. Someone is sick, so a sacrifice is offered, quite simple, no further questions.[4] This is not the case with Leviticus; to conform to its rules one would want to know which kind of sacrifice is called for, and what sort of transgression lies behind the present misfortune. Whether to offer a thanksgiving sacrifice, or an offering to fulfil a vow, or a sin or a guilt offering is quite a technical matter.

KNOWING WHEN TO MAKE A PRIVATE SACRIFICE

The order of doing, the number of times, the exact positioning in space, the rules for a sacrifice, are like a choreography for a ballet. Take note of the balance of Leviticus chapter 4. A principle of descending order gives first the case of a sin by an anointed priest (Lev 4: 3), then sin by the whole congregation (Lev 4: 13), then the case of the sin of a ruler (Lev 4: 22), and then the case of the sin of one of the common people (Lev 4: 27). (Some might want to take this order as a sign of elitism, but notice that the sin of the whole congregation ranks before that of the ruler.)

For the priest's sin the specified offering is a young bull, for the whole congregation, likewise, a bull, for the ruler a he-goat, and for the private person, gender specified, a she-goat or a ewe-lamb, or if the person cannot afford either, a bird. Throughout chapter 4 sins are not further specified than as 'any of the things which the Lord has commanded not to be done' (Lev 4: 2). Specific sins are instanced in chapter 6: 'deceiving his neighbour in a matter of deposit or security, or

[4] Evans-Pritchard 1956.

through robbery, or if he has oppressed his neighbour, or has found what was lost and lied about it' (Lev 6: 2–3). Though these are not cult matters, evidently God does take them seriously enough to require restitution and a guilt offering (Lev 6: 1–7). After all this, how can anyone say that the priestly editor of the first part of the book shows no concern for social justice?

What is to be offered depends on who did the sin. It would be naïve to suppose that that is not a matter of dispute. A history of accusations and counter-accusations will lie behind the decision. If it is a ruler or a priest who is accused, political factions will normally be aligned behind the charge, if a commoner, it is costly to accept the verdict, and reputation is at stake. The unwelcome verdict will be resisted. Tribunals rarely have enough authority to settle even minor disputes, appeal to higher authority is necessary, and everywhere appeals to God's judgement is the last authority. When this is rejected, there is nothing left but to fight or secede.

These lists in Leviticus chapter 4 of kinds of sins and kinds of sinner cannot have been politically bland in their functioning. Decisions can be challenged. To reduce dissension is what divination is for, to settle disputes about facts. But the facts can matter too passionately and the disagreement can go too deep for the oracle findings to be accepted by all the contenders. New rival oracles can be set up, people needing to prove their case may travel far to a distant shrine to get the truth, rivalry between oracles sets in, one oracular shrine may become a court of final appeal. It is hard to understand how the system of free-will offerings described in Leviticus works without a supporting system of divination. The two generally go hand in hand (and woe to the ruler who does not control both).

Biblical commentators who write about divination do not come down into this level of practice. One scholar claims that the oracle gave only the expected answers, and that its function was 'to offer reassurance, to give divine legitimation of the obvious choice, and to incorporate a dangerous and unpleasant task into the religious schema'.[5] Important issues

---

[5] Huffman 1983.

may be at stake, such as the decision to fight or not to fight in Judges 20, for example. The task the oracle commanded was to punish the brother tribe of Benjamin by military destruction, certainly dangerous, and certainly needing divine justification, and reassurance. But the idea that the oracle gives obvious and reassuring answers underestimates the uncertainties and surprises that attend on oracular consultation. It implies that the answers were engineered, almost saying that the oracle worked by a priestly hoax, the priests in collusion with the leaders. But as Cornelis Van Dam says, speaking from the angle of faith: 'it seems unlikely that Yahweh would have given an official means of communication . . . that could in any way have been manipulated for certain priestly or other interests.'[6] And from the angle of anthropology, why not credit the followers with some critical faculty? If there was an official oracle, there would have been private oracles as well. When oracles are consulted privately about individual matters, truth is being sought. Presumably this sometimes applies in affairs of state. Rulers cannot always expect to be vindicated by the oracle, its judgements can overturn dynasties.

This is the fascinating thing about oracles: how can they work unless they are rigged? Sometimes they are.[7] But much intensive study by field anthropologists shows that the consultants and their clients exert tremendous effort to prevent manipulation. Even the self-operated system is protected as far as possible from unconscious subjective bias.[8] One reason that oracles are authoritative is that the possible disasters and explanations are pre-packaged, and also the possible answers, so that a prior plausibility is built into the system. For example, Yoruba divination gives the client a chance to ask more questions after hearing the first response. If, for example, a blessing has been predicted, the client can ask in a fixed order:

---

[6] Van Dam 1997: 211.

[7] V. T. Turner's graphic account of a divinatory session among the Ndembu explains how the diviner used sleight of hand to find a tooth planted in the blood from the patient. (Turner V. T., 1967).

[8] Evans-Pritchard 1937.

Is it a blessing of a long life?
Money?
Wives?
Children?
A new place to live?

If evil has been predicted, the questions will be:

Is it death?
Disease?
Loss?
Fight?
Court case? [9]

Notice how stereotyped are the possibilities of disaster or good fortune.

Oracles work because they draw upon local theories of causation to do the double work of finding truth and promoting peace. Curses are causes, so are moral delicts; the problem when disaster happens is to know who would have cursed, or who sinned. The effect on theories of causation is to stereotype kinds of harms and their causes in a moral framework. Divination adjudicates between contested claims, and indicates the sacrifice that can make a truth for the people to live by. It works by pre-packaging all the important things that can happen.

The diviners who work more complex oracles use the best understanding they can muster of the local situation, so as to select the right divinatory materials for casting the dice and to give the results of the throw a relevant reading.[10] Some oracles are so complex that the diviner cannot manipulate them without obvious cheating and is obliged to read off the results quite mechanically.[11] They can be so technical that it needs fine mathematical skills to operate them.[12] In the first case, the problem for the person seeking truth is how to keep his or her own influence out of the process, and how to command credibility when an answer has been obtained. In the second case the problem is the opposite, mastery of the technicalities is so exacting that the diviner has to abdicate any personal input. This impartial operation is the pride of the

[9] Bascom 1980: 8. [10] Turner, V. T., 1967. [11] Bascom 1969.
[12] Jaulin 1966.

complex system, but it means that knowledge of local factors, political and personal, so valuable in other systems, is discounted: the operator does not so much divine as read the results. The process is mechanical and impersonal and the answers have to be equivocal so that the enquirer can put in his own interpretation.

PLAUSIBILITY OF ORACLES

An oracle is part of a cybernetic system. The experience of misfortune interacts with the possibility of consultation, which interacts continuously with the possibility of action, which is probably in the form of sacrifice. The feedback structures how disaster is perceived. It becomes blameworthy, a failure in the duty of a kinsman, not to ascertain the causes and the action to be taken. The cycle starts with a puzzle, some responsibility needs to be located, names are selected which might reasonably be expected to carry the responsibility, the names are fed into the oracle, when the lot falls on one name the answer is already *prima facie* plausible and the way for action indicated. The cycle energizes a feedback between morality, misfortune, and blaming.

Moral ideas demand vindication one way or another. The weather is a great justifier and omen. In the Bible thunder and rain respond to evil-doing in the usual way (1 Sam 12: 18; 1 Kings 18: 40–5). The ailing body is a telling portent. When her son was ill, the widow who sheltered Elijah immediately believed that her sins were responsible (1 Kings 17: 18), thus in a sense reading his body as a sign. Just as often the victims do not search their own consciences but look for someone else to blame. Guilt is suspected in advance of trouble and the expected misfortunes are in the air, ready to be used as sticks to beat ill-doers. Sometimes the victim is blamed. The disaster which befell the old priest Eli's two sons, both killed in the one day, is traced back to their exorbitant demands, their neglect of their priestly duties, and general debauchery (1 Sam 2: 12, 22, 30–6; 4: 11), but we can be sure it was predicted knowingly by all who saw them defying God's law.

To illustrate how easily omens are instituted: in the villages of the Lele in Zaire the occasion of the communal hunt became a kind of proto-oracle thanks to the belief that if there had been physical violence in the village or even secret anger, the hunt would be unsuccessful. This would be supplementary to the usual consultation of specialized oracles about whether to have a hunt and when and where to go. So when the huntsmen were gathered and about to set off, infirm old men or women would totter up to the meet and disclose their grievances, insisting loudly that in spite of all the insults and cruelty they had suffered they felt no anger, concluding with a blessing on the hunt.[13] If they did not give this blessing and the hunt failed, the rubbing oracle would hold them liable and they would have to pay a fine. If the hunt was successful, it was eagerly hailed as a portent of the good spiritual state of the village, an augur of future prosperity.

Sometimes the sacrifice itself has oracular functions. There can be ways of telling whether it has been accepted or not. In such cases sacrifice and divination are one, the sacrifice is an oracle and the decision to make a sacrifice in the first place is influenced by the need for an answer about the auspiciousness of the occasion. Some communities elaborate the bodies of the members as proto-oracles. The limbs and organs, skin and bone, blood and milk, are coded for different social obligations; when one part suffers, the locus of pain has oracular effects, indicating what duties have been neglected or which relatives may be cursing the victim.

So among the Buissi of the Lower Congo, the body is intricately coded for reference to social categories, and illness indicates automatically what has been done wrong, lack of respect, failure to pay a debt, and to whom. Are father's kin or mother's kin the offended party? The divination seance is the occasion of a review of past dealings of the patient's clan with the relevant other clans; private illness is a public affair, large sums will have to be raised to settle old inter-clan debts, and sacrifical rites must be performed before the patient can be expected to recover.[14] This is complex, it turns the bodies of all the members of a clan into maps of the social system,

---

[13] Douglas 1963.   [14] Jacobson-Widding 1990: 31–58.

dynamically registering promises broken and other forms of ill-doing.

Sometimes divination maps the cosmos on the house and the body on both, by a conventional alignment of body and house with the cardinal points. A Hausa group in Nigeria regard the cardinal points as powers, each with four sides, front, back, right, and left, the object of much ritual being to bring the powers and their sides into propitious alignment. A person and a person's body are also oriented to the cardinal points and allocated between the four quarters. The fundamental direction is the east, the word for which is derived from the word for chest and front. The east and the most masculine and virile aspect of the body are contrasted with the two weaker, feminine, directions, the back and the left.[15] Consulting their house oracle richly unfolds the family's destinies, body, society, and cosmos interlocking at every level; and the oracle is always plausible.

Such complex divination would only be possible in a culture that has been coherently articulated, at least enough, as Philip Peek says, 'to provide knowledge for an orderly, meaningful human existence'. He insists, as anyone who has studied divination will admit, that kinship and political structures depend on divination, not vice versa.[16] Half a century earlier Junod had said of the southern Bantu: 'divination materials are a resumé of the whole social order.'[17] They would have to be. It is one of the truths which before it was said was not recognized, but once said, it is obvious.

The converse is equally obvious that a severe political shock, invasion, conquest, famine, war, exile, any major catastrophe, would make it impossible to use the old divinatory instruments. This could lead to the system of divination becoming unworkable, irresponsible, and dangerous. By the same token, if the Bible was being edited in a period which had lost an earlier functioning divinatory system, it would be very difficult for the editors to reconstruct what that previous society had been like. Its knowledge base would be missing, difficult for the writer describing the old practices and even

[15] Nicolas 1975: 228–9. [16] Peek 1991: 69–71. See also Bascom 1969.
[17] Junod 1927: 571.

more difficult for us, the readers, which explains why it is so difficult to make sense of the priestly oracle.

It is not truth in general, academic or intellectual or spiritual, that is sought in oracles, but an eminently practical truth of morals and character as the protection of frail human purposes. One family suffers a loss, their friends gather round in sympathy, and all ask why it happened. The friends and kinsfolk constitute a 'therapeutic community'[18] round the sufferer, they want to know who was responsible. Was it an accident, or should someone be arraigned? Is there compensation to be claimed? If the finger of blame points at a neighbour, another therapeutic community will be mustered by the family of the accused, to turn the blame back on the victim's supporters or on the victim. To a very large extent all societies negotiate answers to these questions, and their institutions are affected by the kinds of answers they want. Fortunate are those communities not driven by animosity. Some deflect blame from their members by holding the dead responsible, or by blaming capricious demons or ghosts. In others the system is driven by vindictive desires to bring disgrace upon a neighbour or kinsman.

When the community is divided bitterly no closure to disputes is within sight. This means that no criminal can be brought to book while at the same time the suspects are desperate to be exonerated. This is the point at which divination can render its public service, it can either repair the social fabric,[19] or intensify hostilities. Which way it works, for reconciliation or for revenge, depends on the community that works it. Fears of civil breakdown would give Deuteronomy and Leviticus and their supporters good reason to outlaw divination in the already divided communities of Israel or Judah.

PRIESTLY DIVINATION

When all the possible forms of private divination were eliminated, there still remained the theoretical possibility of

---

[18] Jantzen 1978.   [19] Devisch 1991.

priestly divination. It was performed with the two small objects called Urim and Thummim. In Exodus the Lord tells Moses how to make the 'breastpiece of judgement'. It was a square textile on which four rows of precious stones were attached, each of the twelve stones engraved with the name of one of the tribes of Israel (Exod 28: 29–30). It is a bejewelled pocket in which the two divinatory objects, Urim and Thummim, sometimes called the 'sacred lots', are kept. There is nothing about how they are used. When Leviticus recounts the consecration of Aaron, it duly says how he is robed in all the priestly paraphernalia prescribed in Exodus: 'And he placed the breastpiece on him, and in the breastpiece he put the Urim and the Thummim' (Lev 8: 8). Most of the commentaries on biblical divination discuss the working of simple binary oracles which were evidently in common use. Some have thought that the priestly oracle involving the Urim and Thummim was also binary. The recent meticulously comprehensive study of the Urim and Thummim by Cornelis Van Dam shows that from rabbinic times and onwards through the medieval research, no one knew how it worked. In spite of immense scholarly labour, even to the present day no one knows. This may be unsurprising, since oracular consultations are usually confidential[20] and the actual working of the oracles are often well-kept professional secrets. Cabbalistic interpretations of the twelve precious stones, explicitly representing the twelve tribes, and the extension of their significance to colours, seasons, the zodiac, suggest scope for complex divination, but we know most about this, tantalizingly, from documents dating a thousand years later.[21]

Van Dam concludes that it was not a lot oracle, nor based upon a Yes/No binary questionnaire.[22] It could have been a complex oracle, possibly using the so-called lots in conjunction with the twelve gems on the breastplate. But Van Dam himself doubts that it was anything so mechanical, partly because of the great length of the reported answers. He falls

[20] Van Dam's interpretation of expressions such as 'Let us draw near to God' (1 Sam 14: 37) etc. not withstanding. Van Dam 1997: 223.
[21] Séd 1981: Appendix 'Le Symbolisme Zodiacal des Douze Tribus', 293–317.
[22] Van Dam 1997: 210–13.

back on prophecy as the means of communication.[23] The
Urim and Thummim would be the means of inspiration, and
the inspired priest would say the words that God put into his
mouth. This conclusion has the merit of continuity with the
prophetic tradition in the Bible.

One of Van Dam's arguments is based on the direct and
lively style of the oracular pronouncements, given very
quickly in time of urgent need, as no lot oracle could.
Another is that the sheer length of some of the responses
could not be produced out of a binary oracle. However, a
number of stock answers and stock solutions are sometimes
held as resources of the oracle, from which the divinatory session indicates a selection.

For example, the Yoruba have a divining system called
'sixteen cowries' which is used by everyone for their own
affairs.[24] The task of the diviner, often a woman, is to cast
sixteen cowrie shells into a basket or tray, to count how many
land with the hole up. This gives one of a limited number of
possible figures with each of which a set of legends of mythological persons is associated. The diviner, having seen the figure, starts to recite the appropriate set of legends; the client
listening selects a verse that seems applicable to the case, and
stops her there. The diviner, then makes a calculation to tell
the client what would be an appropriate sacrifice based on the
mythological case. The system gives the client some control
of the session, which helps the credibility of the outcome.

Try transferring this type of oracle impressionistically to
the Urim and Thummim. Throws of numbered dice could
be combined with the twelve stones of the Urim and
Thummim. Since each number corresponds to a letter of
the alphabet, three throws would produce a Hebrew word
in a restricted and specialized lexicon, and the word would
already be associated in advance with a punishment. Subsequent throws could indicate one of the precious stones, so
a tribe, a month of the year, or a biblical excerpt about the
members of the tribe could be called up, or even all three at
once. The diviner would need to know these references, from
which he would have to compose a message from God that

---

[23] Ibid.: 217.   [24] Bascom 1969.

fitted the occasion, and couch the judgement in impressively elegant language. Of course the same pronouncements would tend to be repeated. A practice of this kind would account for the lapidary ring of Leviticus' legislative statements and even for the occasional *non sequitur*.

A good example of a mysterious oracular reply is the case of the blasphemer in chapter 24: 10–23. The people who heard the Name of God cursed seized the man, brought him to Moses, and then put him into custody until the will of the Lord should be made known to them. At first glance the answer seems quite clear, but a second look shows a lack of connection between the punishment and the the law of talion that follows it.

13. And the Lord said to Moses,
14. 'Bring out of the camp him who cursed; and let all who heard him lay their hands upon his head, and let all the congregation stone him.
15. And say to the people of Israel, Whoever curses his God shall bear his sin.
16. He who blasphemes the name of the Lord shall be put to death; all the congregation shall stone him; the sojourner as well as the native, when he blasphemes the Name, shall be put to death.'

So far, so good. The oracle might have had a prepackaged text connecting insult to the Name and the penalty of stoning. But then the Lord weighs in with the 'eye for eye, tooth for tooth' quote from Deuteronomy, which does not seem connected with blasphemy. Deuteronomy says: 'it shall be life for life, eye for eye, tooth for tooth, hand for hand, foot for foot' (Deut 19: 21); Exodus says: 'you shall give life for life, eye for eye, tooth for tooth, hand for hand, foot for foot, burn for burn, wound for wound, stripe for stripe' (Exod 21: 23–5). The version of the Leviticus oracle in chapter 24 is:

17. He who kills a man shall be put to death.
18. He who kills a beast shall make it good, life for life.
19. When a man causes a disfigurement in his neighbour, as he has done it shall be done to him,
20. fracture for fracture, eye for eye, tooth for tooth; as he has disfigured a man he shall be disfigured.
21. He who kills a beast shall make it good; and he who kills a man shall be put to death.

None of these laws mentions blasphemy. We can read them carefully but do not find name for name, insult for insult, or stoning for stoning; there is no obvious equivalence that would bring the case of the blasphemer into the category of retaliatory penalties. So why is this the point in the book chosen to expound the law of talion? This question will be taken up again in the next chapter. God said about Moses, 'With him I speak mouth to mouth, clearly, and not in dark speech' (Num 12: 8). 'Dark speech' the oracle often is, enigmatic and disjunct.

Leviticus is full of phrases ambiguous to us now but which make sense if restored to an original context of oracles and retaliatory justice. For example, the commonly recurring phrase, 'shall bear his iniquity' (7: 18; 17: 16), suggests a judicial context. 'To bear iniquity' would mean carrying the guilt and being responsible for restitution or punishment. This is the literal meaning: it is expressed more forcibly by Baruch Schwartz when he insists that 'to bear a sin' means precisely to hold up, haul about, to carry sin for oneself or for someone else.[25] Usually the perpetrator's family group or 'his people' would have to bear it with him, in the sense that they would be expected to contribute to the fine, or in their persons they might be liable to revenge. If he has to bear the iniquity alone it would normally mean that his people have no obligation to help him out, a very severe judgement, expressed by the 'cut off' punishment: 'he shall be cut off from his people' (Lev 7: 21, 25, 27; 17: 9, 14). It means what it says, that he himself will have to bear the penalties, alone. But it is not necessarily the same as: 'I myself shall set my face against that man, and will cut him off from among his people' (Lev 20: 3, 5, 6), which would mean that no one has to take direct action, the Lord himself will single out that man, follow up the crime and punish him directly. This may be a gloss upon 'Every man shall be put to death for his own sin' (Deut 24: 16; Ezek 18: 4, 20; and cited in 2 Kings 14: 6).

Only an oracle can say whether the tree that later will fall upon him, or the bull that will gore him, or the lightning that will strike him, is the result of the Lord's action to cut him

---

[25] Schwartz 1995.

off. But in the end he will pay the penalty in his own person. At least his kinsmen hearing this will not incur any responsibility to follow up his death with demands for compensation. For certain grave offences the congregation is empowered to inflict capital punishment. The phrase 'I shall cut him off' is quite different again from 'his blood is upon him' (Lev 20: 5, 9, 11, 12, 13, 16). This means that whoever kills him for doing this dreadful thing, his father or his brothers, or anyone else, his blood is not upon the avenger.[26] After his death the people will probably need to consult the oracle to confirm the cause of his death. These cryptic clauses lay the trail for the explanation which is delayed until the end of the book. But at this point they still would read less cryptically if they were placed in the double context of collective responsibility[27] and oracular confirmation.

INADVERTENT SIN

The same context should be the background of the discussion of sins and sin offerings in chapter 4. What does the word 'unwitting' or 'inadvertent' mean? Here is another problem which may be solved by referring to the missing oracles in judicial contexts. The modern person's first reaction is to suppose that the unintended or inadvertent sin is not very serious. It seems fair enough that the sinner does not have to do anything about his inadvertent sins until he has discovered what he did.

If anyone sins unwittingly in any of the things which the Lord has commanded not to be done, and does any one of them, if it is the anointed priest who sins, thus bringing guilt on the people . . . (Lev 4: 2–3)
If the whole congregation of Israel commits a sin unwittingly and the thing is hidden from the eyes of the assembly, and they do any one of the things which the Lord has commanded not to be done and are guilty . . . (Lev 4: 13)
When a ruler sins, doing unwittingly any one of all the things which the Lord his God has commanded not to be done, and is guilty. . . (Lev 4: 22)

---

[26] Schapera 1955.   [27] Gellner 1969.

If any one of the common people sins unwittingly in doing any one of the things which the Lord has commanded not to be done, and is guilty, when the sin which he has committed is made known to him he shall bring for his offering . . . (Lev 4: 27)

What is strange is that in the account of sins each of the offences has to be drawn to the attention of the sinner. He is apparently not aware of them, he can even swear an oath or blaspheme without being aware of it! The words are a bit ambiguous:

If any one commits a breach of faith and sins unwittingly in any of the holy things of the Lord, he shall bring, as his guilt offering to the Lord, a ram without blemish . . . (Lev 5: 14)

Unwitting sins are the only kinds of sins which call forth the rituals of sacrifice, and no other sins are mentioned. Does it mean that God only forgives the ill-doing that is inadvertent? Is this supposed to be the loving and merciful God of Israel? Can it be that the repentance of the hardened sinner does not count? In that case there really would be a major difference between the doctrines of Christianity and Leviticus.

Look more closely at the sins listed in chapter 5. One might touch an unclean thing inadvertently, but surely the scenario for failing to come forward as a witness, or for uttering a rash oath without knowing, would have to be ingeniously contrived. It is not impossible; he might have gone away and not heard of the case which he had witnessed, or, more far-fetched, he might not have known the words which turned out to be an oath, or his tongue said them without his meaning them. Also in Leviticus chapter 6, with reference to financial fraud, lying, robbery, and oppression, it would be just possible to be unaware of committing any of these, but the claim of ignorance would be questioned in any normal tribunal. There are two possible explanations, which do not conflict with each other, a psychological one and an anthropological one.

Jacob Milgrom offers a psychological explanation: being guilty is not the same as feeling guilty, and the proper translation would be about subjective feelings of guilt. The text says:

When one has sinned and become guilty, he shall restore what he took by robbery, or what he got by oppression, or the deposit which was committed to him, or the lost thing which he found, or anything about which he has sworn falsely; he shall restore it in full, and shall add a fifth to it, and give it to him to whom it belongs, on the day of his guilt offering. And he shall bring to the priest his guilt offering to the Lord, a ram without blemish out of the flock, valued by you at the price for a guilt offering; and the priest shall make atonement for him before the Lord, and shall be forgiven for any of the things one may do and thereby become guilty. (Lev 6: 4–7)

The translation which gives 'becomes guilty' in English sounds like a legal conviction of guilt, whereas Milgrom eloquently argues that not legal guilt but subjective guilt is at issue. The sinner comes to feel guilty, he is afraid of punishment and aware of the suffering he has caused, he regrets what he did. Here is what he can do to put himself right with himself, as well as with God and man: just repent and do the prescribed ritual.

On these lines Milgrom elaborates on 'the priestly doctrine of repentance'.[28] It means that repentance mitigates crimes against God such as false oaths. Repentance alone is not enough, there must also be sacrifice. Since all sins, however grave, can be classed as unwitting if remorse and repentance follow, a benign technicality allows them all to be forgiven. The idea is well-based in religious understanding. Remember the unexpected response of the poor of London when John Wesley preached to them in the 1740s. He only told them to be assured their sins were forgiven: 'Some were seized with trembling; others sunk down and uttered loud and piercing cries; others fell into a kind of agony. In some instances, while prayer was being offered for them, they rose up with sudden change of feeling . . .' [29]

Conscience, as Milgrom says, is recognized by the priestly writer as 'a legal force which can convert a deliberate sin against God, always punishable by death, into an involuntary sin, now expiable by sacrifice'.[30]

The subjectivity of this explanation could be a problem for anyone taking the view that the Leviticus writer is insensitive to ethical issues since it relies on ethical sensibility of the

---

[28] Milgrom 1976.   [29] Watson 1885.   [30] Milgrom 1976: 17.

priestly writer as well as on that of his theory of repentance. It goes against anything we have said earlier about the analogical style as well as against the source critics' idea that the first part of Leviticus is by the hand of a formal, distant P writer. From an anthropological point of view there is another problem. Something about how to discover hidden sins is being taken for granted. The effect of an oath is to bring these man-to-man offences within the scope of priestly authority by making them into offences against God. The accused is only too likely to deny the sin. How can a person be convinced that he has lied, robbed, or oppressed? Jonah was convinced of his fault when the sailors drew lots. The answer is by divination of course, or by ordeals.

Consider the daily practice of divination. One person is being accused by another of having robbed or defrauded or lied or given false witness; if he claims innocence, secular law has come to an impasse, but the accused can clear himself by taking an oath or ordeal. Or he can resort to divination to prove he has been unjustly accused. Either way, he may resist conviction, rejecting the oracle, or he may cry off responsibility saying: 'Well, if I did do it I didn't mean any harm.' Or: 'I didn't know that would happen, I had no idea that the victim was standing there when I threw the stone', etc. Or: 'No, the defendant did not pay me to keep quiet, it just escaped my mind that I had witnessed the crime.' Or: 'No, they never beat me up, no one told me to go out of town until the case was over.' Witnesses who stick firm to their lies make the law a fool. One of the functions of the oracle is to create credibility for the prosecution.

The anthropological view is that the priestly writer has anticipated just this. The law of sin offerings says that regardless of your knowledge or intentions, when you have discovered (by divination), what you did wrong, you must make restitution plus one fifth of the value of the thing stolen, and pay up a ewe lamb, or a she-goat, or a bird, so as to get atonement done for your sin. Whether you knew about it or did not know about it is irrelevant, the oracle has convicted you and you must do the ritual. By this device arguing and protesting innocence can be quickly dismissed, and the validity of the oracle is not brought into question. This strongly suggests a practice of quasi-judicial divination. There was no doctrinal distinction between witting and unwitting sins, the regular mention of 'unwitting' was not a theological but a practical matter. The oracle would be brought into action when matters came into the jurisdiction of the priests. 'Unwitting' would merely be a convenient term for the principle of brushing aside the usual endless protestations against the oracular verdict.

SACRILEGE

It is impossible now to work out how divination would have been organized previously, and perhaps it was impossible for the Leviticus editor. If he was at work during the exile and after, the sacrifices that he was prescribing would have been suspended. He might not have suspected the connection of private sacrifices with divination. But he would surely have known the connection between the offence called 'a breach of faith' (Lev 5: 14 ff.) and the working of the priest's tribunal.

A 'breach of faith' would be a sin against God himself. Blasphemy would be a breach of faith, so would an act of sacrilege, like stealing the church plate, desecrating the altar, trespass on forbidden spaces. The tabernacle was to have been richly furnished, and it would have been tempting to go off with the candelabra or the golden vessels. Sacrilege has to be expiated by the offering of a ram. The ram of sacrilege is called a guilt offering, not a sin offering, and distinguishes the two kinds of offences, common sins of person against person as distinct from sins of mortal persons against God. The ewe for the common person's sins against other common persons is in contrast with the ram, for the sins of common persons against God.

If a crime of simple dishonesty is mixed up with swearing falsely the oath brings the lesser case into the grave class of sacrilege, misappropriation of sacred things, and so requires it to be dealt with more severely (Lev 6: 2–6). This has been interpreted as an illustration of how the judgement of the priests favours cultic over social and moral concerns.

The text of the law implies that the Priestly authors deemed the subject worthy of their consideration and required the bringing of a sacrifice, only because, in addition to the monetary damages, a false oath had been sworn. Had there been no oath sworn, the case would have been considered like that of any other sin committed by one man against his fellow man, and would have been of no concern to the priesthood, who were interested only in the ritual cultic sphere . . . the ritual experience is detached from the sphere of social morality.[31]

'Worthy of their consideration . . . only . . . because an oath had been sworn . . . interested only in the cultic sphere.' The mild sarcasm conforms with a long tradition of P-baiting.[32] The impression given is that the priestly writer of the first part of Leviticus did not spontaneously support ethical principles. P's idea of holiness did not entail righteousness; he would have been surprised when Isaiah spoke of holiness and righteousness in one breath (Isa 5: 16) .

Both Knohl and Milgrom suggest that Isaiah would have inspired the second Leviticus writer (not P, but H by now) to mend his ways and develop a revolutionary programme to right the abuses of the social order. Milgrom says, 'stung by their fellow Jerusalemite's rebuke' he adopted 'Isaiah's revelation that the Lord's holiness implies that Israel must be ethical'.[33] According to Knohl the priestly writer (P) was convinced that, 'God ordains Moses to institute a cultic system detached from social arrangements or justice; God does not intend to satisfy the needs of the individual or the congregation—neither their physical needs nor even their spiritual ones.'[34]

Several things have gone wrong with this complicated argument from silence. This criticism of the priests uses a modern, dilute idea of holiness in which the old power and terror have been replaced by a care for individual needs. Second, the idea of right order (discussed earlier in Chapter 2) has been replaced by a modern concept of individual ethics. Further, it does not allow for the division of labour

[31] Knohl 1995: 139–40.

[32] Knohl quotes Milgrom on the same biblical passage: '. . . all that matters to the priestly legislator is to enumerate those situations whereby the defrauding of man leads, by a false oath, to the "defrauding" of God' (Milgrom 1976: 89–108).

[33] Milgrom 1996: 74.   [34] Knohl 1995: 141.

that has allocated social administration and cult to Deuteronomy and Leviticus respectively. Lastly, it is naïve about how the worshipper's conscience is activated in religious practice. Some fundamental understanding has been missed of how the worshipper's conscience is manifest in religious practice.

Anthropologists try to frame their questions so as to bring what looks like a conflict between cult and conscience down to a lower key. Ultimately all conflicts about principle are conflicts between persons and probably between persons in rival institutions in which rights and duties have been differently constructed. A cult depends on the worshippers, so it normally expresses the conscience of the people. The worshippers decide what to believe and what not to believe. If they say they believe that God will come down on them with terrible punishments, it will certainly be because they want to dissuade their fellows from some specified deeds. If they allow it to be said that God does not really mind about a particular misdeed, it is because they have no particular interest in dissuading other people, kin or neighbours, from doing it. This or that view of God, whatever it may be, is acceptable to a given historical set of people, or acceptable at one time but not at another.

Everywhere God's image is battered about in the name of true religion. Sometimes God is more involved with moral issues as we recognize them, and sometimes less, because religions change their focus. People change the way they feel about some problem, say the crime wave and their ability to deal with it. If they feel very helpless, they may start to talk about God's anger, hoping thus to exert pressure on would-be criminals; if later they feel the crime wave has passed and everything is under control, they may use God for something else. Whatever else happens, God is going to be used.

Some of the shifts in uses of God may depend on shifts and gaps in the regular system of policing. For example, sometimes God comes out strongly against all kinds of homicide, and sometimes it is only fratricide that really angers him. To explain his changed concerns we should look to the concerns of the worshippers: they may have a well-oiled mechanism of self-help and blood-revenge which effectively punishes killing of outsiders, each clan mustering its avengers, clan by clan; in such a case self-interest may be sufficiently co-ordinated for justice not to need God as arbiter. But there may be gaps: a system which depends on brothers to do the punishing may be useless to restrain killing of brother by brother; then they will tend to invoke God's aversion to frat-ricide and look to his secret punishments to act as indirect and long-term deterrence for a crime they are powerless to sanction directly.[35] God is everywhere used to supplement gaps in the legal system; the Bible is no exception.

Another example. An ancestor cult may be efficient for controlling misdeeds by descendants of the dead, but power-less to punish inter-lineage fighting. If the people are worried enough about the inadequate kinship constraints, they can develop a doctrine of blood pollution[36] that punishes homi-cide wherever it happens. They will institute sins against the earth to complement sins against the ancestors, and priests of earth shrines will exact heavy fines from anyone who pollutes the land by shedding blood on it. The belief supplements a gap in policing. In Leviticus the idea that the land itself will vomit idolators illustrates the case in point (Lev 18: 27).

JURIDICAL USES OF THE OATH

Let us propose a new scenario for the use of the oath in chap-ter 5. The plaintiff, suspecting he is not being judged fairly, can ask the defendant to swear his innocence; the oath auto-matically turns a minor case between persons into a major case for priestly enquiry and priestly justice, which involves heavier sanctions. In declaring that anyone has committed a breach of faith if they have deceived or robbed or oppressed their neighbour, etc., and also sworn falsely, the Levitical text uses the oath to raise a civil crime to the level of sacrilege. It is a standard technique for appealing to a higher court. So far from being concerned exclusively with the cult it reflects a care to protect the system of justice, like our penalties for perjury.

[35] Schapera 1955.   [36] Goody 1962.

A similar practice in nineteenth-century Ashanti was used to check corruption and official malpractice.[37] The belief was that anyone taking in vain the name of an ancestor of the reigning Asantahene was in dire danger of death, or he should be executed forthwith, and until he had been punished the Asantahene himself was endangered by the anger of his own royal ancestor. Consequently a person who found he could get no justice by the normal means might be driven to this perilous course, swearing on the name of an ancestor of the king. Of course such a sacrilege had to be reported to the king at once, and he had to institute an urgent inquiry into the circumstances. If the swearer was proved to have right on his side, he would be vindicated, his injuries would have redress and his oppressor, not he, would face capital punishment. You might say that the only thing that mattered to the king was the honour of his ancestor, but that would be to miss what was going on.

In conclusion, the study of oracles reveals a misunderstanding about the ethical views of the Leviticus writer. A technical legal institution has been mistaken for a doctrinal position. The passages on sin and sacrilege from Leviticus 4: 1– 6: 8 definitely signify what we would call ethical concern. They attest to an effective priestly concern for the integrity of the legal system and for ways to protect the litigant oppressed by abuses of the law. Once the uses of divination are understood, the claim that two supposed writers of Leviticus, P and H, have different moral values has to be dismissed. It is even possible that the whole practice of divination had lost its importance in Israel so long before the editors went to work that they really did not know much about it. On the other hand, if the practice had been recently abolished and driven underground, it would be indiscreet to know too much. Either way, the chapters on sin offerings give an impression of having been patched over gaps in information.

Complex divinatory systems can map a body on a building and orientate both to the fixed stars and the paths of the planets. Divination hangs moral and political meanings on astro-

[37] Busia 1951.

nomical or medical conditions. If the Leviticus writer tried to put the various pieces together, he would have had to delve deeper into the philosophical background of his training, and perhaps even to compose quite freely on the basis of the three principles of the religion, the justice of God, the covenant, and blood as its sign.

(7)

Land Animals, Pure and Impure

> Behold, I establish my covenant with you and your
> descendants after you, and with every living creature
> that is with you, the birds, the cattle, and every beast of
> the earth with you, as many as came out of the ark. (Gen
> 9: 9–10)
>
> For thou lovest all things that exist, and hast loathing
> for none of the things which thou hast made, for thou
> wouldst not have made anything if thou hadst hated it.
> (Wisdom 11: 24)

God met his people on Mount Sinai and continues to meet
them in the tabernacle. In sacrifice the body of the sacrificial
animal becomes another microcosm in its own right, corresponding to the tabernacle and the holy mountain. Then the
sequence of cultic laws is interrupted by the narrative in
chapters 8–10. When the law-giving is resumed it develops a
different bodily microcosm. This time the body of the worshipper is made analogous to the sanctuary and the altar.
Whatever will render the altar impure will do the same for
the Israelite's body. The laws of impurity sketch out the parallel in meticulous detail over chapters 11–15. The animal is
taken into the body by eating corresponds to that which is
offered on the altar by fire; what is disallowed for the one
is disallowed for the other; what harms the one harms the
other. One thing that the book never says is that it is bad for
the health of the body to eat any of the forbidden animals.

LAND ANIMALS UNDER THE COVENANT

Chapter 11 is probably the best known in Leviticus because
it deals with the Mosaic dietary laws. It has been taken to

imply that the forbidden animal meats are abominable, detestable, or unedifying in one way or another. Taking account of the full context, which is the rest of the Pentateuch, it would be difficult to overlook one biblical principle: God is compassionate for all living things; not only to the humans, he is good to all his creatures (Psalm 145: 8–9). So if he himself does not detest them, why should he tell humans to detest any of his animals? This is a serious and central doctrinal problem.

Two kinds of covenant are the basis of chapter 11. First the covenant with Noah and his descendants in which God said he would never again punish the land and the living things on it for the evil things done by mankind, and made the rainbow its sign. It is emphatically also a covenant with the animals: 'This is the sign of the covenant which I make between me and you and every living creature that is with you, for all future generations' (Gen 9: 12) . . . 'I will remember my covenant which is between me and you and every living creature of all flesh . . .' (Gen 9: 15, repeated in vv. 16 and 17). A few verses earlier in the same chapter God has required a reckoning for the life-blood of humans. 'Only you shall not eat flesh with its life, that is, its blood. For your life-blood I will surely require a reckoning; of every beast I will require it and of man' (Gen 9: 4, 5). In Genesis God gave man dominion over animals. Robert Murray[1] has argued persuasively that dominion for Genesis always entails responsibility. Leviticus presents the further implications of human dominion over animals. A one-sided pledge from God cannot quite be called a covenant: the animals are not bound by any counter-obligations, unless by a stretch of the imagination the command to them at the creation to go forth and multiply counts as such.

Later, the covenant with Abraham is a promise of fertility to his descendants. It does not mention the animals, but extravagantly it says that his descendants will be as innumerable as the dust (Gen 13: 16). It echoes the blessing of Genesis to Noah and his sons, 'Be fruitful and multiply, and

---

[1] Murray 1992.

fill the earth' (Gen 9: 1), and 'Be fruitful and multiply, bring forth abundantly on the earth and multiply in it' (Gen 9: 7), the very words used for his blessing on the creatures of the water and the air after they had been created (Gen 1: 22). There is no doubt that this God is concerned with fertility, and that his promise is linked with their obedience.

The covenant with Moses on Sinai is the explicit assertion of God's overlordship over the people of Israel and their livestock. It specifically includes the servants and the cattle in the sabbath observance (Exod 20: 8). From householder to children, to servants, to cattle, the animals come under the lines of authority drawn by the Sinai covenant. Sabbath observance only affects the work animals, the ox that treads the husks off the grain, that draws the cart, that turns the waterwheel.[2] Exodus also makes the point strongly by requiring that the male first-born of the domestic animals be offered to the Lord just as the first-born of humans. 'Consecrate to me all the first-born; whatever is the first to open the womb among the people of Israel, both of man and of beast, is mine' (Exod 13: 2). 'You shall set apart to the Lord all that first opens the womb. All the firstlings of your cattle that are males shall be the Lord's' (Exod 13: 12). The rule for land animals which always sounds so complicated is quite simple when the covenant is seen to be its guiding principle. God is the feudal Lord. From this it follows that no one is allowed to harm God's people or use God's things, nor must his followers harm each other, or harm the other living beings on his territory without his express permission. This he gives for the killing of herd animals in sacrifice, and use of their carcasses.

The question of whether they do or do not come under the covenant is paramount. Leviticus divides land animals into two categories, first, the herds and flocks which share the lives of their owners, travel with them, and provide their sustenance, and second, all the rest. The pure animals come under the terms of the covenant of their masters, and their treatment is strictly regulated. The feudal relationship extends from God to his people and to their livestock.

---

[2] The ass that carries loads and persons is not mentioned here. A half-way category, it is given a half-way treatment when it comes to offering the first-born to the tabernacle: 'Every firstling of an ass you shall redeem with a lamb . . .' (Exod 13: 13).

The teaching about the sanctity of blood derives from this feudal relationship. God protects the people of Israel, his rites give them covering, sacrifice is the means he has given to them for expiation. Sacrifice protects them from the consequences of their own behaviour, even from his just anger. They are never, ever, allowed to eat blood, but he has given them the right to consecrate the lives of their herd animals, to use their blood to make atonement to him for their sins, and to eat the blood-free flesh for their own nourishment (Lev 17: 11). This solemn injunction teaches the sanctity of life (the life is in the blood). In religious terms, the mosaic dietary code is an invitation to Israel to join in the divine work of creation by living a life that honours the way God made the world and the covenants God has made with his people.

THE TWO TEXTS

The two texts in Leviticus and Deuteronomy start by running in close parallel. They give a perfectly logical classification which echoes the opening chapters 1–7 on sacrifice with a description of the domesticated ruminants of their herds, cattle, sheep, goats, which may be consecrated for offering on the altar. Then follows in both texts a careful set of rules to discriminate near-misses, candidates for entry into the class of domestic ruminants which fail because they show one but not both the required criteria.

Marching in step, the two texts say that the unclean animals are only 'unclean for you'. Because the dietary rules about land animals derive from the covenant, they only apply to the people of Israel. Deuteronomy seems to say by its prefatory remark that abominable things are the things forbidden as unclean in 14: 7–8. The equation of unclean with abominable in Deuteronomy is the source of the idea that the forbidden animals have some detestable characteristic, the focus of so much scholarly ingenuity. But in Leviticus the unclean animals are not abominable.

The microcosm is based on the body of anyone of the congregation of Israel about to take nourishment; the body is equivalent to the altar and so is his hospitable board round

Table 7.1.   Land animals, pure and impure, Deuteronomy 14: 3–9 and Leviticus 11: 2–8

Deuteronomy	Leviticus
3. You shall not eat any abominable thing. 4. These are the animals you may eat: the ox, the sheep, the goat, 5. the hart, the gazelle, the roebuck, the wild goat, the ibex, the antelope, and the mountain-sheep. 6. Every animal that parts the hoof and has the hoof cloven in two, and chews the cud, among the animals, you may eat. 7. Yet of those that chew the cud or have the foot cloven you shall not eat these: The camel, the hare and the rock badger, because they chew the cud but do not part the hoof, are unclean for you. 8. And the swine, because it parts the hoof but does not chew the cud, is unclean for you. Their flesh you shall not eat and their carcasses you shall not touch.	2. These are the living things which you may eat among all the beasts that are on the earth. 3. Whatever parts the hoof and is cloven-footed and chews the cud, among the animals, you may eat. 4. Nevertheless among those that chew the cud or part the hoof, you shall not eat these: The camel, because it chews the cud but does not part the hoof, is unclean to you. 5. And the rock badger, because it chews the cud but does not part the hoof, is unclean to you. 6. And the hare, because it chews the cud but does not part the hoof, is unclean to you. 7. And the swine, because it parts the hoof and is cloven-footed but does not chew the cud, is unclean to you. 8. Of their flesh you shall not eat and their carcasses you shall not touch.

which he gathers his family and friends. Way back in the time of the Leviticus writer the body was already the analogue of the altar. Not a secular analogue, for in a total religious system (such as that of Leviticus) the word secular does not have much meaning. The table, and all who eat at it, and everything that has been cooked for them to eat, are under the same law of holiness.[3] Body for altar, altar for body, the rules

[3] After the destruction of the temple when the Mishnah substituted the cleanness of the worshipper's body and food for that of the altar and sacrifice, they already had a strongly developed precedent in Leviticus, chapter 11. Neusner 1977.

which protect the purity of the tabernacle are paralleled by rules which protect the worshipper. What he can eat without contracting impurity and what can be offered to God in sacrifice are the same.

An interesting difference between the texts of Deuteronomy 14 and Leviticus 11 is that the Leviticus opening, with its reference to living beings on the earth (Lev 11: 2), recalls the account of the creation in Genesis, 'Let the earth bring forth living creatures according to their kinds: cattle and creeping things and beasts of the earth, according to their kinds' (Gen 1: 24). The opening verses of Leviticus 11 are only the beginning of a larger survey of land animals (the beasts of the earth) which is not featured in Deuteronomy.

Table 7.2.   Living beings on the earth

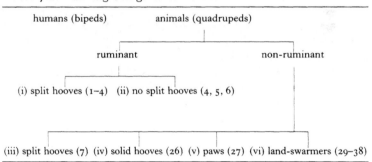

When Leviticus has listed the different types of land animals that are impure and must not be eaten, look round and see what is left—nothing! All these land animals are either clean or unclean, pure or impure. Now that verse 26 is taken to refer to animals with solid hoofs, we can use the following comprehensive typology of the land animals:

   (i) animals of the flocks and herds, ruminants, split hooves;
 (ii) ruminants without split hooves, e.g. camel, rock badger, hare;
(iii) non-ruminant with split hooves, pig;
(iv) solid hooves, e.g. asses, horses;
 (v) paws, e.g. lion, civet cat, dog, hyena;

(vi) list of eight land animals that go on their belly: the mole, the mouse, the great lizards, the gecko, the land crocodile, the lizard, the sand lizard, and the chameleon.

The zoological criteria are good enough to make an exhaustive list of land animals. By the end of the chapter everything living on the land has been included: going on hoofs, going on paws, gliding on the belly—what else is there? Everything has been accounted for.

Deuteronomy makes a point of allowing the killing and eating of wild counterparts of domestic herds (Deut 14: 5). Leviticus does not say anything about gazelle, roebuck, or antelope, but we saw above that it recognizes that there are wild animals which can be hunted and eaten (Lev 17: 13). But they cannot be offered in sacrifice. We scarcely need to repeat that it is no part of Deuteronomy's business to legislate for sacrifice.

The first set are under the covenant, and clean. All other land animals, excluding the first set, are unclean or impure, and their dead bodies not to be touched or eaten. Deuteronomy makes a point of allowing the killing and eating of wild counterparts of domestic herds (Deut 13: 5), of which Leviticus does not speak. Were Leviticus explicitly to permit secular slaughter, it would undermine the covenant basis of the Levitical rules constraining humans from eating animals that they have not reared. A similar silence covers what is to be done with blemished animals from their flocks and herds which are not allowed to be sacrificed. Presumably they are quietly eaten.

Many four-footed animals are not specifically mentioned in the catalogue; for instance, rodents such as squirrel, rabbit, rat, cat, do not need to be listed since they are covered by the rules for animals that go on their paws. Finally, not on the chart above, there are other land-dwellers indicated as 'swarming things that go on the belly, go on all fours, or with many feet' (Lev 11: 42), including land-dwelling insects, snakes, worms, spiders, centipedes. Leviticus calls these by a word that is translated as abominable, but Leviticus uses a different word from that used by Deuteronomy and also translated the same way. Leviticus also confuses the issues by applying a general defilement term for land-swarmers: the people must not 'defile' themselves by contact with their carcasses (Lev 11: 43–4). The sanction for infringing the rule is not severe. Though uncleanness is very contaminating, the sanction is just to wait till sundown (Lev 11: 31, 39). If someone has gone further than just touching an unclean corpse, the sanction is still mild, he must wash his clothes and remain unclean until evening; and anyone who carries its carcass shall wash his hands and remain unclean until evening (Lev 11: 40). We should not exaggerate the penalties or the severity of the rules.

The rule of uncleanness only affects contact with the dead carcass. In this respect contact with the carcasses of land animals are accorded a similar, though lesser, impurity as contact with human corpses. The people of Israel are enjoined to have towards their livestock some of the responsibilities of a feudal lord to his followers. Both humans and livestock are called to be separate and pure in the interior circle of a world of unclean nations or unclean animals. Milgrom says that the effect of the criteria for edible quadrupeds (Lev 11: 3) is to limit Israel to three domestic species: sheep, goats, and cattle.[4] But there is more to it than just not eating. Notice some of the tacit restrictions that follow from these rules. All land animals have been classified within the system. They can all be touched alive, but the only ones that can be touched after death are the classified ruminants. This means that only the latter can be killed for sacrifice. While they are alive camels and asses can be harnessed, loaded, ridden, dogs can be beaten, cats can be kicked, mice can be trapped, without incurring impurity, but once they are dead they convey uncleanness.

In effect the rule against touching a dead animal protects it in its lifetime. Since its carcass cannot be skinned or dismembered, most of the ways in which it could be exploited are ruled out, so it is not worth breeding, hunting, or trapping. These unclean animals are safe from the secular as also from the sacred kitchen. The rule is a comprehensive command to respect the dead body of every land animal. If

[4] Milgrom 1989.

anyone were to take it seriously it would be very restrictive. The verb to touch has also the idea of harming, damaging, laying hands upon as if to steal or strike. An example is in Genesis when Abimelech commands his followers not to harm Isaac: 'Whoever touches this man or his wife shall be put to death' (Gen 26: 11), and says to Isaac: 'We have not touched you and have done to you nothing but good' (Gen 26: 29). The rule of not touching the corpse makes the skins useless for fur coats or fur blankets, no leather waistcoats or bags, no shoe leather or wine-skins. Their bones and teeth cannot be carved for combs, buttons, containers, dice, jewellery, utensils. Their gut cannot be used for stringed instruments, or their stomachs or bladders for bags, or their sinews for sewing. In practice the penalty is so light that the rule would hardly prevent a taxidermist or tanner from pursuing his trade, so long as he purified his clothes and himself before approaching the tabernacle. Nonetheless it is still unequivocally forbidden to touch these creatures when dead. The tremendous domestic complications entailed by the high degree of contagiousness might deter the furrier, and it would be awkward for the wearer of a mink coat to have to keep washing, and no one else could so much as shake hands with the wearer without afterwards performing the same ablutions. To be classified unclean ought to be an advantage for the survival of the species.

INTERPRETATIONS OF UNCLEANNESS/IMPURITY

Though Moses admonished Aaron and his sons to distinguish between the holy and the common and between the clean and the unclean (Lev 10), he did not explain what is meant by unclean, or holy. The sages did not make much sense of it at all. Why pig is counted unclean in the Bible has been the subject of much speculation. Changing the word to 'impure' does not really help. Why ever should a non-ruminant with cloven hoofs be counted impure?

Some scholars favour the idea that pig has to do with cults of the dead in Egypt or Canaan, but this does not explain the uncleanness of the other three animals named with it. When the classification is so comprehensive it cannot be sound to take the animals as if they were separate items in a catalogue without headings or sub-headings. If some of the rules have the effect of banning predators, or blood, or carrion-eaters, it is not a comprehensive explanation. It is also too Hellenistic, too oriented to feelings, for this book. The same for the idea of Philo, the first-century CE Jewish philosopher,[5] that the forbidden species each signifies a vice or virtue. In a long, rambling homily he takes each forbidden animal separately and explains its prohibition in terms of symbols. His fanciful allegories are not rooted anywhere in the Bible text, only in the imagination of the philosopher, and so inevitably his moral preoccupations dominate the reading. He derives from Leviticus 11 a lesson to control gluttony, passions, and desire. The animals that go on the belly are forbidden so as to teach the people not to pay attention to their bellies. It is not a naturalist explanation, he does not consider the forbidden animals to be bad in themselves, rather the contrary:

All the animals of land, sea or air whose flesh is the finest and fat-test, thus titillating and exciting the malignant foe pleasure, he sternly forbade them to eat, knowing that they set a trap for the most slavish of the senses, the taste, and produce gluttony, an evil very dangerous both to soul and body.

Philo was not working from any tradition that was close to the writing of the text, for he does not draw on the rest of Leviticus or Deuteronomy to construct his sermons.

Some moralizing interpreters have regarded the laws as oblique commands that will restrain human 'omnivorousness and ferocity';[6] others again as arbitrary commands to test obedience.[7] Others give up on interpreting at all, treating the rules as inexplicable, though deriving from an ancient time when they presumably once made some kind of sense. Some treat the Levitical scheme as a relic of a pastoral way of life.[8] For this to be serious there would need to be a theory of why some relics remain strong when their supporting context has passed away, while others are forgotten. In default of such a theory it can still be argued that the Leviticus writer

[5] Philo 1939: 99–102.   [6] Kass 1994: 12.   [7] Maimonides 1881.
[8] Houston 1993.

could not betray all the pastoral tradition. His commitment to the idea of the ancient covenant would preserve rules about herd animals. However, the general disarray among rival interpretations testifies to the lost tradition. Not surprisingly the general public is ready to believe that there is something abhorrent about the creatures which the book tells them to abhor. To this day it is common to hear distinguished scholars explain ritual purity by natural reactions:

Many people wince at having to pick up a dead animal; most people (except two-year-olds) try to avoid touching defecation; corpses inspire a natural feeling of awe, and we hesitate to touch them; washing off semen and blood is almost natural, and certainly not hard to remember. Even gnat-impurity, which sounds picky, is not hard to understand. Who wants a fly in one's soup?[9]

Most of the discussion is based on the Deuteronomy formula, not on Leviticus. The first mistake in this quotation is to have used lines from Deuteronomy as if they came from Leviticus and as if they all meant the same thing. Deuteronomy says that winged insects are unclean, but not Leviticus. Humans are constantly under their attack, flies feast on babies' eyes, they breed their maggots in the larder, walk contemptuously over food, they suck blood and sting to frenzy. It is plausible that invasive insects and creepy-crawlies might be disliked universally. Another mistake is to use supposedly natural or 'almost natural' reactions to justify all the uncleanness rules. The nuisance value of insects makes this explanation plausible, but the rules are not mostly about insects. Why revile shy animals like hares and useful animals like camels by classifying them with the naturally dislikeable? The naturalist explanation must be wrong for a book so sophisticated as Leviticus, and for anthropologists it is always wrong to take natural as a universal category, forgetting that nature is culturally defined.

Again, the text itself specifically says that these are rules made for the people of Israel; what is designated as unclean for them is not unclean for the whole of humanity. Thus the rules of impurity are not a way of promoting a universal hygienic principle or pronouncing a general health warning.

---

[9] Sanders 1990: 145.

The only explanation will be in the rest of the rule system. Many civilizations have been built on camel meat, or pork, and though hyrax is hard to get, there is nothing bad for you in adding hyrax or hare to your diet; some people habitually eat blood, and the dietary value of suet fat can be underestimated. One popular explanation for the banning of the water-swarmers (which in Leviticus are not unclean) is that they are scavengers: pigs will eat carrion; shrimps and crabs feed upon dead fish; so dirty feeders are forbidden. This explanation is weak because a lot of animals would opportunistically consume carrion if they found it, and anyway the text says nothing about carrion-feeding animals.

The concept of dirtiness has contaminated the conceptual field; the idea of disgust at eating unclean things dominates interpretation. The kitchen, medical, and bathroom senses intrude. Leviticus certainly plays upon disgust at bodily exudations in its long disquisition on uncleanness of bleeding and leprosy in chapters 12–15. If impure was not originally a term of vilification it certainly has become one. Appeals to medical and aesthetic principles are not the way to interpret an enigmatic law in Leviticus: the only safe path is to trace the contrast sets and parallels the book itself develops. The impurity of an animal kind is part of the technical meaning of ritual purity.

In itself the idea of impurity is not difficult to translate. The word is well chosen from secular contexts where unclean, defiled, impure, dirty correspond to a situation which calls for an act of cancellation. But washing, polishing, burnishing, are too superficial to carry all the meanings of purification. In Christianity impure is used for the defilement of sin, with frequent reference to the parallel with a soiled garment, it is taught that the repentant soul requires a cleansing rite. But the listed uncleannesses of Leviticus are not sin in general, they are a separate set of sins, they depend on physical contact only, and the central principle is that the contaminated body has contagious power, which entails that all its future physical contacts convey contamination. The rules prescribe how the object spreading defilement must be washed, destroyed, or somehow stopped, according to the gravity of the defilement.

The word for impure, *tame*, is worked very heavily in Leviticus and used sparsely elsewhere in the Bible.[10] We may ask why it became such a favourite word for the priestly writer, but the first question is how it relates to holiness. Once again, the most illuminating passage to explain what it is about is the warning that God gave to Moses about the sanctity of Mount Sinai. In Exodus 19: 10–24 he tells Moses to make a fence round the mountain and to prevent the people from approaching the mountain, not even to touch the edge of it. He tells Moses to tell them to purify themselves, to wash their clothes and be ready for the day when he will appear to them, but to wait until they are summoned by trumpet: 'Go down and warn the people, lest they break through to the Lord to gaze, and many of them perish. And also let the priests who come near to the Lord consecrate themselves, lest the Lord break out upon them' (Exod 19: 21–2). The danger is two-edged: the people might break through or the Lord might break out, and in either case, people will die. This is the effect of holiness. The holy thing that is not correctly guarded and fenced will break out and kill, and the impure person not correctly prepared for contact with the holy will be killed. Furthermore, a person who has had the misfortune to 'contract' holiness, to use Milgrom's term, may inadvertently contaminate other unprotected things or persons, merely by contact.[11]

The nearest usage in European languages for the idea of contagion is in the discourse of honour, especially with reference to the virtue of women or the honour of a knight. The taint of dishonour gives a fair idea of impurity and violation. In Mediterranean cultures a woman's honour must be protected at all costs; if she is defiled her violator must be killed; if her father or brothers fail to cancel the offence they will be dishonoured too, and the whole family. It is not a metaphor, it is a concept about behaviour that has practical consequences: none of her sisters will be able to marry, no

---

[10] *tame*, impure, occurs 89 times in the Bible; 47 times in Leviticus; 8 times in Deuteronomy, and not at all in Exodus.

[11] Milgrom 1991: 443–56 argues that in Leviticus holy things do not transmit holiness to persons, but contact kills them, whereas Ezekiel following an older tradition taught that holy things could transmit holiness to persons as well as to objects.

respectable person will do business on equal terms with the menfolk, they will not be able to hold up their heads at a meeting, the contaminated family is ruined.[12]

Israel had a patronal society in which the patron–client relation is expressed by the client's respect for the honour of the patron. At meetings between lord and vassals the latter bring specified gifts of food to be ceremoniously shared. Leviticus says that the cereal offering must expressly be given with the 'salt of the covenant' (Lev 2: 13), which suggests that the terminology and values of covenant would have been current and easily interpretable for the people for whom the book was written. Defilement as a violation of holiness is a particularly apt expression for an attack on the honour of God perceived as a feudal lord. The word for holy has the sense of 'consecrated', 'pledged', 'betrothed', as 'sacrosanct' in modern English, something forbidden for others,[13] not to be encroached upon, diluted, or attacked. A key text for understanding impurity in Leviticus would be: 'For you are a people holy to the Lord your God; the Lord your God has chosen you to be a people for his own possession, out of all the peoples that are on the face of the earth' (Deut 7: 6). This is followed by a reference to the principle of requital on which the covenant rests (Deut 7: 9–10). A few verses later the same text goes on to say what being holy or reserved to the Lord entails in terms of behaviour. It corresponds to the requirements of chastity and fidelity in the discourse of honour and betrothal, which is similar to, or rather, modelled upon the discourse of alliance and covenant. 'You shall therefore be careful to do the commandment, and the statutes, and the ordinances, which I command you this day' (Deut 7: 11).

In addition to obedience the covenant with the overlord requires protecting his honour, or abstaining from insult. His power protects his people or his things and places, and to insult any of them is an insult to his honour. The parallel with the discourse of honour explains why sins cause uncleanness to adhere to the sanctuary and to the altar. Jacob Milgrom is curious to know why the altar should need atonement when the altar has not sinned. He develops a convincing theory of

[12] Campbell 1964.   [13] Tigay 1996: 86.

contagion from sin clustering on and around the holy places until it is washed off by the rite of atonement.[14] His analysis of contagious impurity is impeccable, but one can notice that the language of dirt and ablution is unnecessarily materialist. In the courts of chivalry a warrior would recognize that his armour is dishonoured if he himself is impeached: as well as his children, and father and mother, his helmet, his coat of arms, his house, all are tainted and made worthless by the contagious dishonour. Blood washes off the major taint, a noble gift cancels a minor fault. In the same way, bringing uncleanness into the Lord God's sanctuary makes it impure since the place shares in the insult to God.

Leviticus has first described the pure animals as ruminant hoof-cleavers, and then has gone on to exclude 'ruminants' which do not cleave the hoof and the one non-ruminant species which does (the pig). This order of listing gives the impression of excluded animals trying to get into the privileged enclosure so that they too could be consecrated and share in the Lord's cult. There would have been pressure from enterprising cooks seeking to alleviate the monotony of the menu. The sense of pressure to be included adds to the meaning of the animals excluded for having only one but not both defining features.

In the midrash the image of a reclining pig stretching out its cloven hoofs and saying: 'Look, I'm pure,' while concealing the fact that it does not chew the cud, is used to characterize the hypocrisy of the Roman empire, which posed as being dedicated to law and justice, while actually oppressing the peoples it ruled.[15]

Frivolously one can ask why pig or any other animal would seek to be accounted pure when the pure animals are destined for early death and the fire of the altar. On a secular view, having one but not both the criteria for purity would be a saving blessing, but the context is religious.

The meaning of purity depends on the sense of God's awful majesty, manifest in his creation. Exodus describes it in a narrative of volcanic explosion, thunder, fire. Deuteronomy describes it with words about God's power, and with verbal warnings of disaster. Leviticus conveys it by

---

[14] Milgrom 1983.   [15] Tigay 1996: 139.

double, triple, multiple microcosms. The people, with their children and their servants and their domestic animals too, benefit from his covenant. As vassals of God their unworthiness is immeasurable, but yet they are invited to eat at his table, and may eat the food that is offered to him. Sacrifice is a communal feast. Theoretically the people of Israel never eat meat except in God's company, in his house and with his blessing. They have been singled out for the honour of being consecrated to God, to be his people. The height and the depth of this honour is inexpressible. At another level it is a parallel honour for their flocks and herds, the cloven-hoofed ruminants, to be singled out of all animal kinds to be consecrated to God. This paradigm turns the covenant animals into vassals in relation to the people of Israel, as are the people of Israel the vassals of God.

SACRED CONTAGION

We still can ask what interest Leviticus could have had in elaborating the concept of holiness and impurity in these ways. The full answer must relate to the fact that belief in the maleficent power of demons has been demolished. The theodicy has to be changed: his friends will no longer be able to tell a sick man that he has been seized by a leprosy demon or a women that her child has died because a female demon took it. Suffering and sorrow still remain, and death. The priests are expected to explain, give comfort, and help. This is what the doctrine of purity does. If you fall sick, it could be that God has broken out on you because you unknowingly incurred holiness or impurity. This is a close parallel to the superseded idea that a demon might have caught you. A sacrifice will put it right, or a wash and waiting till evening, according to the gravity of the transgression. The word 'unclean' is particularly apt for relating the field of demonological medicine to the new regime, it affords a theory of pain and suffering free of demons and affords an alternative explanation for bodily afflictions.

So why should touching unclean animals provoke a dangerous breaking-out of this kind? The insult to God is to have come into his sacred place after profane and contagious contact with the corpse of one of his creatures. Taken together the food purity rules and the touch purity rules are part of a unified doctrine in which corpse pollution, bloodshed, and unsanctified death are classed as breaches of covenant.

It has been a puzzlement to Christian readers that Leviticus puts unclean contact into the same bracket as breaches of the moral code. However, there is nothing puzzling about both kinds of disobedience to the Lord's command being treated together. To touch an unclean thing and then to approach the tabernacle puts the person in need of atonement. Leviticus in chapter 5 begins the topic of uncleanness:

Or if anyone touches an unclean thing, whether the carcass of an unclean beast or a carcass of unclean cattle, or a carcass of unclean swarming things, and it is hidden from him, and he has become unclean, he shall become guilty (Lev 5: 2). When a man is guilty in any of these, he shall confess the sin he has committed and he shall bring his guilt offering to the Lord for the sin he has committed . . . and the priest shall make atonement for him for his sin. (Lev 5: 5–6)

And again in the summing up, chapter 7 emphasizes the contagions principle:

Flesh that touches any unclean thing shall not be eaten; it shall be burned with fire. All who are clean may eat flesh, but the person who eats of the flesh of the sacrifice of the Lord's peace offerings while an uncleanness is upon him, that person shall be cut off from his people. And if anyone touches an unclean thing, whether the uncleanness of man or an unclean beast or any unclean abomination, and then eats of the flesh of the sacrifice of the Lord's peace offerings, that person shall be cut off from his people. (Lev 7: 19–21)

This is very emphatic language, repetitive, classificatory, and redolent of mytho-poetic analogy. Such a statement from an archaic thought style cannot be decoded into modern terms. The interpreter must not read emotional quality into language which is primarily cast in a spatio-temporal mode. The contact has been forbidden, and the person who has become contagious shall not carry the contagion sacrilegiously to defile the holy place or to eat the flesh of the Lord's peace offerings; he will be punished. A domestic ruminant is the designated medium of atonement and the priest following the instructions for a sin offering in chapters 4 and 5 will make atonement for a sinner and he will be forgiven. He can live his ordinary life in this contagious state, but because of the contagion he and other persons he may contact will commit sacrilege if they take part in the cult of the tabernacle. He can expect to be criticized by his believing fellows and be made to take the blame for a community-wide disaster, and possibly expelled, like Jonah by the sailors.

Unclean is not a term of psychological horror and disgust, it is a technical term for the cult, as commentators have often pointed out. To import feelings into the translation falsifies, and creates more puzzles. The technique of delayed completion postpones the meanings until chapter 17. At that point Leviticus commands the people not to eat blood, not to eat an animal that has died an unconsecrated death, that is, an animal that has died of itself, or an animal torn by beasts, presumably with its blood still in it (Lev 17: 8–16; see also Deut 14: 21). The dietary laws thus support the law against unconsecrated killing. The Leviticus writer's reverential attitude to life, animal and human, explains the animal corpse pollution rules. 'Thou shalt not stand upon [profit from] another's blood' (Lev 19: 16). The case of the animal's blood and the case of the human's blood are parallel. Ritual impurity imposes God's order on his creation.

((8))

Other Living Beings

Thou makest darkness, and it is night, when all the
beasts of the forest creep forth.
. . . the earth is full of thy creatures. Yonder is the sea,
great and wide,
which teems with things innumerable, living things,
both small and great.
There go the ships, and Leviathan which thou did form
to sport in it.
These all look to thee, to give them their food in due season.

(Psalm 104: 20, 24–7)

Thinking on the lines of binary opposition, the Leviticus
writer finds the world divided into two kinds of humans,
those under the covenant, and the rest, and two kinds of land
animals, those under the covenant and the rest. But the rest
are not evil, the picture is not painted in black and white. It
was the work of the later commentators to read good and bad
into the divisions between pure and impure.

In the book of Leviticus only land animals (but most land
animals) are unclean or defiling. For covenant some territorial principle is necessary, or at least ownership. Creatures of
the air and water are not named as specifically unclean. A
separate set of rules forbid touching their dead carcasses,
backed by the word translated as 'abominable'. Taking this
difference seriously has produced a completely new reading.
Jacob Milgrom has argued from close perusal of the text
that impurity and abomination in Leviticus cannot be equivalent terms as they trigger different sequences of action.[1]

---

[1] Milgrom 1992. Milgrom says that these two concepts are different in Leviticus.
Since he does not consider the book to be one composition he can attribute divergences to the first author, P, or to the second author, H.

Uncleanness or impurity is a contagious condition of a person, place, or thing, incompatible with the service of the cult. After touching an unclean corpse the person has to wash and be unclean until evening. Contact with the corpse of a water-swarmer or air-swarmer is not unclean, it is an 'abomination'. No action at all is required.

This puts a very different complexion on all previous commentaries that have tried to combine Deuteronomy 14 and Leviticus 11. The former organizes the dietary rules under the uncleanness rubric, and the latter organizes them under two separate rubrics: uncleanness and unholiness.

Table 8.1.   In the waters

Deuteronomy 14: 9–10	*Leviticus 11: 9–23*
9. Of all that are in the waters you may eat these: Whatever has fins and scales you may eat. 10. And whatever does not have fins and scales you shall not eat, it is unclean for you.	9. These you may eat, of all that are in the waters. Everything in the waters that has fins and scales, whether in the seas or in the rivers, you may eat. 10. But anything in the seas or in the rivers that has not fins and scales, of the swarming creatures in the waters and of the living creatures that are in the waters, is an abomination to you. 11. They shall remain an abomination to you; of their flesh you shall not eat, and their carcasses you shall have in abomination. 12. Everything in the waters that has not fins and scales is an abomination to you.

The division of living beings between two dispensations is fraught with consequence for understanding the dietary laws and much else in Leviticus besides. In its much simpler code Deuteronomy only divides clean from unclean and counts all unclean things as 'abominable'. It uses a different Hebrew word from that used in Leviticus though both have been translated according to the Deuteronomy meaning. (Of this more below.) Table 8.1 shows that Deuteronomy uses the same criteria for forbidden water creatures as Leviticus, but says that they are unclean, whereas Leviticus only uses that word for land creatures. Leviticus holds the forbidden water beings in 'abomination', but says not a word about their being unclean. The same for the creatures of the air. Deuteronomy applies the word unclean to the airborne beings, as well as the word 'abominable', using the terms interchangeably. In Leviticus the terms are not interchangeable. Certain air creatures are translated as 'abominable', not unclean.

In Table 8.2, the colourful names of birds of prey, carnivorous, carrion-eating and fish-eating, are imagined transla-

Table 8.2. In the air

Deuteronomy 14: 11–20	*Leviticus 11: 13–19*
11. You shall eat all clean birds.	13. And these you shall have in abomination among the birds, they shall not be eaten, they are an abomination: the eagle, the vulture, the osprey,
12. But these are the ones which you shall not eat: the eagle, the vulture, the osprey,	
13. the buzzard, the kite, after their kinds;	14. the kite, the falcon according to its kind,
14. every raven after its kind;	15. every raven according to its kind,
15. the ostrich, the nighthawk, the sea gull, the hawk, after their kinds;	16. the ostrich, the night hawk, the sea gull, the hawk according to its kind,
16. the little owl and the great owl, the water hen,	17. the owl, the cormorant, the ibis,
17. and the pelican, the carrion vulture and the cormorant,	18. the water hen, the pelican, the carrion vulture,
18. the stork, the heron, after their kinds; the hoopoe and the bat.	19. the stork, the heron according to its kind, the hoopoe, and the bat.
19. And all winged insects are unclean for you; they shall not be eaten.	
20. All clean winged things you may eat.	

tions. No one knows for sure what they were, they cannot be identified ornithologically. The translations have been made up from careful examination of etymologies, and post-biblical usage has been guided by the assumption that they are winged predators and that their carcasses could be identified by beaks and claws designed to grasp and tear. Tigay says: 'Virtually all the forbidden winged creatures are birds of prey or scavengers.'[2] The implicit reasoning is moralistic, something like: 'These creatures are forbidden because they are cruel predators, or these animals eat blood and carrion, they are dirty scavengers, so they must be the ones we are taught to avoid.'

Here is support to the argument that Leviticus has been read through Deuteronomy and the interpretation made to conform to it when possible. The traditional interpretations of Leviticus' chapter 11 follow Deuteronomy in treating 'abomination' and 'uncleanness' as synonyms,[3] making no difference between the two terms: what is unclean is abominable and what is abominable is unclean. Leviticus does make a difference. As Milgrom says of the so-called dietary laws: 'They are part of P's complete, comprehensive and universal *Weltanschauung* whose roots are in creation and whose compass embraces all creatures.'[4] In Genesis God said on the fourth day of creation:

'Let the waters bring forth swarms of living creatures, and let birds fly above the earth across the firmament of the heavens.' So God created the great sea monsters and every living creature that moves, with which the waters swarm, according to their kinds, and every winged bird according to its kind. And God saw that it was good. And God blessed them, saying, 'Be fruitful and multiply and fill the waters in the seas, and let birds multiply on the earth.' (Gen 1: 20–3)

The Leviticus chapter 11 is woven from two distinct threads, impurity applied to the land animals, and abomination applied to swarming air and water creatures. In Leviticus 11 the land animals are not abominable and animals that 'swarm' are not unclean. This holds throughout the exposition. There are two apparent exceptions, both in perorations

---

[2] Tigay 1996: 139.   [3] Levine 1989: 65.   [4] Milgrom 1992.

Table 8.3. Living beings

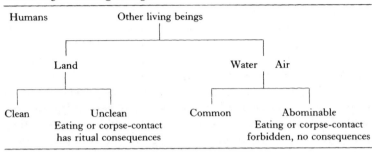

rounding off a long passage. In Leviticus 11: 43–5, unclean-ness and abomination are associated: with the command to abominate:

> You shall not make yourselves abominable with any swarming thing that swarms; and you shall not defile yourselves with them, lest you become unclean. For I am the Lord your God; consecrate yourselves, therefore and be holy, for I am holy. You shall not defile yourselves with any swarming thing that crawls upon the earth. For I am the Lord who brought you up out of the land of Egypt, to be your God; you shall therefore be holy, for I am holy. (Lev 11: 43–6)

Later, Leviticus 20: 25 refers to 'unclean birds'. Since the two exceptions both appear in perorations it would be legitimate to summon source criticism to defend the main principle: some later editor must have put in these items which go clear against the substance of the preceding chapters. Milgrom upholds the principle by having recourse to the theory of two writers, attributing the elision of the two separate elements to the holiness writer. This may be correct and only source criticism can tell. Certainly holiness is very much to the fore in these last verses. Another recourse is to parse the ideas of cleanness and holiness according to what they do in the text and not according to a speculative assumption about authorship. It is fully in accord with Leviticus' literary style to weave together two strands, one about the cult, one about life, and to bring them together at the end. It consistently teaches that both cult and life come under the rubric of holiness.

GOD'S CARE FOR HIS CREATION

The effect of reading Leviticus as if it was saying the same as Deuteronomy is to lose the context of Levitical purity rules. Thus it gives ammunition to criticism from other religions. For two millennia Christian children have been taught that their God is loving and merciful, unlike the God of Judaism. The God of Leviticus is supposed to be obsessed by impurity, impure bodies, sex, and food. The contrast made between Leviticus on the one hand, and Genesis, Exodus, the psalms, and wisdom writings on the other, seems to imply a different theological perspective, but that is implausible since the priestly writer is freely credited with being the final editor of the whole Pentateuch.

Why did God ever create the unclean animals? Was it not arbitrary and capricious to make creatures he did not like? Why did he declare harmless animals to be unclean or abominable and tell his people to abhor them? The likeliest answer is that feelings of detestation and abhorrence are not being invoked at all in Leviticus, the rule is not to hate but to avoid or shun, and the do-not-touch rule protects the listed creatures. It is the same feudal Lord who said: 'For every beast of the forest is mine, the cattle on a thousand hills. I know all the birds of the air, and all that moves in the field is mine' (Psalm 50: 10–11).

In telling the people that land-dwelling quadrupeds that are not brought into the covenant are unclean and that other animals are abhorrent or abominable, Leviticus is using the same classification as in Genesis, where God quite obviously took a benignly protective view of all his creatures. Go back to the story of Noah to see how the whole of animal creation is classified at a time before sacrifice was instituted. There we find expressed the divine concern for 'every living thing'. God instructed Noah to bring into the ark three classes:

of every living thing of all flesh . . . Of the birds according to their kinds, and of the animals according to their kinds, of every creeping thing of the ground according to its kind . . . (Gen 6: 19–20)

Of clean animals, and of animals that are not clean, and of birds, and of everything that creeps on the ground, two and two, male and female, went into the ark with Noah . . . (Gen 7: 8–9)

they and every beast according to its kind, and all the cattle according to their kinds, and every creeping thing that creeps on the earth
according to its kind, and every bird according to its kind, every
bird of every sort. They went into the ark with Noah, two and two
of all flesh in which there was the breath of life . . . (Gen 7: 14–16)

Water creatures did not have to be rescued from the water, of
course. The flood was a disaster for land and air animals and
creeping things.

And all flesh died that moved upon the earth, birds, cattle, beasts,
all swarming creatures that swarm upon the earth, and every man;
. . . He blotted out every living thing that was upon the face of the
ground, man and animals and creeping things and birds of the air
. . . (Gen 7: 21, 23)

Notice that the language and classifications of Genesis are the
same as those on which Leviticus 11 has laid out the dietary
laws. In each environment teeming swarmers complement a
range of more differentiated creatures: in the waters, fish
with fins and scales; in the air, birds with wings and two legs;
and on land the various four-legged animals, and finally the
whole series crowned by the ruminants with proper hooves,
the domestic flocks and herds set apart for consecration.

Putting the dietary laws of other religions into the same
context, gods often impose dietary rules upon their worshippers. The thing to notice is that if an animal is forbidden as
food, it is not because there is anything wrong with the
animal, anything abhorrent or disgusting about it. Rather
the other way, the animal often turns out to have featured in
the mythology as a strong or talented being which has rendered a service to the god, or in some prehistoric exchange a
human ancestor incurred a debt of great magnitude towards
the ancestor of an animal species. They formed a pact of ever-
lasting friendship and in consequence the human descendant
of the first beneficiary is forbidden to eat the animal descendants of an ancestor's benefactor, it would be an act of gross
ingratitude and impiety. Taboos often work like game laws
restricting the devastation of poachers.[5] Comparisons teach

---

[5] In Mesopotamia a term, *nig-nig*, corresponds closely to the idea of biblical
uncleanness in the sense of setting bounds to human action. Geller 1990: 109–10.

us to look for explanations somewhere other than in harmful or unattractive features of the animal itself.

Leviticus and Deuteronomy, whatever else divides them, agree on the fundamental meaning of the covenant to the people of Israel; it is a promise of fertility. According to Deuteronomy's view of the covenant God promises to multiply the people of Israel in return for their obedience.

And because you hearken to these ordinances, and keep and do them, the Lord your God will keep with you the covenant and the steadfast love which he swore to your fathers to keep; he will love you, bless you, and multiply you; he will also bless the fruit of your body and the fruit of your ground, your grain and your wine and your oil, the increase of your cattle and the young of your flock . . . there shall not be male or female barren among you, or among your cattle. (Deut 7: 12–14)

The promise of fertility demonstrates God's compassion, it is the reward of covenanted obedience and loyalty, 'that the Lord may turn from the fierceness of his anger, and show you mercy, and have compassion on you, and multiply you, as he swore to your fathers, if you obey the voice of the Lord your God, keeping all his commandments' (Deut 13: 17–18).

TRANSLATING SWARMING AS TEEMING

If the anthropology of the Do-not-eat rule is to influence the modern reading of Leviticus 11, another set of entrenched translations needs to be challenged. The word which is commonly translated as 'swarming' is closely associated in Hebrew with breeding, bringing forth, and fertility in general.[6] But in translations of Leviticus 11 its relation to fertility is ignored. The connection between breeding and swarming must have seemed to Maimonides difficult to interpret literally. He presented a far-fetched theory that the swarming creatures in Leviticus 11: 42 breed within seeds or fruits,[7] the label pointing not to their own fertility but to the fruitfulness of their breeding ground. Levine acknowledges a

---

[6] 'To bring forth moving creatures.' Jastrow 1950: 2, 1633.
[7] Cohen, P., 1985: 91.

connection with germinating when he says that it means 'to come to life, crawl, swarm'.[8] But the connection with fecundity, abundance, and proliferation in a good sense, which is so prominent for that word in Genesis, has been dropped in interpreting Leviticus.

Genesis clearly connects the word with fecundity. It is the verb for God's command to the waters to bring forth. The words from the same stem in translation are underlined in the next passage:

God said: 'Let the waters *bring forth swarms* of living creatures . . .' God created the great sea monsters and every living creature that moves, with which the waters *swarm*, according to their kinds, and every winged bird according to its kind. And God saw that it was good (Gen 1: 20–1)

After the flood, when he made his covenant with Noah, he said again:

Be fruitful and multiply, *bring forth abundantly* on the earth and multiply in it. (Gen 9: 7)

When this word is used in Genesis fecundity is positive, in the good sense of blessing, as in God's blessing to Abraham. Somehow in Leviticus the meaning of the word has been shifted to a negative sense. The Leviticus writer has a literary trick of using a closely matched pair of words in spiralled apposition. He writes about creatures which are 'brought forth' in 'swarms' as if they are assimilated to the living things that 'creep' on the earth. In Hebrew the meanings of the two terms, creeping and swarming, are distinct, but in English they have come together, very likely as a result of the great influence of the Bible on the English language. Yet, in Leviticus the class of the abominable contains not only swarming but also creeping. Both words will have to be closely examined, but first consider swarming.

Chouraqui's recent translation of Leviticus[9] gives the French for swarming as *foisonnant*, an extremely interesting term because of its ambiguous double value, as shown in the last item in this quotation from Harrap's *French–English Dictionary*:

[8] Levine 1989: 67.   [9] Chouraqui 1993.

Foison: Abundance, plenty, great numbers.
Foisonner: verb, to abound with: '*la lande foisonne de gibier*', 'the heath is alive, swarms, teems, with game'; of earth, lime, etc., to increase in volume, to swell, to expand.
Foisonnant:
1. abundant, plentiful, '*Partout des fleurs à foison*'.
2. festering and swollen, '*Masse foisonnante de cadavres*'.

In English 'teeming' would translate the aspect of fertility: to bring forth, produce, give birth to, bear (offspring), to be prolific, or fertile; to abound, teem, swarm (OED), but it hardly does much for the second, sinister, meaning of festering and rot. There is an English word that does exactly catch both the meaning of the Hebrew and the two meanings of the French *foison*: it is the verb 'to pullulate'. Though it is not obsolete it is so little used that it is only worth mentioning here to support indirectly the argument that follows. The OED gives:

Pullulate, intrans. verb: to sprout out, spring forth, spread, grow, increase,
(a) of a growing part, shoot, or bud,
(b) of a seed, to sprout, to germinate, to breed, to multiply,
(c) to put forth morbid growths.

It also means to teem, to swarm, to spring up abundantly: 'beggars pullulate in the place', or 'the mind pullulates with superstition'. A citation from OED 1621 has Levitical resonances: 'the swellings and diseases of the body whose root remaineth still within.' Another citation from 1891: 'those rampant, many-footed things that pullulate in damp and darkness under big flat stones.'

The contrary view, pursued here, is that in chapter 11 Leviticus uses 'swarm' in the positive sense, in line with the commands in Genesis to bring forth abundantly. There is another sense of excessive proliferation, a threatening encroachment on the land, which Nahum Sarna finds implied in Genesis 1: 25: 'the proliferation of animals, especially the wild variety, constitutes a menace. This idea is actually expressed in Exodus 23: 29 and Leviticus 26: 22.'[10] The latter reference is a curse conditional on breach of

[10] Sarna 1989: 11.

covenant, which explicitly presents animal fertility as inimical to human numbers : 'And I will let loose the wild beasts among you, which shall rob you of your children, and destroy your cattle, and make you few in number, so that your ways shall become desolate' (Lev 26: 22). So we have two connotations, one, positive, a respect rule, endorsing and extending God's command to humans and animals to be fruitful, the other contrasting animal fecundity with human barrenness. Typically, commentators on Leviticus 11 have tended to adopt the darker meaning. Maimonides interpreted Lev 11: 44 to refer to 'creeping things which breed in decayed or mouldering matter.'[11] The interpretations tend to elide the two words, as if swarming and creeping were synonymous. There is a traditional assumption that insects, which creep, constitute the prime swarmers of animal creation: 'This collective noun includes all small creatures that go about in shoals and swarms, insects that fly in clouds, such as gnats and flies generally (cf. Ethiopic, germinate), and small creatures such as weasels, mice and lizards that are low on the ground (cf. Aramaic, crawl)'.[12] But this assumption depends entirely on the dubious translation of 'to creep'.[13] The Genesis commentary says that 'creep' is: 'A general term for creatures whose bodies appear to move close to the ground. Here it seems to encompass reptiles, creeping insects and very small animals.'[14] This is true of land animals, but does not help with translating the term, as Leviticus applies it, for air- or water-swarmers. Creeping does not necessarily have a negative sense, though it often suggests furtive, hidden movement, and so can be used in a sinister context. As a translation it has lost the main idea of the Hebrew word, the idea of motion and life. The Hebrew dictionary says that either the ground or an animal can be the subject of the verb 'creep'. An animal may 'move lightly', 'move about', 'prowl' on land, or 'glide about' in the waters. And the ground itself can creep or teem, for example in the expression 'all with which the ground creeps (teems)'. These translations open it to apply to the signs of life as it does in Genesis, where it refers to any breathing thing. 'And to every beast of the earth,

[11] Cohen, P., 1985: 93.   [12] Snaith 1967: 5: 2.
[13] *remes* (noun), *ramas* (verb).   [14] Sarna 1989: 11.

and to every bird of the air, and to every thing that creeps on the earth, everything that has the breath of life' (Gen 1: 30). When 'moving' is taken to be the sign of life, the sensitive translator has used 'moved' or 'stirred' instead of 'crept' (Gen 7: 21–2).

The two words come so close together in modern English that 'teem' is found in the dictionaries both for swarming and for creeping. By referring to the generative principle that belongs to 'swarming' and to the life principle that belongs to 'moving', the word 'teem' bridges the two meanings. It would help the reinterpretation if instead of 'swarming' with all its distracting pejorative senses we could use 'teem', and for 'creeping', to come closer to the Hebrew, we could simply say 'moving'. Then the questions about why the carcasses of teeming, living things should be avoided can be posed afresh. Tracing the idea through the classifications of Leviticus, teeming is fulfilling God's command to multiply, it is fertility exemplified; the rule that teeming things cannot be presented on the altar derives from this fact. Leaven and honey, for example, partake of the qualities of teeming life, and this is enough, according to analogical reasoning, for them to be classified as antithetical to consecrated things. Remember that the holy of holies is traditionally a place of fertility. There can be protection for, but no covenant with, teeming things. If they cannot be offered to God, it is that they are his already: 'All that moves is mine' (Psalm 50: 11), which is: 'All that has life in it is mine.'

LEAVEN AND HONEY AS TEEMING LIFE

At the beginning of the book it was ruled: 'No cereal offering which you bring to the Lord shall be made with leaven; for you shall burn no leaven nor any honey as an offering by fire to the Lord. As an offering of first fruits you may bring them to the Lord, but they shall not be offered on the altar for a pleasing odour' (Lev 2: 11–12). Many unconvincing explanations have been tried for the one or the other. Some recall that the prohibition on leaven was made in Exodus when the people of Israel about to leave Egypt were commanded to eat

unleavened bread. Thereafter, avoiding leaven for sacrifice
would be a memorial rite. This explanation is selective, it
leaves the prohibition on honey dangling, since honey does
not figure in the Exodus story. We have to look for a pre-
existing principle to explain the command in Exodus.

There was an understanding in Late Antiquity that leaven
was a metaphor for corruption and evil. Milgrom says,
'Leaven itself comes from corruption and corrupts the dough
with which it is mixed, in general fermentation seems to be a
kind of putrefaction.' Although the instances of this view
come from much later Christian, rabbinic, and Hellenistic
sources, Milgrom applies it to the Leviticus case, excusing
the leap by saying: 'undoubtedly they reflect an older and
universal regard of leaven as the arch-symbol of fermentation, deterioration, and death'.[15] Against this argument
another commentator on Leviticus remarks drily that it is
implausible that corruption, souring, and spoiling should be
so strongly associated with leaven since many highly
esteemed foods were made with it.[16]

However, Milgrom is right, there is a sinister side to fermentation. European women until very recent times believed
in an antagonism between menstruation and certain food
processes. The menstruating woman could not expect to be
successful in making conserves such as jam or emulsions such
as mayonnaise. Old country women in France believed that
during menstruation they should take care not to approach
near to anything that might ferment, wine or pickled meats
for example, or the process would instantly be spoilt.[17] There
is evidence of an ancient belief that spontaneous fermentation is inauspicious. Herodotus gives an account of an occasion when after a sacrifice, 'jars full of meat and water, they
bubbled of themselves, without fire, and overflowed'. It was
taken to be a sign of disaster.[18]

As to honey, there is some argument about whether the
prohibition is just for honey of bees, or whether it bans date
and grape nectars, but that detail does not make any difference to the levels of disagreement. None of the proferred
explanations say why honey and leaven are named together,

[15] Milgrom 1991: 189.   [16] Levine 1989: 12.   [17] Verdier 1987.
[18] Herodotus 1: 59.

but a good explanation for leaven ought also to work for honey.

Notice that it is burning them on the altar that is specifically wrong.[19] When first-fruits offerings are described, there is no objection to leavened bread being offered, but if the cereal is to be burnt on the altar it consists simply of crushed grain with salt, oil, and spice (Lev 2: 14–16). The acceptable explanation must take account of both honey and leaven and should note that this rule opposes them to the covenant gifts, cereal, oil, spice, and salt.[20] So we can expect yeast to be in some way beyond covenant. The answer invokes the major division of the biblical world-view: on the one hand, natural generation, including sexual reproduction of humans, and on the other, divine generation by the covenant, symbolized by circumcision of the people of Israel. Honey and leaven work in the natural mode of generation, sacrifice works in the divine mode, and to teach the lesson they are kept apart.

Honey and leaven are partners in the bread-making process. This is why the same explanation does for both. Antique bakery did not depend on packets of processed yeast. Leaven was kept in the dough, and at each baking a portion was reserved to start off the next batch. The leaven in yesterday's dough would be kept somewhere cool so that it would be quiescent until needed. Then honey and warm water and some new flour would be added to activate it again.[21] It makes no difference if the sugar element is from date syrup or from bees' honey. Gradually the warmth and the sweetness reawaken the old dough and the lump starts to swell; when it has risen to a certain size the baker knocks it down and sets it to rise again, the second time increasing its size still more. It may be put to rise several times according to the fineness or lightness of the bread texture desired.

[19] 'It is clear that leaven and honey were not unsuitable for all offerings, only for those burned on the altar' (Levine 1989: 12).

[20] 'Sacrifices: . . . Salt: The purpose of salt would have been simply to prevent premature putrefaction of the covenantal fare. It is not improbable, however, that the real purpose—at least originally—was to avert demons, for the belief that salt, being an incorruptible substance, is immune to such corrosive influences and can impart this immunity to any who consume or hold it, is widespread in folklore . . .' (Gaster 1962: 157).

[21] Marx 1994.

Should he fail to cut it down, the activated dough will steadily go on rising until slow pustules push through and pimple the surface, eventually the tumid lump erupts, and the smooth ball of dough disintegrates. It is an exemplar of teeming life. Under its benign aspect it exemplifies the multiplying, sprouting, bringing forth, and increasing that was blessed in Genesis. The reason for forbidding honey is the same as for leaven. There is nothing bad about either. They combine to create fermentation, and by that action they are examples of teeming life which lies outside the covenant between God and his people. The prohibition is another example of the rule that only sacralized materials can be offered to be burnt on the altar, and teeming things are never to be consecrated.

TRANSLATING ABOMINATION

Leviticus is translated as saying that eating a teeming swarmer is an 'abomination' in the eyes of the Lord. 'Swarmer' means an abundantly fertile creature. No reason is given for the swarmer being abominable, and Leviticus does not use any of the vivid Hebrew pejoratives, or any pejoratives at all, for the animals banned in this chapter. We are therefore going to take 'abomination' here as a word from the same root as a more common word for 'abomination', but used idiosyncratically, in a form which does not have its detestable and idolatrous associations.[22] The word is very rare outside Leviticus.[23] It seems to have been specially chosen by the Leviticus writer, or even specially coined, to avoid the pejorative association. There is therefore a case for seeking to establish a new translation instead of 'abomination'. The dictionary gives 'detestable', or 'abhorrent', as of idolatrous practices. Here it would seem to be used in a 'tech-

---

[22] Leviticus evidently uses the form *sheqets* in preference to the heavily pejorative term, *shiqquts*. The noun *shiqquts* has a form which clearly associates it with nouns like *piggul* (Lev 7: 18) and *gillul*, (Lev 26: 30). Cf. Sawyer 1967: 42 n. 2.

Deuteronomy uses *toeba*, also translated as 'abomination'. *Sheqets* is never used in Deuteronomy. In the Pentateuch it is only found eleven times, of which nine are in Leviticus.

[23] Only Ezekiel 8: 10 and Isaiah 66: 17, both clearly exceptional.

nical' sense, as a specialized Levitical concept. 'Detest' and 'abhor' are emotional terms, warm and sticky, but laws (especially Levitical laws) are rendered in a cool, dry context of defined action in defined space. A legal injunction would need a more directive and precise term than 'abominate', less emotional than 'revulsion or 'detestable'. A more kinetic and spatial translation might be: 'You shall completely shun', or 'You shall utterly reject', rather than 'You shall abominate'. Doing honour to the archaic rhetorical style with this precautionary shift of vocabulary, the test line would then read, 'You shall absolutely shun everything that swarms, etc.'

This shift would resolve one of the initial problems of chapter 11: why God ever made abominable things. On this reading they are not abominable in the sense of the Deuteronomic word for abomination. If the Leviticus word wrongly translated as 'abominable', when stripped of its subjective quality means emphatically to avoid or shun, then God would simply be telling his people to avoid certain things, keep out of their way, not harm, still less eat, them. Deuteronomy uses the other word, also translated as abomination, to indicate that an action is wrong. For example: 'You shall not do so to the Lord your God; for every abominable thing which the Lord hates they have done for their gods' (Deut 12: 31). Likewise Leviticus 11: 43 points the same way when it condemns 'making yourself abominable with them'. The JPS translation suits the present argument even better: 'You shall not draw down abomination upon yourselves'. In other words, what is held to be abominable in that text is the doing. In English we can say that cannibalism is abominable or even that human flesh is abominable, and it does not mean that the victim is abominable or to be detested. Eating is the ultimate predation. The theological problem about God's arbitrariness would be resolved if what is abominable is the action of eating or mutilating the carcasses. The animals in question are a part of God's beautiful creation, saved from the flood by his express command, and it is forbidden to attack them. 'Anything in the seas or the rivers that has not fins and scales, of the swarming creatures in the waters and of the living creatures that are in the waters, is *an abomination* to you [to be shunned by you]' (Lev 11: 10).

And these you shall have *in abomination* [avoid] among the birds, they shall not be eaten, they are *an abomination* [to be shunned] . . . (Lev 11: 13–19)

All winged insects that go on all fours are *an abomination to you* [to be shunned by you] . . . (Lev 11: 20–3)

Every swarming thing that swarms upon the earth is *an abomination* [to be shunned]; it shall not be eaten. Whatever goes upon its belly, and whatever goes on all fours, or whatever has many feet, all the swarming things that swarm upon the earth, you shall not eat; for *they are an abomination* [to be shunned]. You shall not make yourselves *abominable* [to be shunned] with any swarming thing that swarms; and you shall not defile yourselves with them, lest you become unclean . . . (Lev 11: 41–3)

If this usage can be accepted it means that, though contact with these creatures is not against purity, harming them is against holiness. Surely it is not puzzling that these abounding creatures which proliferate freely, and glide lightly in the water or over the land should not be harmed? They are symbols of fruitfulness in animal creation. Eating the teeming creatures offends God's avowed concern for fertility. The ancient association of the temple with fertility supports the idea that harming the teeming creatures is wrong. The fertility principle is central enough and important enough to be balanced against the principle of cultic purity throughout chapter 11. Procreation and cult, the two principles of creation and covenant make a double-stranded twist through the chapter. This is the new theodicy which sapped the power of the Canaanite demons. Their evil programme of spreading disease and infertility is bypassed by the new version of religion.

Leviticus specifies that anything that lives in the waters and has not fins or scales must not be eaten: it is 'an abomination to you' (Lev 11: 10, and repeated in vv. 11 and 12). The law does not say there is anything inherently abominable about shrimps or eels or octopus, or even that they are universally to be abominated. They are just an 'abomination' to the people of Israel. Interpreting the law as a mark of respect for these creatures would mean that God protects swarming water animals from being preyed upon by his people. Scaly covering is a protective armour, fins guide locomotion, being without them is a disadvantage. Without scales the octopus or the eels are as vulnerable as the shoals of young fish. The graceful sea horses and timorous shrimps frisking in their scaly coats, spiky lobsters and crabs lurking in their plated armour, without fins are unable to escape. The Hebrew word used for fish scales in Leviticus 11: 9, 12 and in Deuteronomy 14: 9–10 is used for Goliath being clothed in a coat of mail (1 Sam 17: 5) and for Pharaoh in his armour, under the figure of a scaly crocodile (Ezek 29: 4).[24] Reading the text again, the prohibited water creatures, which include the monsters of the deep from Genesis' creation, are all swimmers, blessed to bring forth abundantly. In some species absence of fins and scales exposes the bare skin and assimilates the whole species into the class of foetus and young. Water-swarmers excite compassion as well as signify fertility, they are vulnerable. But more importantly, they teem, and as teeming creatures they cannot be sacrificed at God's altar, or eaten by the Israelite, whose body is a figure of that altar.

CREATURES THAT SWARM IN THE AIR

Leviticus does not introduce a new set of rules for air creatures. It is reasonable to expect that as well as insects there are forbidden bird species which qualify as swarmers. Birds that nest on the ground are extremely prolific compared with tree- or wall-nesters. The ground pullulates where they jostle with their unfledged young, and the sky darkens and reverberates as their dense swarms fly by. Some walk, but some creep.

Take the case of quail: the rabbis declared them clean: otherwise the Lord would not have provided them to the people of Israel to eat in the desert.[25] This would be good Deuteronomic reasoning. In Leviticus the concept of uncleanness applies only to land animals, so the issue for that book could not be whether quail are clean or unclean. The

---

[24] The Persian soldiers 'wore on their heads loose caps called tiaras, on their bodies sleeved tunics of blended colours, with iron plates, something like fish scales' (Herodotus 1987: 7.61).

[25] Levine 1989: 68.

question is settled by the thought that the Lord would not have sent 'abominable' birds to the desert travellers. Quails are tiny birds that seem to fly in vast flocks, but their narrow wings can only take their fat little bodies on short quick flights. The birds tend to get blown off course. They nest on the ground; prolific breeders, they lay from twelve to twenty eggs in a clutch. How's that for teeming? They run in a characteristic crouching posture, neck stretched forward and head low; in the long grass they do not seem to use their legs. How's that for gliding, moving lightly on the earth, creeping?

If quail count as teeming creatures of the air, this would explain God's wrath when the Israelites snatched them up to eat when the wind drove them over the desert. The Book of Numbers says:

And there went forth a wind from the Lord, and it brought quails from the sea, and let them fall beside the camp . . . And the people rose all that day, and all night, and all the next day, and gathered the quails . . . While the meat was yet between their teeth, before it was consumed, the anger of the Lord was kindled against the people, and the Lord smote the people with a very great plague. (Num 11: 31–3)

Why was he so angry? and so quickly? Gluttony is a favourite rabbinical explanation, but it seems possible that the arrival of meat from the sky in swarms of quails was a trap or a curse in response to their continual murmurings.[26] The anger in the words of God to Moses about the people having rejected the Lord and preferring to go back to Egypt (Num 11: 18–20) suggests they were being led into a test of obedience. They fell on the meat and ate it, without even asking to be dispensed from the law.

The Numbers text says nothing about quails being associated with teeming things. But the psalmist on the same incident describes the quantities of quails in terms that recall God's promise of multitudinous progeny to Abraham: 'He caused the east wind to blow in the heavens, and by his power he led out the south wind; he rained flesh upon them like dust, winged birds like the sand of the seas' (Psalm 78: 26–7). Like dust! Like sand! Remember how being innumerable,

---

[26] Milgrom 1990: 92.

like dust, like the sand of the seas, signified desirable fertility in the promise of God to Abraham.

If this is a fair interpretation of the Numbers passage it might help to confirm the antiquity of the dietary laws. The text did not have to have been written down. Numbers does not need to mention why God was angry because it was obvious. The psalmist saw the connection and only needed to half-spell it out. Swarms of quails showed all the signs of a well-known protected form of life; teeming birds were forbidden like teeming water-life—that should have been enough.

COMPETITION IN THE HOLINESS STAKES

These puzzles arise in part because the books of Moses give the impression of the people of Israel confronted by their God alone in a vast desert; no one else is there except hostile Canaanite armies whom God keeps at a distance. But a religion that bothers to put down its doctrines in writing is very likely to be in confrontation with other religions. There are always rival preachers seeking to attract the faithful to other shrines. A competition in holiness would be the context we should expect, and that unleashes a competition in doctrinal comprehensiveness. How animals are regarded in the religion would become one of the selling-points, as it were, a test of the goodness of its doctrines.

In the sixth and fifth centuries BCE, when the priestly books are supposed to have been edited, the whole world as it was known to those who lived between the Mediterranean and the Aegean and on through Asia Minor to the Himalayas, was engaged in theological controversy about the right to take animal life. Holiness was a competitive business, and kindness to animals one of the obvious gambits. In addition to protecting human life, most religions forbid other killings. Hinduism protects cows, Buddhism goes better and protects all animals; if animals are to be ranged according to their vulnerability, insects score highest. Oriental ascetic movements which make a point of not killing could make respect for insect life the test case. 'You are forbidden to kill cows. *We* are forbidden to kill insects!' could be an effective ploy in competitive claims to spiritual worth.

Leviticus does not forbid killing them, but it does forbid eating. Individually, insects are the easiest living beings to kill, the most provocative and likely to be attacked, with power to annoy but not to protect themselves. The spies sent by Moses to scout out the promised land returned saying it was peopled with giants compared with whom they seemed to themselves as grasshoppers (Num 13: 33). Being likened to insects struck fear into the hearts of the people of Israel.

Jainism is supposed to have been founded in the sixth century BCE and, along with Buddhism, claims to have links with more ancient pre-Vedic movements. This is the religion which requires its followers to look carefully where they walk, to sweep the path in front of them and to examine the place where they are going to sit, lest they carelessly crush a living insect. 'A monk should remain undisturbed even if bitten by insects. He should not scare them away nor keep them off. He should not kill living beings.'[27] After inspecting his cloth, the Jain monk should fold it, and remove any living organisms that are there with his hand:

one who is careful in his inspection protects the six kinds of living beings, e.g. the earth bodies, the water bodies, the fire bodies, the wind bodies, plants and animals;[28]

if crawling animals feed on his flesh and blood, he should neither kill them nor rub the wounds; even if these animals destroy the body, he should not stir from his position.[29]

Herodotus mentions some Indians situated very far to the south of the Persians, perhaps a religious community: 'There are other Indians again, and another style of life. These will not kill any living thing, nor do they sow anything or possess houses; and what they eat is herbs.'[30] There is no reason to suppose the earliest written accounts of extreme ascetic movements coincided with their origin. Asceticism would go back as far as the beginning of religion. We should not conclude that this ascetic community only started in the year that Herodotus reported it, or that it was unique. Such move-

---

[27] Jain 1974: 133.   [28] Ibid.: 140.   [29] Ibid.: 151.
[30] Herodotus 1987: 3.100.

ments could have been as ancient as Israel. Nor can we assume that the priestly editors did not know the old oriental controversies about the sanctity of animal life. After all, there had been millennia of water-borne and land traffic over the region. They were not recluses; they had been to Egypt, they had been to Babylon. They would have been familiar with the Egyptian reverence for animals described by Herodotus. They would have known that the Egyptian priests scrupled to kill any living thing save the animals they sacrifice,[31] they would have met or heard of various minority religious groups. There is no way, to make a historical case against this argument while the dating of Leviticus remains so insecure. They might have had news of the dietetic precepts of Empedocles (490–430) in Sicily, and of his philosophy of the unity of all living things and the transmigration of souls. Empedocles would not have been the first to teach the iniquity of killing animals. At Kandahar in India an inscription records the precepts of the good king Asoka, who decreed that piety required abstention from the flesh of living beings. The fact that the inscription was third century BCE and in Aramaic and Greek makes the point.[32] Alfred Marx daringly interprets the central place given by Leviticus to cereal offerings as a sign of a utopian vegetarian philosophy, a reconciling reference to the vegetable offering of Cain in Genesis 4: 3, or at least as a symptom of conflicting ideologies presented in the same book.[33]

Some parts of Leviticus could well have been composed as a manifesto *against* seductive foreign religions. There would have been some competition in the purity stakes where devotees of dozens, or hundreds, of sects were scoring against each other as is their wont with more and more austere paths of renunciation. Every one of the religions would be involved in proving themselves the holiest; showing respect for life, like asceticism, was and still is taken as a prime sign of spirituality. It is unlikely that in this ferment of religious argument Israel could have stood completely apart and that none

---

[31] Ibid.: 1.140.   [32] Pouilloux 1960: 165, inscription 53.
[33] Marx, Alfred, *Les Offrandes*, chapter V, A 'Un conflit d'idéologies' (1994), 134–49.

of what her learned men heard from Babylon or Egypt or India influenced their writing.

Here they were, priestly exponents of a monotheistic religion committed to animal sacrifice, making claims to holiness which had to be stronger than other such claims from other religions. What were the priests to do in such a scenario? Were they to join the extremists, go the whole way and denounce killing animals? No, it would have been unthinkable to deny their ancient traditions. How could they honour their historical identity if they stopped consecrating their herds, if they stopped celebrating Mount Sinai in the zoning of the sacrificial carcass, and stopped using blood for anointing the priests, for cleansing from sickness and for forgiveness?

When the dietary laws of Leviticus are re-examined in this perspective the improved translations help to see that chapter 11 was much simpler than had been supposed: an overall survey of land animals classed all except the flocks and herds of the people as unclean, not to be eaten or offered for sacrifice . . . that is all. And the animals classified as unclean turn out to be not abominable at all. Leviticus is analogical thinking, highly classified, intellectually subtle, theologically all-encompassing. Deuteronomy is rational thinking, emotional, politically sophisticated, theologically superficial. It is essential to see the two books separately, each with its own burden to deliver, each in its own way.

Leviticus makes sense of animal creation when it is read as a sermon on God's pattern of the universe. In this reading covenant and fertility are two contrasted principles. Covenant gives the paradigm of the laws at Sinai and the tabernacle, hedged by purity rules expressing God's overlordship and his justice. His kindness toward teeming things belongs to the other dispensation that has to do with chapter 1 of Genesis, his blessing on abundant fruitfulness. The protective laws that tell humans to avoid teeming creatures demonstrate God's compassion. The balance between the divine attributes, justice and mercy, gives a more intelligible reading than does the idea of God's horror of impurity. It is more in harmony with the style of Leviticus, and more in keeping with the rest of the Pentateuch.

,

CONCLUSION

The chapter is buckled into a ring with a great peroration taking us back to the beginning, not just to the beginning of the chapter, or just to the beginning of the book, but beyond Exodus, back to the beginning of Genesis. Compare the two quotations:

God made the beasts of the earth according to their kinds and the cattle according to their kinds, and everything that creeps upon the ground according to its kind. And God saw that it was good. (Gen 1: 25)

and:

This is the law pertaining to beast and bird and every living creature that moves through the waters and every creature that swarms upon the earth, to make a distinction between the unclean and the clean and between the living creature that may be eaten and the living creature that may not be eaten. (Lev 11: 46–7)

The chapter has been closely studied for two millennia, but the double strand, so obvious once it has been pointed out, has been disregarded. Astonishingly, this polished piece of antique prose is still intact enough for us to admire its patient argument by classification, the elegant helical twist, covenanted justice balanced by divine compassion, and their smooth merging in the triumphant return of the chapter to its own opening phrase, echoing Genesis.

(9)

Atonement for Sick Bodies

> Who shut in the sea with doors, when it burst forth from
> the womb; when I made clouds its garment, and thick
> darkness its swaddling band, and prescribed bounds for
> it, and set bars and doors, and said: 'Thus far shall you
> come, and no farther, and here shall your proud waves
> be stayed'? (Job 38: 8–11)

The first chapters of Leviticus have introduced a microcosm
at three levels, with the tabernacle and Mount Sinai transposed on to the dismembered trunk of the sacrificial animal.
The worshipper's body has already been paralleled to the
altar by shared restrictions on animal foods and animal sacrifice. Now another microcosm of the sanctuary in danger of
defilement is to be built from the human body prone to sickness.

Chapter 11 of Leviticus went into the topic of impurity of
animal species in depth and introduced the concept of teeming life. The next four chapters take off from the theme of
reproduction to form a distinct literary unit. Chapter 12 is
about blood impurity of a woman menstruating or giving
birth, then two chapters on leprosy, 13 and 14, are followed
by chapter 15 on genital discharges from men or women, all
sources of impurity. The peroration at chapter 15: 33 closes
a ring by referring back to the opening of chapter 12, impurity of menstruation. With this reading the whole section
becomes a formal a–b–b–a pattern.

> a Reproduction, a woman, birth of children of both sexes, ch. 12
>   b Leprosy, diagnosis, ch. 13
>   b' Leprosy, cleansing, ch. 14
> a' Reproduction, genital discharges of adults of both sexes,
> ch. 15

It is a mistake to ignore the connections between these chapters. The first and last, on discharge of blood (chapter 12) and discharge of sexual fluids (chapter 15), are directly about the reproductive process. God's compassion has been demonstrated in the preceding chapter (11) by the rules declaring it 'abominable' to harm corpses of the teeming, fertile creatures of water and air. The next set of rules returns to impurity, hence they are about the tabernacle. The writer has returned to the theses of chapter 11 on the dangers of impurity in the approach to the tabernacle, the danger that holiness will break forth and destroy, or that impurity will break in and contaminate.

In Leviticus' favourite literary form, chiastic composition, the meaning is at the pivot or the middle of a series of parallel verses. On either side of the sections on leprosy there stand supporting verses on human reproduction like steps or like framing pillars. Within the series on a leprous person, two additional afflicted objects are introduced, a leprous garment, and a leprous house. The alternation makes an a–b–a–b pattern as follows:

a   Leprosy of a person, diagnosis, 13: 1–46
  b Leprosy of a garment, diagnosis, 13: 47–59
a′ Leprosy of a person, declaring clean and atonement, 14: 1–32
  b′ Leprosy of a house, diagnosis and cleansing, atonement,
  14: 47–53

When body, garment, and house are found in a carefully constructed set of rules, we have been warned. It signals a return to the body/temple microcosm. The reading is also returned to the early conceit of the 'house-that-Jack-built', the concentric pattern of one thing placed upon another and another. Neither the stricken garment nor the stricken house is a trivial member of the series. The body, the garment, and the house are given the same diagnostic treatment and the cleansed house gets atonement as does the body. They have not cropped up by accident, and they cannot be ignored without losing the sense of the whole passage.

Of leprosy, more below; first, to study the supporting framework, the loss of genital fluids, blood and semen. Recall the antithesis so important in Leviticus between natural and cultural reproduction. Obviously loss of these fluids is hostile to natural reproduction. A woman does not menstruate when she is pregnant, so menstrual blood and haemorrhage signify absence of pregnancy. In symbolic structures female blood loss is frequently counterpoised to symbols of fertility.[1] Similarly on the male side, in the Bible culture the loss of semen is antithetical to conception (Gen 38: 8–10). In this section (Lev 12–15) the loss of these vital fluids provides a discourse on reproduction which is interrupted by the long section on leprosy. At first glance it is difficult to see what leprosy has to do with reproduction. But when Leviticus frames one case of impurity within another, the system of extended exemplification makes the meaning transparent.

LOSS OF VITAL FLUIDS

It does not follow from the laws of corpse pollution that any contact with blood entails impurity. The solemn law is that blood must never be eaten, and dead bodies must never be touched, both actions convey impurity. However, blood flowing from a live body, such as a bleeding nose or a scratched knee, is not impure—so long as no one is proposing to eat it and so long as there is no contact with a dead body. So why should the blood of childbirth and the blood of menstruation be impure? Some analogical reasoning is evidently at work and we know already that Leviticus' mode of explaining is to cite exemplars.

The Leviticus writer has a bad name as a formalist, intent on minute observance of ritual, also as excessively preoccupied with sex and disease. Here it may be remarked that religions which ritualize sex are usually more in favour of it than against. To suppose that the numerous sexual regulations of Leviticus exhibit a narrowly puritanical attitude to sex would be like expecting a culture with numerous food rules to condemn good food. It is where sex is recognized as a potent elemental force, at once the source of desire, fulfilment, and danger, that religion seeks to appropriate sex and to bind it

[1] Turner, V. W., 1967.

with rules. Compared with other religious teachers the Leviticus writer is not unusually high-minded, obsessed with cleanliness or sex-denying. Toilet practices, discharge of fluids, and physical impurities do not interest him as such. True to God's compassionate concern with fertility his strong interest is in reproduction. He has used a strict principle of selection to focus exclusively on three topics: on a woman's discharge of blood, menstruating or post-parturient; on leprosy; and on male and female genital discharges. These are the only medical topics in the book.

Some religions legislate for private bodily functions, but what counts as private depends on the culture. Herodotus was impressed that the Egyptians of the fifth century BCE defecated and urinated in private, in their houses, apparently a marked contrast with the Greeks.[2] Deuteronomy teaches that defecation in the war camp is against holiness (Deut 23: 12–14) and that every soldier should go outside the camp, carrying a stick (in addition to his weapon) to bury his excrement. And Deuteronomy actually gives a reason: 'because the Lord your God walks in the midst of your camp'. Here is another difference between the two books. Leviticus does not suppose that God is at all annoyed by the sight of his creatures' defecation. Leviticus' ideas of ritual impurity have no connection with the regular inflows and outflows of the functioning body. Nor does the idea that God would be offended by the sight of human excreta connect with anything else anywhere in the Pentateuch.[3] It does seem to be a surprising concern of the writer of Deuteronomy, the transcendental theologian and promoter of the 'Name theology', who is supposed to have a less material conception of God's presence. However, Deuteronomy is not quite on its own in this for the theme is also explicit in the religion of the Essenes.[4] A. Baumgarten comments on the contrast between the primitive sanitary arrangements of the Essenes, the ditch in a field, and the arrangements of the temple priests, who at least in the

[2] Herodotus 1987: 2.35; quoted in Baumgarten 1996: n. 32.

[3] Baumgarten, A. I., 1996 notes Ezekiel 4: 12–15, and Prov 30: 12, as objections to making use of human faeces, and notes also that though Deuteronomy 23: 12–14 has a rule to protect God walking in the camp from sight of human faeces, no sanctions are mentioned.

[4] Baumgarten, A. I., 1996.

time of the Mishnah provided a private latrine chamber[5] in the surrounding temple precincts. According to Josephus on the Essenes:

[On the Sabbath] they do not even go to stool. On other days they dig a trench a foot deep with a mattock—such is the nature of the hatchet which they present to the neophytes—and wrapping their mantle about them, that they may not offend the eyes of the deity, sit above it. They then replace the excavated soil in the trench. For this purpose they select the more retired spots. And though this discharge of the excrements is a natural function, they make it a rule to wash themselves after it, as if defiled.[6]

The purity rules of the Essenes may have been derived from the Bible, but Sara Japhet's study of Leviticus, Deuteronomy, and other biblical sources shows considerable differences between their practices.[7]

In short, there is nothing unusually far-reaching, intimate, or strict about the Levitical rules for ritual purity, rather the contrary. What is unusual is that these topics should be selected and presented in such a highly systematic form. But that is the style of a writer preoccupied with building microcosms of the world.

The beginning of chapter 12 links up with the end of chapter 11 and the idea of teeming fecundity by saying: 'If a woman conceives, and bears a male child, then she shall be unclean seven days; as at the time of her menstruation, she shall be unclean' (Lev 12: 2). The verb which is translated as 'conceives' is the same as for seeding and bringing forth young in Genesis 1: 11–12. Chouraki's French translation appropriately succeeds in associating pregnancy with seed in one word: '*une femme qui est ensemencée*.'[8] A more literal English translation would be: 'If a woman has been inseminated and brings forth a male child, then she shall be unclean.'[9]

As with uncleanness of animal carcasses, the uncleanness of the inseminated woman is strictly ritual, it only affects

---

[5] Baumgarten, A. I., 12, citing Mishnah, Yoma 3.2.

[6] Josephus 147–9. This and the unusually far-reaching prescription of their toilet practices does not necessarily suggest prudery so much as that the Essene members were concerned to monitor each other's behaviour.

[7] Japhet 1993: 69–87.   [8] Chouraqui 1993: 141.

[9] Levine 1989: 73 (following LXX and emending the text).

contact with the tabernacle. After her delivery she is technically impure for a fixed period, after which she must make atonement, but apart from this there is nothing unpropitious in her condition, and nothing shaming or undignified in the requirement of atonement. Like the case of the impure animals, impurity is a matter of territorial definition, a question of separating holy precincts and objects from profane activities. The new mother's separation does not mean that there is anything wrong in itself with blood-loss. The book does not give a reason for placing her in a liminal status, it simply ordains that for a set period after the birth of a child she is impure, which means that she cannot touch a hallowed thing or come into the sanctuary.

Ritual disablement is not a hardship; indeed, she needs the privilege of rest. A male child must be taken away to be circumcised after eight days, but the period of her seclusion goes on until full forty days are accomplished. For the birth of a girl Leviticus doubles the period so that her mother gets eighty days' seclusion.[10] The boy child by his circumcision becomes party to the covenant with Abraham in a way a girl child can never be. Interestingly, he does not contract impurity by contact when returned to his mother for nursing. The rite of circumcision almost certainly would have prophylactic powers for mother and child. This may be one reason for the doubling of the time of the mother's impurity after birth of a girl. We should not discount protective powers attributed to the rite. Before modern medicine made childbirth less risky the woman had a high probability of not surviving, or of losing her child, and would have been in danger of her life for some time following delivery. Circumcised male child and mother would be safer afterwards and allowed to venture abroad sooner, whereas the mother of the female child has to lie low and avoid danger for a much longer period. Safer from what? From demons? No, not now. The people may be still afraid of demons, still liable unofficially to attribute their harms to them, but in this religion no seeking out of causes,

---

[10] Magonet 1996. Magonet's research and speculation about why the birth of a girl child may involve double seclusion is based on the central idea that what is impure is menstrual blood, and that a girl child may exceptionally be born menstruating, hence double pollution.

still less propitiation of demons, is allowed. Whatever the dangers that menace new male babies, the rite gives them some protection. Leviticus cannot say that outright because of the eschewed magicality, but the religion which it super-seded would not have minced words and the congregation would have been in the habit of expecting health from rituals. Is it fanciful to suggest that the vulnerable person who is declared impure is under the same kind of ban that protects impure animals from human predation, but that this time the predators who are warned off are the unmentionable demons?

When the stipulated time of her impurity is ended, the woman needs to bring a lamb for a burnt offering, and a bird for a sin offering, so that the priest can make atonement for her (Lev 12: 8) but there is no suggestion that she has com-mitted a sin. The law suggests a different gloss on these sac-rifices. Like circumcision it is likely that the rite of expiation or atonement also has a prophylactic effect, protecting the vulnerable mother and child, or in the case of a leper, ward-ing off the recurrence of illness. Needing atonement is the main theme which links human reproduction with leprosy. The leper must make a guilt offering (Lev 14: 18, 21) and a sin offering (Lev 14: 22, 30–1) for expiation. The discourse on leprosy has many things in common with that on the inseminated woman. One, in a minor key, is the association with fertility by birthing and teeming, burgeoning, swelling, and reproducing; others are the concept of impurity and the recuperative and prophylectic powers of the rite of atone-ment.

LEPROSY

These chapters 13 and 14 are usually taken as medical. Fair enough, they deal with disease, and the form of the writing is modelled on Mesopotamian diagnostic treatises.[11] Problems with the Hebrew word translated as leprosy are well known.

---

[11] '21: Si, couvert de boutons blancs, son corps est noir . . . il en a était atteint alors qu'il était au lit avec une femme . . .

22: Si couvert de boutons rouges, son corps est noir, il (en) a été . . .' (Labat 1951: 71).

In the following pages the word leprosy will be retained because it is the traditional translation, but it should be clear that it does not refer to modern medical definitions of leprosy. Used here it refers to the group of diseases (whatever they may have been) intended by the Leviticus writer. Milgrom and Levine use the term 'scale disease' instead of the word leprosy,[12] which they regard, with reason, as medically misleading. A form of leprosy goes through a phase of drying and flaking of the skin, leaving the body covered in white scales. The Bible word translated as leprosy in Kings and Numbers is associated with characteristic whiteness: when Elisha's servant was turned into a leper: 'He went out from his presence, white as snow' (2 Kings 5: 27); when Miriam was struck with leprosy: 'there was Miriam, stricken with snow-white scales' (JPT translation, Num 12: 10). These two cases sound as if turning white is an early symptom of leprosy. But this does not correspond well with the symptomatology of Leviticus 13, where white skin is identified as the end of the infection, the sign of a cure, contrasted with raw red skin, the sign of being stricken :

If the leprosy breaks out in the skin, so that the leprosy covers all the skin of the diseased person from head to foot, so far as the priest can see, then the priest shall make an examination, and if the leprosy has covered all his body, he shall pronounce him clean of the disease; it has all turned white and he is clean. (Lev 13: 12–13; and also 13: 16 and 17; and 13: 38–9).

According to Leviticus the whiteness indicates remission, the eruptions have stopped and the skin is white.[13]

Leviticus' description of the symptoms gives an idea not of one, but of various skin diseases grouped together in various stages. Along with what modern medicine calls leprosy other disorders seem to be indicated by the diagnosis, perhaps skin cancer, which comes out in big red pimples, makes scabs and

---

[12] *tsara'at*, translated as scale disease in Milgrom 1991: 768–889; Levine 1989: 75–6.

[13] The whiteness of the dried pustules are diagnostic of the cure, but the whiteness of the pimples and the hair in the spots are diagnostic of the disease (Lev 13: 8 passim).

Levine 1989: 78. 'Skin turned white is new skin that has grown over the "raw" area.'

dries out; perhaps psoriasis; probably tropical ulcers and
yaws; the major infectious diseases, plague, smallpox,
mumps, chicken-pox, measles. There are symptoms of
Hansen's disease which the Leviticus writer does not emphasize, the gross swelling of the limbs, the local numbness,
eventual loss of toes and fingers, and facial deformity, just as
there are other symptoms of the infectious diseases, such as
the high temperatures of scarlet fever and measles, of which
he says nothing. The Leviticus writer is particularly interested in the ebb and flow of the disease. Someone can be
declared cured and afterwards can relapse, the patient can
pass from the state of clean to unclean, and back again, needing the pronouncement of the priest each time to allow him
to re-enter the community. This is what happens in the slow
development of certain forms of leprosy as we now use the
term; there are active phases in which the patient suffers
acute pain, the flesh swells and the skin erupts; in the passive
stage the pain abates, the swelling goes down somewhat, the
skin heals blotchily, the patient's strength returns, even if
only temporarily. In Leviticus the declared leper is unclean.
He must live outside the camp, wear distinctive dress, and
warn others of the risk of contamination by calling out
'Unclean' (Lev 13: 45–6). Even so, he can hope to be cured;
ritual cleansing and atonement are available when he is
healed and ready to come back into the camp. Thinking
exclusively of our experience of the medically identified leprosy we tend to suppose that the affliction was incurable and
fatal. However, this is not Leviticus' view. It assumes that
the leper leaves the community, and comes back when the
sores are dried up, re-entering temporarily if they were due
to a remisssion of psoriasis or yaws, permanently if the case
was chicken-pox, or never coming back if the patient dies.

The text of chapter 13 uses swelling, spreading, and erupting as diagnostic for the sickness in question. The RSV
translation uses 'eruption', which fits excellently to
Leviticus' description of most of the symptoms. The same
word also means to blossom.[14] The book describes an erup-

---

[14] See Levine 1989: 78, note to 13.12: ' "If the eruption spreads out over the
skin", Hebrew p-r-h means "to blossom". Compare Exodus 9.9, "dermatitis breaking out into boils".'

tive condition and focuses attention on the active eruption of spots and carbuncles.[15]

When a man has on the skin of his body a swelling or an eruption or a spot . . . if the diseased spot is dim and the disease has not spread in the skin, then the priest shall pronounce him clean; it is only an eruption; and he shall wash his clothes, and be clean. But if the eruption spreads in the skin, after he has shown himself to the priest for his cleansing, he shall appear again before the priest; and the priest shall make an examination, and if the eruption has spread in the skin, then the priest shall pronounce him unclean; it is leprosy. (Lev 13: 2, 6–8)

The emphasis on an eruptive condition as diagnostic of leprosy reintroduces the idea of teeming fecundity, but in this chapter blossoming and erupting are morbid.

When chapter 13 has described the process of diagnosis, chapter 14 explains the cleansing of the person: a sin offering is required, and a guilt offering. Again, the notion of the offerings as prophylactic is reasonable. There is no attempt to identify a sin that caused the disease. This is very striking. Nowhere does Leviticus say that the disease can be attributed to sin of the victim. In the sweep of comparison with other religions this is noteworthy. In Africa leprosy is widely associated with incest. Deuteronomy uses the idea that such diseases as 'the boils of Egypt' are caused by sin. Typically Leviticus avoids blaming and accusations. It says that if the priest has pronounced the man unclean, 'the disease is on his head' (Lev 14: 44), which means he is responsible for keeping the rules of seclusion imposed on him. The Lord actually says that he himself may put the leprous disease into a house (Lev 14: 34). Leviticus is not at all inclined to search out causes of disasters or attribute blame. These chapters have other objectives.

REPRODUCTIVE DISORDERS

The short series of chapters on breach of the body's limits concludes by coming round to its beginning, for it started

---

[15] Since the etymology of the word is doubtful, and since the symptoms described are heavily focused on spots or boils, there is a lot to be said for the suggestion that it comes from the similar word for wasp or hornet's sting. Sawyer 1976.

with a woman's normal blood of birthing, went through the long discussion of leprosy, and now ends with discharge of vaginal fluids. Pause for a moment to appreciate the larger balance: chapter 11 was about animals, chapter 12 was about a woman with genital bleeding, chapters 13 and 14 were about a male leper, now chapter 15 is about first a man, then a woman, who has a genital discharge. The law is the same, both for the man and for the woman, and at the end of seven days, atonement is available for both on the usual terms. It is typical of the priestly writer to be carefully balancing gender as well as topics. The impurity of the genital discharge is highly contagious. Starting with the man:

Every bed on which he who has the discharge lies shall be unclean; and everything on which he sits shall be unclean. And any one who touches his bed shall wash his clothes, and bathe himself in water, and be unclean until the evening. And whoever sits on anything on which he who has the discharge has sat shall wash his clothes, and bathe himself in water, and be unclean until the evening. And whoever touches the body of him who has the discharge shall wash his clothes, and bathe himself in water, and be unclean until the evening. . . . And any saddle on which he who has the discharge rides shall be unclean . . . (Lev 15: 4–9)

The second law is that when a couple has sexual relations involving a seminal emission, both are required to bathe and are impure until evening (Lev 15: 18). Third, the same rules are repeated for a woman who has a discharge of blood (Lev 15: 19–30). The female flows of blood and the male flows of semen are meticulously matched. In both cases, male and female, the end of the discharge must be followed by a rite of atonement (Lev 15: 14–15, 29–30).

The law of bodily discharges in Leviticus is in some respects less onerous than in Deuteronomy or in the Community of the Renewed Covenant in Qumran in the second century BCE. Japhet shows the different focus in Deuteronomy[16] which requires the man who has experienced a nocturnal emission to be removed out of the camp: 'If there is among you any man who is not clean by reason of what chances to him by night, then he shall go outside the

---

[16] Japhet 1993.

camp, he shall not come within the camp' (Deut 23: 10). Japhet explains that the Leviticus writer does not send him out of the camp because he is not writing about the camp but about the normal life of the congregation. The law in Deuteronomy refers only to the war camp, and to only one aspect of that law: men's nocturnal emissions. The narrowing of focus would be explained, Japhet suggests realistically, by the fact that women were not likely to be present in a war camp. As to the time of impurity and the requirements for removing it, Deuteronomy simply says, 'When evening comes on, he shall bathe himself in water, and when the sun is down, he may come within the camp' (Deut 23: 11).

The same rule for washing after a nocturnal emission is given in Leviticus 15: 16–17. But when a man with a genital discharge becomes clean (Lev 15: 14) he undergoes the same purification rites as the woman after childbirth (Lev 12: 6–8), and as the cleansed leper (Lev 14: 30). He waits eight days after washing, and then takes two birds to the priest for the offerings for atonement. By these rites Leviticus gives a coherent exposition of the meaning of bodily impurity. Clearly the lesson teaches the parallels between impure and holy for the body of the person and the body of the tabernacle. Like the laws of leprosy the laws of bodily discharges depend on the doctrine of sacred contagion, whereby any contact with the polluted thing will transmit the pollution just as virulently, and on, and on, indefinitely, from contact to contact. The line of dangerous contacts will eventually impinge on sacred food or place.[17]

The next chapter is the law for the purification of the sanctuary. The parallels between the rite of Yom Kippur and the rites for the cleansed mother, the cleansed leper, and the cleansing after genital discharge are striking. This time it is Aaron who has to bring two animals, one for a burnt offering and one for a sin offering, and two he-goats; and after their slaughter he sprinkles the shrine with blood seven times on the east side and in front (Lev 16: 14, 19), and it is Aaron who has to stay secluded for seven days (Lev 8: 35).

---

[17] Milgrom 1983.

In Deuteronomy the danger affects the whole camp where the Lord God walks with his people, but though Deuteronomy suggests that it would be wrong for God to see humans evacuating their bowels or to meet them when they have had nocturnal emissions, its only justification is the tacit assumption that such things would be offensive to any refined and sensitive person. Leviticus uses the rules to develop the parallel of body with tabernacle. All this emphasis on contamination and uncleanness means that the body and the tabernacle are analogues one of the other. Washing the body is an enactment that replicates atonement for restoring the sanctity of the tabernacle. The replication justifies the vocabulary of washing and dirt for the cult, because it does for both contexts. Like sacrifice, washing is a form of learning and knowing by doing.

It would be an unwarranted stretch of the imagination to classify leprosy as a reproductive disorder. True it is that the words for the symptoms of the disease are the same as those which were used in Genesis for the command to the teeming beings to bring forth, to erupt, spread, and be fruitful on the earth. The diseased pustules of leprosy are described as spreading, erupting, and blooming. But this does not explain convincingly why leprosy is placed here, in the middle of the two reproductive disorders. There are more telling considerations. One is comprehensiveness of the pathology; by gathering the gravest internal and external afflictions of the human body into one series, the typification of diseases is complete. God's care and control is comprehensive. The rites of atonement are implicitly effective for the total range of well-being. Persons who are impure should not be walking round with everyone else, infecting them by contact, and it could be disastrous to neglect to purify. The unity of the series is asserted by the verbal repetition of the language of purity in case after case. Like the animals, and like the tabernacle, no sin has caused the impurity, leprosy is not a punishment any more than a nocturnal emission is a sin.

To get a different kind of understanding, recall Leviticus' project to establish a new religion, cleansed of kings and ancestral spirits, freed from control by demons, not even recognizing evil spirits, unlike any known foreign cults.

Chapters 12–15 describe three exposed and risk-prone conditions, that of a newly delivered mother, that of anyone suffering from leprous diseases, and that of anyone who has had
a genital discharge of any kind. These same three conditions
were attributed to dangerous demons in Mesopotamia. . . .
whether this can count as evidence for how they were attributed in the Palestine region before the reform of the religion
is not clear. But it is at least interesting to know that in
Babylonian beliefs there was a dreaded goddess who systematically preyed on pregnant women and babies, a god of
epilepsy who was also god of leprosy, and the belief that
demons could be manufactured from nocturnal emissions
collected in a bucket.[18] Medical learning of the Mesopotamian sages was focused on charms and spells and potions to
cure victims of attacks from these sources.

Lamatshu was the daughter of Anu, a depraved goddess
who attacked young women and babies: 'both miscarriages
and cot deaths were attributed to her. Slipping into the house
of a pregnant woman, she tries to touch the woman's stomach seven times to kill the baby.'[19] The moon god, Sîn, controls the rays of moonlight which bring on madness and also
leprosy:

Very clear is the effect of the Moon-god on the skin of human
beings. A patient who has red pustules or boils, suffers from the
'Hand of Sîn', according to a variety of texts. A person suffering
from the skin disease *garabu*, associated with leprosy, has to perform a ritual invoking the name of Sîn. Whoever commits perjury
against the Moon-god and the Sun-god will be full of 'scales' . . .
the standard curse formulae telling what the Moon-god will do to
the sinner: Sîn will 'clothe' him with the skin disease *saharšubbu*,
'like a garment'. This disease is loosely translated 'leprosy' in
Assyriological literature, and it was indeed notorious and feared
like leprosy in other societies and times; people having it were
shunned.[20]

These are only three examples that fit the selected cases. The
Leviticus writer would have chosen his three topics with the
intention of covering the whole range of bodily sickness. To

[18] Saggs 1978: 104.
[19] Black and Green 1992. Foster 1993: vol. ii, 864–6.
[20] Stol 1993: 128.

the modern reader demons specifically associated with these afflictions need to be brought to mind to recall the overwhelming scope of demonic agency in the region in which Morton Smith invited us to find the bearings of the religion of Israel.

The microcosm of the body is part of the store of shared background knowledge which is demonstrated in other parts of the Pentateuch. The text itself does not explain that the tabernacle is at some level of thinking equivalent to the body, it makes the point by putting kinds of bodily condition together. For a leper to approach the tabernacle is a more serious breach of purity than for a person to eat a forbidden species. The latter offence requires the body and the clothes to be washed, but no sacrifice. In this respect leprosy ranks at the same level of seriousness as a woman's loss of blood after childbirth and as genital emissions of a man or a woman. In moral terms they seem at first to be very different, but in body logic terms they are equivalent threats to the integrity of the living being. The breach of the body's containing walls evidenced by escape of vital fluids and the failure of its skin cover are vulnerable states which go counter to God's creative action when he set up separating boundaries in the beginning.

Spatial separations made in the name of purity enact the humble bowing down of his creatures before the overwhelming majesty of the Lord. Everything in creation is arranged in order; each thing on a lower rank to be kept apart from one above, contact between them to be mediated by sacred powers given for the purpose. First he separated the waters above and below the firmament (Gen 1: 7), and then he gathered the waters together in one place and let the dry land appear (Gen 1: 9–10). When he was angry he released the waters from above to flood the earth (Gen 6) and 'the fountains of the great deep burst forth and the windows of the heavens were opened' (Gen 7: 11). It was the pleasing odour of Noah's burnt offering (so often cited in Leviticus) that made him decide never again to destroy every living creature and to restore the order of the seasons. This was the first covenant he made with the people. 'While the earth remains, seedtime and harvest, cold and heat, summer and winter, day and night, shall not cease' (Gen 8: 22). His power over the waters is the favourite sign of his greatness. The body that releases its waters in a disorderly way is not a faithful model of the world he made.

Attend again to the logic of the festering skin, notice how the body of the afflicted person has to be taken to the priest for diagnosis, how many days it is tested, the sign of spreading or not increasing as the decisive symptom, and notice the uniform requirement of atonement. Then notice the extensions from the body to the afflicted garment, to the house, each with the same vocabulary of festering and discoloration, each taken to the priest, each with the same tests and same periods of testing, and the same pronouncements.

First the teeming ground with the teeming animals breaking forth upon it and burgeoning, then the body's skin erupting with burgeoning pustules, then the affliction with the same name erupting upon the garment upon the skin, then the leprous house that is upon the garment that is upon the skin that is upon the body. Remember that a house in Hebrew is the word for a building, a domicile, but also and perhaps primarily the word for a line of kinsmen, as the house of Jacob or the house of Israel. This is another concentric construction in the house-that-Jack-built style that distinguished the first series of chapters 1–3. Each cover for the person inside is covered again by another covering.

The three analogies of leprosy (pustulating body, garment, house) lead up to the fourth, the tabernacle. This is where the series of spoilt covers converges. If the leprosy in the garment is cured, the garment is washed and put back into service (Lev 13: 58). The healed leper is declared clean (Lev 14: 9) after a ceremony with two birds, one sacrificed and the other to go free. The same ceremony of the two birds counts as atonement for the leprous house (Lev 14: 53). But the human has to make further offerings to have atonement done for himself, a guilt offering of two male lambs and one ewe lamb (Lev 14: 10–32). If there is no cure, the incurably defiled house must be destroyed (Lev 14: 39–42), as also the incurable leprous garment (Lev 13: 52), and eventually the incurable leper can expect to be destroyed by the disease. In the last case, defilement of the tabernacle, chapter 16 enjoins the rite of atonement for the tabernacle. If the defilement of the tabernacle were not remedied, the people could expect the curses of chapter 26 to be unleashed upon them as a punishment for failing to keep the covenant.

The chapters 12–15 have prepared the approach to atonement. Moreover, the whole construction of the book up to this point turns out to be a deliberately wrought ring with the instructions for making atonement for the tabernacle as its grand climax. The first seven chapters are about offering pure unblemished animals for free-will offerings or for atonement for sins which are listed (and which include contact with unclean things). The laws are interrupted by the narrative of the consecration of Aaron and his sons, the desecration of the sanctuary by the two sons of Aaron and their punishment by death. Then the laws are resumed, starting with chapter 11, pure and impure animals, chapters 12–15, impure humans needing atonement, and finally, chapter 16, the rite of atonement itself described.

When the circle is complete, it is clear that everything that has been said so far was designed to converge on the doctrine of atonement. The next chapter, 17, closes the ring with a latch on to the beginning. In chapter 17 the lesson of the opening verses is repeated: that all animals to be slaughtered

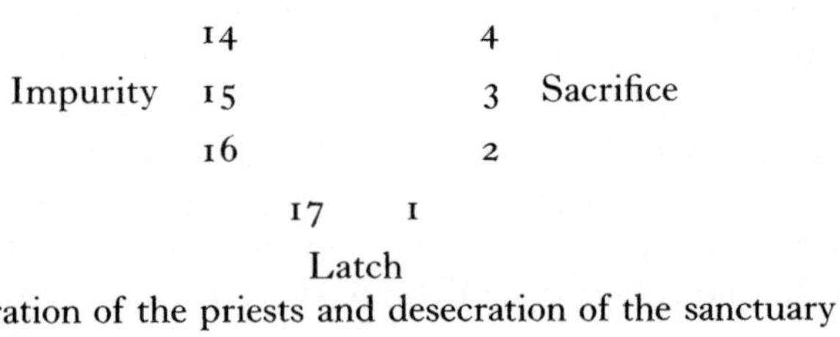

<pre>
                    Screen
                 10   9   8
            11   7
            12   6
            13   5
            14   4
  Impurity 15   3   Sacrifice
            16   2
                 17   1
                   Latch
</pre>

Consecration of the priests and desecration of the sanctuary

Figure 9.1. The ring closed

Table 9.1.   End recalls beginning

If any man of the house of Israel kills an ox or a lamb or a goat in the camp, or kills it outside the camp, and does not bring it to the door of the tent of meeting, to offer it as a gift to the Lord before the tabernacle of the Lord, bloodguilt shall be imputed to that man. (Lev 17: 3–4)	Speak to the people of Israel and say to them, When any man of you brings an offering to the Lord, you shall bring an offering of cattle from the herd or from the flock. . . . he shall offer it at the door of the tent of meeting . . . (Lev 1: 2–4)

must be brought to the tabernacle to be consecrated. See in Table 9.1 how the opening and closing verses echo one another.

Though the book goes straight on from chapter 15 to the chapter on atonement, the modern reader needs a pause. Everything so far has led to this rite; when it is described, the rite itself gives no resting-place for the interpreter, it points on to the doctrine of blood, the meaning of life, and of God, as the covenant-maker.

It will be best to postpone looking at the chapter on atonement until chapter 19 has been reached, for so much elucidation is withheld until then. The rites of consecrating Aaron and his sons as priests, and the echoes of this with the reconsecrating of the tabernacle, the cleansing of a leprous house and a cleansed leper, the scapegoat and the scapebirds, none of these are finished with until Leviticus has completed its account.

The first half of the book is as constrained as a sonnet, rhyming its meanings back and forth, withholding the completion of a thought, teasing with ironies, tender and grotesque, always holding the overall pattern. Its confident artistry astonishes. It is powerful and controlled, meticulous in following conventional rules. Yet it is bold in imagery, its scope running from the grandiloquent law of sacrifice to intimate details of anatomy and disease, from the familiar livestock to the curious little creatures with feet and no legs, from high style to bathos. Throughout it sustains its set direction and delivers its message. The first part of Leviticus looks so firm and complete, no loose ends, a perfect ring, no wonder that chapters 1–16 have been thought to be a separate piece. Its very compactness invites the questions about whether Leviticus is two compositions or one; if two, which was written first? and are the two authors at odds with each other on important doctrines? However, the questions are premature. When the book has unwound its whole length, the two halves of the book complete a single composition written in a tradition of binary halves.

(10)

The Two Screens

The solid letters of the world grew airy.
The marble serifs, the clearly blocked uprights
Built upon rocks and set upon the heights
Rose like remembered columns in a story.

Seamus Heaney[1]

Leviticus consists almost entirely of divine laws. It is interrupted twice by narratives, only twice, and both about encroachment on the divine prerogative. There is no accepted explanation for why they should occur where they do. The explanation here proposed is that the structure of law and narrative cuts the book to the shape of the controlling paradigm. This means that the book of Leviticus itself is structured as a tripartite projection of the tabernacle, and thus also as a projection of Mount Sinai.

LEVITICUS A PROJECTION OF THE TABERNACLE

On this reading the two stories would correspond to the two screens which, according to the instructions given in the Book of Exodus, divide the desert tabernacle into three sections of unequal size. The narratives interrupt the movement through the laws as the two screens interrupt the movement through the tabernacle and divide it into three sections. Scholars wonder why the two narratives occur just where they do: the answer is that their position in the book is an element of structure. They have to be placed exactly where they are in order to make the text correspond to the three spaces of the desert tabernacle. Individual laws are placed

---

[1] Heaney 1996: 45, 'Remembered Columns'.

where they are so that the reader can locate the corresponding point on the procession round the inside of the tabernacle, or up and down and round the outside of Mount Sinai. Each literary section thus separated off by a narrative has a certain completeness of form and homogeneity of matter; furthermore each section so defined deals with topics that relate appropriately to the corresponding part of the building: the first part deals with what happens in the court of sacrifice, the last part deals with what is contained in the ark of the covenant in the holy of holies, and the middle deals with the sanctuary, the precinct preserved for the priests.

To support these claims for the literary structure of Leviticus, consider the evidence in antiquity for the use of spatial positioning as a technique of memory. Romans are known in the first century BCE to have practised an art of memory by which orators preparing a complex speech were trained to locate their thoughts with reference to a building. The sources of architectural mnemotechnics are in Cicero's *De Oratore* and Quintilian's *Institutio*. Cicero attributed the origin of the mnemonic technique to Simonides. The latter had just left a banqueting hall before the roof collapsed, killing all who were in it; because Simonides could recall the location of each person's seat at the table he was able to reconstruct the guest list. This was hailed as a clear example of the benefits to memory of placing images in an orderly spatial background. In the first century CE different memory arts were a topic of lively debate, which was revived again in the Middle Ages[2] and again in the Renaissance.[3] Before these later discussions, there was evidently in antiquity a sophisticated awareness of the role of spatial experience for storing information.

Leviticus has more profound purposes for the architecture of the tabernacle. After all, the *aide-memoire* only plays a humble role in artistic creation. To expound a complex metaphysical doctrine is an altogether nobler function. This book of Leviticus, regarded traditionally as written down by Moses at God's direction, has a literary structure also modelled on the plan of the tent designed for God's meetings with

---

[2] Carruthers 1990.   [3] Yates 1969.

his people. With this double role the text is much more than a memory system: it is itself a microcosm. It holds together the meanings of many levels of existence. It is likely that Europe had once had a much richer tradition of cosmological literature, oral and written, based on the architecture of temples and bodies. By the time of Cicero the ancient cosmology had been blurred and diffused, and with it the grand tradition of microcosmic thinking might well have been reduced to a lowly technique of memory recall.

It has not been easy to find other examples of the genre which organizes itself on the organization of a limited space. The text of Leviticus is not related to the building as a guidebook, nor is it a shape extracted from another text by mysterious, almost numerological, methods.[4] The role of the narratives in Leviticus are comparable to their role in articulating the structure of the Book of Numbers, which is based on a regular alternation of narrative and law. The distribution of narratives in Numbers may be an exemplar followed by Leviticus where the narratives are also clear dividers of structural units.[5] The resultant structure is more like a 'pattern poem' in the Greek Bucolic tradition, in which the pattern of lines on the page made by variation in the number of syllables per line gives an illustration of the topic of the poem. A poem on a dove is in the shape of dove's wings, a poem on an axe or an egg is in the shape of an axe or egg, the outline of the poem on the shepherd's pipe looks like a pipe.[6] Most directly relevant is the poem 'Dosiadas: the first altar', in iambic metre, the lines arranged in the form of an altar.

Kathryn Gutzwiller, has proposed a test for a truly distinctive genre. She says that 'true genres', not subgenres, are distinguished not by content, subject matter, theme, or by form, prosody, figures of speech, or even by external structural arrangement. A genre is a form that moulds its material to produce a unique inner structure, with a coherent analogy as the structure.[7] In this strict sense, Leviticus is a genre. The structure of the written text is an analogy of the structure of the desert tabernacle.

[4] Rabanus 1831.   [5] Douglas 1993c.   [6] Edmonds 1912: 501.
[7] Gutzwiller 1991.

ΔΩΣΙΑΔΑ ΔΩΡΙΕΩΣ

ΒΩΜΟΣ

Εἰμάρσενός με στήτας
πόσις, μέροψ δίσαβος,
τεῦξ᾽, οὐ σποδεύνας ἶνις Ἐμπούσας μόρος
Τεύκροιο βούτα καὶ κυνὸς τεκνώματος,
χρυσᾶς δ᾽ αἴτας, ἄμος ἐψάνδρα
τὸν γυιόχαλκον οὖρον ἔρραισεν,
ὃν ἀπάτωρ δίσευνος
μόγησε ματρόριπτος·
ἐμὸν δὲ τεῦγμ᾽ ἀθρήσας
Θεοκρίτοιο κτάντας
τριεσπέροιο καύστας
θώυξεν αἶν᾽ ἰύξας
χάλεψε γάρ νιν ἰῷ
σύργαστρος ἐκδυγήρας
τὸν δ᾽ αἰλινεῦντ᾽ ἐν ἀμφικλύστῳ
Πανός τε ματρὸς εὐνέτας φὼρ
δίζῳος ἰνίς τ᾽ ἀνδροβρῶτος Ἰλοραιστᾶν
ἦρ᾽ ἀρδίων ἐς Τευκρίδ᾽ ἄγαγον τρίπορθον.

DOSIADAS

THE FIRST ALTAR

THIS *puzzle is written in the Iambic metre and composed of two pairs of complete lines, five pairs of half-lines, and two pairs of three-quarter lines, arranged in the form of an altar. Of the writer nothing is known; he was obviously acquainted with the* Pipe *and also with Lycophron's* Alexandra. *The poem is mentioned by Lucian (Lexiph. 25), but metrical considerations point to its being of considerably later date than the* Pipe. *Moreover, the idea of making an altar of verses presupposes a change in the conception of what a poem is. It was now a thing of ink and paper; and Dosiadas seems to have interpreted the* Pipe *in the light of the pipes of his own time, as representing the outward appearance of an actual pipe.*

Figure 10.1. The first altar

Edmonds, J. M., *The Greek Bucolic Poets* (1912), 506.

For another biblical example of a text plotted on a building, there is the house that Wisdom built on seven pillars. Patrick Skehan makes the demonstration that the text of Proverbs 1–9 is an elaborate projection of Wisdom's house by an intricate analysis which requires 'seven pillars' to be translated instead as 'seven columns' of stanzas.[8] 'On the traditional and only true reading of Proverbs 8. 30, Wisdom claims she has always been an architect; this, taken with Proverbs 1–9 and the rest of what we have seen above cannot but dispose us to see her at work again, building her house . . ..'[9]

In Leviticus the structure of the text is more than a formal analogy for the matter. The two narratives are more than neutral markers. First there is the fire narrative at chapters 8–10. The story starts with Aaron's consecration, fire from the sanctuary consumes the burnt offerings, two of his sons approach the sanctuary with unholy fire or incense and are forthwith destroyed by the Lord's fire. The second story is the short stoning narrative at 24: 10–22: in the heat of a fight a man blasphemes against the holy Name, the Lord is consulted, the blasphemer is stoned to death at the Lord's command. As analogies for the first and second dividing screens, they are warning clear enough against sacrilegious approach.

These two narrratives explode violently into the majestic sequence of laws. They are not any kind of narrative, each is a story of breach of the ordinances, one is about breach of the holiness of the tabernacle and the other about insult to the holy Name. They share stylistic peculiarities which will be discussed below. It is enough here to say that both are punitive, both short (one much shorter than the other), both brutal, both close abruptly, and when they are finished no further interpretation of them is provided. The sequence of laws seems to continue as if there had been no interruption.

In a book so cunningly wrought it is a mistake to read the two barrier stories separately. They should be read as a matching pair, each a barrier to the next chamber of the tabernacle. On this reading the spatial design of the

---

[8] Skehan 1947.

[9] He also mentions an Egyptian Wisdom text which is known to have direct literary connection with Proverbs, the text being divided into 'houses' by the author: *The Teaching of Amenemope the Son of Kanekht*, cited by Skehan 1947.

tabernacle and the actions which take place in each compart-
mented space endow the book with strong literary coherence.
Using them to stand for barriers against unauthorized entry
is a device for sliding between the ground plan and the text
and back again. The stories themselves are parables about
trespass on forbidden ground.

FIRE FOR FIRE, BURNING FOR BURNING

The first narrative in Leviticus counterpoises three fiery
episodes. The first is when the burnt offering is all prepared
and God sends fire to burn it as a sign of his approval. 'And
fire came forth from before the Lord and consumed the
burnt offering and the fat upon the altar; and when all the
people saw it, they shouted, and fell on their faces' (Lev 9:
24). The second episode is when the sons of Aaron trans-
gressed by offering unholy fire. 'Nadab and Abihu, the sons
of Aaron, each took his censer, and put fire in it, and laid
incense on it, and offered unholy fire before the Lord, such
as he had not commanded them' (Lev 10: 1). Immediately
the Lord retaliated: 'And fire came forth from the presence
of the Lord and devoured them, and they died before the
Lord' (Lev 10: 2).

Divine fire often has a prophetic or oracular role in the
Bible. The first of these fire miracles was a sign from God of
acceptance, a ratification of the sacrifice. Much earlier God
had ratified his promises to Abraham by a flaming torch (Gen
15: 17). He identified himself by flame to Moses (Exod 3: 3).
When Moses was to vindicate Aaron and himself against the
insults of Korah and the captains he told them to get their fire
censers next day and stand ready for the judgement, and
indeed it came with the same lethal swiftness as the burning
of the sons of Aaron, consuming all the two hundred and fifty
intransigent rebels (Num 16: 34).

It is very curious that concerning the execution of the sons
of Aaron no one is sure what they did wrong. It is not clear
what was wrong with the offending fire, translated as
'unholy' or as 'strange' fire. Perhaps the young priests had
gathered up profane fire instead of taking it from the altar.

Perhaps they did it because they were drunk, and perhaps their real offence was drunkenness. Neither offence sounds grave enough for such violent retribution. On some interpretations what the young priests did is not so important as who they are. Their names suggest that their deaths are a sequel to the earlier burning story about their father's sin at Sinai. On this reading the story is a priestly plot to delegitimate the line descended from Aaron.[10] When Moses came down from the mountain and found the people had been burning sacrifices to the golden calf he took it and burnt it with fire (Exod 32: 20). Aaron's lame explanation for what he had done was that when the people despaired of ever seeing Moses again he had told them to bring him gold, and he had thrown it in to the fire, 'and there came forth this calf' (Exod 32: 4), but his responsibility was clearly much more direct since he actually carved the idol, made an altar for it, and organized the sacrifice. He was also responsible for letting the people break loose among their enemies, which unleashed fierce fighting before order was restored (Exod 34: 25–8). On this line of reasoning the story in Leviticus refers back to the sin of Aaron and brings his bad fame forward into the next phase of the Bible story. But if the purpose of the story is to blacken Aaron's name there is more explaining to be done, since in Leviticus God continually gives Moses messages for him and Moses consistently treats Aaron as the revered head of the cult.

Given the chiastic design so prominent in this book and its complex symmetries and piled-up equivalences, we must take note of the triple return of fire for fire. First in chapter 9 the Lord made the gift of good fire that sanctified and consumed the offering on the altar, then in chapter 10 came the bad fire offered by Aaron's sons, negative reciprocity, a return of bad for good. Third, the fire from the Lord settled the score by burning the wrongdoers. It seems to be complete in itself, in classical narrative form, A–B–A, which we will recognize again and again. However, the names of the sons of Aaron give us the hint to read the fire stories together across Exodus and Leviticus. Nadab means 'willingness', Abijah means 'God is my father' (or Abihu, 'He is

[10] Damrosch 1987. Cross 1973: 205.

my father'). This suggests that their deaths are a sequel to an earlier burning story in which their father was involved. Any satisfying explanation needs to account for their names and for two further items that remain unexplained, the strange fire, and the mention of strong drink. The first thing that the Lord himself (not Moses) said to Aaron after the slaughter of his sons was: 'Drink no wine nor strong drink' (Lev 10: 8). This sounds like an irrelevance, and the more surprising in that it is the first and only mention of drink in the story. We had no reason to think that they had been drinking.

Let us treat the Exodus and Leviticus stories as two cases of unholy fire, the first offered idolatrously to a graven image, the second offered blasphemously to God on his holy altar after it has been installed. Both interrupt the giving of laws. In Exodus when the news of the golden calf is heard, God has concluded his instructions for making the tabernacle, and told Moses that the sabbaths are the sign of the covenant of Sinai; he has given him the two tablets of stone on which the commandments are engraved with his own finger (Exod 31). When Moses has restored order after the worship of the golden calf, God rewrites the commandments on new tablets (Exod 34: 1, 28). He repeats the promise of the covenant (Exod 34: 10), and Moses and the people resume the work of making the tabernacle. But the future cannot develop as if that treachery had never happened. We are reminded that the Lord God is merciful and gracious, slow to anger and abounding in steadfast love and faithfulness (Exod 34: 6). He has also said that he will by no means clear the guilty (Exod 34: 7), and that in some future day he will visit their sin upon them (Exod 34: 34). The story cannot stop here with the sense of impending doom. It must go on.

The Leviticus fire story is almost a miniature replica of that of Exodus. This is how Leviticus reminds the reader that the religion is based on the covenant and on God's mercy and justice, and that its own teaching is the continuation of Exodus. The first part inverts each item of the golden calf story.

Exodus	Leviticus
32: 1–5 Burnt offerings are sacrificed to the golden calf	8: 1–30 Anointing of Aaron, first burnt offering in the court of the tent of meeting
6 The people sit down to eat and drink and rise up to dance	31–3 Aaron and his sons are told to eat their portion at the door of the tent, enjoined to stay there seven days
7–11 God's anger burns to consume the people	9: 23 The congregation sees the glory of the Lord
12–14 God's burning anger is quenched by Moses' pleading	9: 24 God sends his fire to consume the burnt offering

Everything that has gone wrong in the Exodus story has gone right in the Leviticus story, so far. But in the next stage when the priests offer unholy fire, God's fire is not quenched but burns them up. The recitals go on to make further equivalences between the two stories. In each case Moses has a clearing-up job to do.

Exodus	Leviticus
32: 15–20 Moses restoring order, burns the calf, grinds up the gold	10: 3 Moses restoring order, arranges for the bodies to be removed. Aaron and remaining sons to stay in the tent of meeting, 'lest you die' (10: 7)
Scatters gold dust on the water, makes the people drink it	9 'Drink no strong drink'
21 Moses reproaches Aaron, people are out of control, fighting ensues, Levites kill 3,000.	16–19 Moses reproaches Aaron
35 God sends plague	
33: 7–12 Order is restored, pillar of cloud at the door of the tent of meeting.	20 Moses accepts Aaron's response

When the two stories are set side by side the injunction to avoid strong drink shows up as a parallel to the enforced drinking in the earlier story. The link between the two stories made by the admonition not to take wine or strong drink needs more attention. Making the people drink the infusion of idolatrous gold dust sounds like a drinking ordeal. It recalls the ordeal applied to the woman suspected of adultery in the Book of Numbers (5: 26–8). God has threatened to punish the actual sinners. He sends a plague because they made the calf (Exod 32: 34–5). We can suppose that the plague attacked those convicted of idolatry by the ordeal.

There is no corresponding ordeal in the story of the unholy fire, the malefactors have been caught in the act and summarily executed. And Aaron is warned against drink. For good reason, if this story is plotted on the drink and doom pattern described by Diane Sharon for biblical and ancient Near Eastern literature.[11] This is an old and common convention which puts four events in a sequence: an *eating event,* an *encounter,* an *oracle,* and an *affirmation* of the doom foretold by the oracle. For example, in Daniel 5 King Belshazzar hosts a banquet and gets drunk (*eating and drinking*); he orders the sacred vessels from the Jerusalem temple to be profaned by being used at his feast; writing appears on the wall, Daniel is called in to interpret it (*the encounter* and *the oracle*), and he pronounces the doom of the king. The oracle of doom is *affirmed* when Belshazzar is killed that very night.

In the same traditional terms we can take the idolaters sitting down to eat and drink as the first event, the encounter with Moses as the second, the forced drinking of gold dust as the oracle, and the destruction of the wicked by plague as its affirmation. It follows that the warning to Aaron not to take strong drink is a vital part of the story about unholy fire. It is necessary not only to cue the reader into the parallelism, but to cue the reader also to know that the second story is not on the hitherto established pattern of the doom of paradise. It is about something new that happened on Mount Sinai.

---

[11] Sharon 1998: 63–79.

Indeed, the search for parallels shows up the story of the unholy fire as a low-key inverted version of the story of the golden calf. Its presence in Leviticus is to emphasize the continuity from Exodus. The theme will be temporarily set aside in the chapters that follow immediately, chapters 11–15. Then it will be taken up again in earnest in chapter 16. It will become clear that the terror and chaos of the golden calf story are prologue to the grand ceremonies for the ordination of Aaron and the ceremony of atonement for the tabernacle. These are the means which God in his mercy has given to the people of Israel for keeping his covenant. When the first barrier story in Leviticus is analysed in reference to the golden calf episode it turns out to be much more than a neutral marker showing where we have reached in the plan of the book. It is about the temple worship of the true God.

This and the other story in Leviticus is about the Lord's justice in general, the very nature of Hebrew law, its symmetry and logical foundation. In a very old and self-consciously literary book, we need to find a literary level of interpretation: the story about the sons of Aaron and the story about the blasphemer are about poetic justice, judgement in its most elementary form. The covenantal principle surfaces in these stories as a rule of reciprocity. The word for covenant is not necessarily used, but the idea of a network of balanced mutual obligations is implicit.

THE CURSER CURSED

The second story bursts in to the calm sequence of laws like an alarm bell. Commentators have scratched their heads in vain to know why it should be just here. The simplest explanation is that it is placed at the point in the book which corresponds to the second screen which stands to guard the most holy place from intruders. This time we do know what has been done wrong, and it is appropriate to the analogy with the tabernacle that it is about the man who blasphemed. For cursing the name of God he was executed by stoning at the Lord's command in chapter 24. Stoning is not an obvious

tit-for-tat riposte for insult or blasphemy, but in the middle
of the short story the law of talion is solemnly recited:

Now an Israelite woman's son, whose father was an Egyptian, went
out among the people of Israel; and the Israelite woman's son and
a man of Israel quarrelled in the camp, and the Israelite's woman's
son blasphemed the Name, and cursed. And they brought him to
Moses. His mother's name was Shelomith, the daughter of Dibri,
of the tribe of Dan. And they put him in custody, till the will of the
Lord should be declared to them. And the Lord said to Moses,
'Bring out of the camp him who cursed; and let all who heard him
lay their hands upon his head, and let all the congregation stone
him. And say to the people of Israel, Whoever curses his God shall
bear his sin. He who blasphemes the name of the Lord shall be put
to death; all the congregation shall stone him: the sojourner as well
as the native, when he blasphemes the Name, shall be put to death.
He who kills a man shall be put to death. He who kills a beast shall
make it good, life for life. When a man causes a disfigurement in his
neighbour, as he has done it shall be done to him, fracture for fracture, eye for eye, tooth for tooth; as he has disfigured a man he shall
be disfigured. He who kills a beast shall make it good; and he who
kills a man shall be put to death. You shall have one law for the
sojourner and for the native; for I am the Lord your God.' So
Moses spoke to the people of Israel; and they brought him who had
cursed out of the camp, and stoned him with stones. Thus the
people of Israel did as the Lord commanded Moses. (Lev 24:
10–23)

The strong retaliatory element does not appear obvious in
the story although it is usually taken to illustrate the application of the law. There is nothing at first glance to connect
cursing with stoning. 'Sticks and stones do break my bones,
but words will never hurt me,' but if it is shifted to the verbal
level a linguistic parallel appears, with scope for possible
word-play. Two words have been used. Verse 15 says:
'Whoever curses his God.' The word for the act of cursing[12]
means to trifle, despise, dishonour, make contemptible. But
in verse 16 it says: 'He who blasphemes the name of the
Lord.' This term is slightly different, it has the same stem as
'to bore a hole', or 'to pierce', and by extension, to specify, to
pronounce explicitly, to identify,[13] and from here by exten-

---

[12] *q-l-l*, dishonour, curse.
[13] *n-q-b*, to pierce, bore through, perforate. Levine 1989: 166.

sion presumably to name insultingly. Usually the two meanings are unconnected, but there is resonance between them.
In the midst of a fight the man did two bad things, first he
cursed, and second he spoke against or pierced with words
the name of God. When consulted what to do (presumably
by the priestly oracle) God commanded that he be put to
death by stoning. The Hebrew stem of the verb which is
translated as to stone[14] actually means to hurl or pelt. In
English it could mean to pelt with anything, cabbages, bad
tomatoes, or dung, but in Hebrew it is always used to pelt
with stones. The oracle does not seem to have chosen a punishment that fits the crime, but if the word play be admitted,
the retaliatory principle works in the literary mode: the blasphemer has hurled insults at the name of God, let him die by
stones hurled at him. In English the nearest double meaning
is the metaphor of mud-slinging. Then the oracle would run
as follows: he has slung mud, let him die by mud slung at
him.

The literary mode might be right. There are some curious
names in this story, which need to be unravelled. We are told
that the blasphemer's mother's name was 'Shelomith', which
might suggest retribution,[15] her father was Dibri, which suggests lawsuit;[16] by his mother he was of the tribe of Dan,
which suggests judgement.[17] By a strongly directed selection
of the meanings of the names the story told to children could
go like this: 'Once there was a man (with no name), son of
Shelomith-Retribution, grandson of Dibri-Lawsuit, from
the house of Dan-Judgement, and he pelted insults at the
Name ... and the Lord said "He shall die, he pelted my
Name, he shall be pelted to death." ' Against this reading it
might be claimed that these happened to be the actual names
of the mother's kin of a historical person whose crime has
become famous. The fact that this person, the blasphemer,
has remained nameless weakens this objection, and to accept
it would be to disregard other cases in the Bible where the
name has something to do with what is related.[18] You would
have to explain why his mother's name is given and those of

---

[14] *r-g-m*, to throw, hurl, pelt.   [15] Cf. *shelummat*.   [16] Cf. *dibrah*.
[17] Cf. Genesis 49: 16: 'Dan shall judge his people as one of the tribes of Israel.'
[18] Garsiel 1991.

his maternal forebears to three generations, why these names have no further references in Leviticus, and why his own name is not given at all. The primary question is not the translation of the names, but why the names should be there at all. The bit of genealogy might be explained by asking what it contributes to the story itself, but in this case, unlike the case of Aaron's sons, it contributes precious little.

The punning on names draws attention to the punning about the punishment. One of its literary effects is to take away any pretence of historicity. Let us consider the name-punning as a framing device which conveys a temporary withdrawal from the main narrative. It would be saying this is not a story about Moses, but a story within the Moses story, a tale within a tale. As with other tales within a tale its function is to highlight the main theme of the book.[19] The play upon names makes it into a fanciful narrative about where retaliation fits into the whole scheme of things. God's words from the oracle, 24: 17–23, explain that the particular case illustrates the general principle of equivalence, that is the basic principle on which the curser of the living God must be cursed to death. This theme will be developed after considering some other instances.

Place the two Leviticus cases of the burners burnt and the curser cursed alongside the fornicator speared through the body with his seductress in Numbers. The fate of Zimri is an obvious case of the punishment fitting the crime. It is often taken to be funny, and yet it is the occasion for a solemn pronouncement about God's honour.

While Israel dwelt in Shittim the people began to play the harlot with the daughters of Moab. These invited the people to the sacrifices of their gods, and the people ate, and bowed down to their gods. So Israel yoked himself to Ba'al of Pe'or. And the anger of the Lord was kindled against Israel; and the Lord said to Moses, 'Take all the chiefs of the people, and hang them in the sun before the Lord, that the fierce anger of the Lord may turn away from Israel.' And Moses said to the judges of Israel, 'Every one of you slay his men who have yoked themselves to Ba'al of Pe'or.' (Num 25: 1–5)

---

[19] The Balaam story is separated from the sequence of events in the Book of Numbers' account of the journey from Sinai to the Jordan by similar literary devices. Douglas 1993d.

This is the preface to the story, and it is worth noting Milgrom's comment that impaling the wrongdoers is a closer translation than hanging, and his interesting notes on the various forms of execution by impaling.[20] If the word[21] has the same sense as impale does in English what Phinehas then did was a form of impaling.

And behold, one of the people of Israel came and brought a Midianite woman to his family, in the sight of Moses and in the sight of the whole congregation of the people of Israel, while they were weeping at the door of the tent of meeting. When Phinehas the son of Eleazar, son of Aaron the priest, saw it, he rose and left the congregation, and took a spear in his hand and went after the man of Israel into the inner room, and pierced both of them, the man of Israel and the woman, through her body. Thus the plague was stayed from the people of Israel. Nevertheless those that died by the plague were twenty-four thousand. (Num 25: 6–9)

In this extraordinary story the text does not specify exactly what Zimri did to excite Phinehas' anger. It has been the focus of ribald speculation from early times, but the sequel and the horrendous toll of dying Israelites that ceased when Zimri died shows it was a grave offence. Perhaps he should never have introduced a Midianite woman to the entrance of the tent of meeting. Perhaps they went through the screen, perhaps they did behave indecently; there are hints of ritual prostitution in the text about how the Moabite women tempted the Israelites to pay cult to their god (Num 25: 1–5). Perhaps the common assumption that the two were actually copulating in full sight of the congregation is correct.

> But let me have bold ZIMRI's fate,
> Within the arms of COSBI!
> Robert Burns[22]

[20] Milgrom 1991: 213, and Excursus 61, 476–80.   [21] *hokah'*.
[22] Song:
I murder hate by field or flood, | Though glory's name may screen us: | In wars at home I'll spend my blood, | Life-giving wars of Venus: | The deities that I adore | Are social Peace and Plenty; | I'm better pleased *to make one more*, | Than be the death of twenty.
I would not die like Socrates, | For all the fuss of Plato; | Nor yet would I with Leonidas, | Nor yet would I with Cato: | The Zealots of the Church, or State, | Shall ne'er my mortal foes be, | But let me have bold ZIMRI's fate, | Within the arms of COSBI!
(Robert Burns)

Whatever it was, Moses was occupied with impaling the ringleaders of the mass apostasy, as he had been commanded by God, and Phinehas decided to impale these two offenders on his own initiative. The plague which was the anger of God stopped at once and the Lord said to Moses:

> Phinehas the son of Eleazar, son of Aaron the priest, has turned back my wrath from the people of Israel, in that he was jealous with my jealousy among them, so that I did not consume the people of Israel in my jealousy. Therefore say, 'Behold, I give to him my covenant of peace; and it shall be to him, and to his descendants after him, the covenant of a perpetual priesthood, because he was jealous for his God, and made atonement for the people of Israel.' (Num 25: 11–13)

The speech is more vivid in the translation used by Milgrom's (JPS) commentary.

> Phinehas . . . has turned back my wrath from the Israelites by displaying among them his passion for Me, so that I did not wipe out the Israelites in My passion. (Num 25: 11)

Or, literally, 'in his becoming impassioned by my passion'. Milgrom says: 'Phinehas' passion matched that of God.'[23] The punishment literally fits the crime in that the lovers were slain in a brutally enforced and lethal embrace. Sexual penetration was punished by the penetrating spear, Zimri the penetrator was himself penetrated. Then, the anger of God was matched by the anger of Phinehas, passion matched passion. Next, God discerning that expiation or atonement had been made, found it the occasion to make a final requital: he announces a perpetual pact of friendship with Phinehas and his descendants. His concluding words about pact and ransom are already replete with the idea of talion. A free reading of the Lord's speech would go somewhat as follows:

> Phinehas did turn away my wrath.
> His passion for his God matched his God's own passion.
> He paid me the ransom for Israel.
> I repay him with my pact.

Again we are gratuitously given the names of the chief actors in the story, who are otherwise completely unknown. Their

---

[23] Milgrom 1991: 216.

names enmesh us in the same kind of courtroom puns that decorate the story of the blasphemer in Numbers 24.

The name of the slain man of Israel, who was slain with the Midianite woman, was Zimri the son of Salu, head of a fathers' house belonging to the Simeonites.
And the name of the Midianite woman who was slain was Cozbi the daughter of Zur, who was the head of the people of a fathers' house in Midian. (Num 25: 14–15)

What are they doing here, all these extra names? Do they get turned up in the course of the divinatory process? The root of the word Zimri indicates pruning knife, pruner, or saw; his father's name, Salu suggests to weigh in Hebrew, very suggestive of scales of justice and well chosen for a story of retaliation and for reference to perfect weights and measures as signifiying justice. Cozbi, suitably enough for her role, suggests lie, falsehood, deceptive thing. Zur is not so easy to choose a meaning for; it could mean adversary, foe, or it could mean narrow, or straightened or distressed. So for a try:

Zimri-Pruner, son of Salu-Weights-and-Measures, penetrated Cozbi-Deceiver, daughter of Zur-Enemy, in the tent of meeting. But Phinehas cut down the Pruner. Phinehas' zeal for God's honour turned away God's zeal for his own honour by penetrating them both at once with his spear.

Is it possible that names which play no further part in the book are there as a framing device? Is their function to announce a tale within a tale? Leviticus 24 is a little tale about a half-caste whose father was Egyptian and his mother an Israelite. Is his marginal ethnic status nothing to do with the case against him? He cursed God's name in the heat of a quarrel. Following the Levitical laws of chapters 4 and 5, he might have been asked whether he repented, then he might have had to pay a heavy fine and have atonement done for him. Why can he not have the forgiveness that can be claimed for the inadvertent sinner? See Chapter 6 above on the judicial uses of oaths: the non-fit between chapter 6 and the account of stoning in Leviticus 24 is another point at which the seam shows in the stitching together of a religion without oracles. The blasphemer's remorse would be credible if he said:

I realize I did wrong, but I didn't mean to, it was quite inadvertent, a slip of the tongue, I was carried away by the excitement of the fight. Now I repent of my unwitting sin. Allow me to take an ordeal to prove it was inadvertent.

As observed already, the case of hurling insults at the name of God fits poorly on the cited examples of matching crime by punishment. Death by hurling stones and sin by hurling insults have a weak literary match, but apart from the pun there is no matching of the punishment with the crime. The idea of revenge is fearful and solemn, but in the priestly writings on *lex talionis* a grim playfulness lurks, both in Leviticus and in Numbers, in the names that decorate suggestively but do no more, and in the puns on punishments fitting the crimes.

SCANDAL OF TALION

This reading suggests that Leviticus 24 is less vengeful and angry than Exodus 21 and Deuteronomy 19. Is it possible that the Leviticus writer is taking a different line on the enigma of divine justice and compassion? He is more of a visionary and poet than a lawgiver, he does not deserve to share the odium that attaches to the law of talion as a primitive and violent system. By quoting it in a jingly form, in a peculiar circumstance where its fit is not clear at all, surrounded with funny names, where it only makes sense as a play upon words, he may be trying to say something else about the measure-for-measure[24] principle. Leviticus is possibly making an opening here for the complex view of retribution celebrated in the Book of Job. What is being tested is the universal validity of the principle of retribution. 'So the Book of Job can be seen as bringing into the spotlight logical fallacies that have attached themselves to the doctrine. Its aim is not merely the systematization of thought; it seeks primarily for the right standards for this estimation of individuals, and perhaps also for the release of the socially ostracized from unjust criticism.'[25]

---

[24] Diane Sharon's help with this theme is gratefully acknowledged.
[25] Clines 19: 284–91.

Surely the idea of exact repayment for injury is against the spirit of Torah, which enjoins forgiveness and compassion. Indeed much rabbinical commentary upon the *lex talionis* has been trying to make that very point: the law does not require exact revenge, it is there to set a limit to the amount of vengeance that can be demanded: if one eye has been lost the victim cannot try to take both eyes of his attacker, still less the life. Feuding is to come to an end. Leviticus supports Deuteronomy, the sons shall not be killed for the crimes of their fathers, and each shall bear punishment only for his own crime. If one life is lost, only one life is allowed in retaliation and no more. If that is correct, there is even less connection between the crime of the half-caste blasphemer and the recital of the eye-for-an-eye tag which is supposed to justify his execution.

In the Exodus and Deuteronomy versions the law of talion is recited without context. In Exodus it reads:

If any harm follows, then you shall give life for life, eye for eye, tooth for tooth, hand for hand, foot for foot, burn for burn, wound for wound, stripe for stripe. (Exod 2: 23–5)

In Deuteronomy it is more awesome but ends with the same string, which is probably a stock oracle response:

then you shall do to him as he had meant to do to his brother; so you shall purge the evil from the midst of you. And the rest shall hear, and fear, and shall never again commit any such evil among you. Your eye shall not pity; it shall be life for life, eye for eye, tooth for tooth, hand for hand, foot for foot. (Deut 19: 19–21)

These passages echo similar laws of the region, but it is not in keeping with the Leviticus writer's strength of purpose to borrow a foreign legal code without adapting the meaning to the Leviticus project.

The subtlety of thought and the high degree of literary control exerted throughout Leviticus, and the general Pentateuchal effort to distance the culture of Israel from other cultures around, combine to suggest that if the priestly writer refers to other people's legal codes it would be in an ironic, if not in an actually disingenuous vein. Here it is argued that for Leviticus the meaning of the old tag about 'an eye for an eye a tooth for a tooth' is embedded in the lesson of reciprocity which underlies the covenant. Leviticus is more interested in the restitutive than in the criminal aspects of law. This study argues against taking the story of the blasphemer punished by stoning too legalistically. It is not teaching the letter of the law but making a literary comment on the letter of the law. The style shows that what should be taken seriously is some kind of general match between offence and retaliation. The general principle is that God's universe runs on reciprocity. In other words, the law is the negative side of the principle of fair dealing on which the covenant is based.

Remember Daniel's judgement on the elders who bore false witness against Susanna. He asked each accuser separately what was the tree under which they saw her with her lover, and ordered punning death sentences for them (Susanna: 54–9). Bernard Jackson's account of the well-known joke is worth quoting:

the climax rests upon the different trees advanced by the two elders as the *locus delicti*. The point is reinforced by a skilful double pun. When the first elder replies 'under a mastick tree' (*hupo schinon*) Daniel retorts that the angel of God has already received instructions to cut him in two (*schisei se meson*) for the lie; when the second testifies that it was a holm (*hupo prinon*), Daniel replies that the angel of God is waiting, scimitar in hand, to saw him in half (*prisei se meson*). Patristic sources debate already whether the existence of this double pun is evidence that Greek was the original language of the story; Origen asked his Jewish associates whether they could reproduce it in Hebrew, but they could not. . . . More recently, the New English Bible translators have, with modest arboreal licence, reproduced the pun in English: ' "Under a clove-tree . . . he will cleave you in two; under a yew-tree . . . to hew you down" .'[26]

Daniel's judgement, which makes a verbal matching of crime and penalty, illustrates the law of retaliation in Leviticus.

The principle of equivalent retaliation is quite blatant in the narrative books. Why did Jezebel die by falling out of a high window (2 Kings 8: 30)? Answer: the false woman built high places for false gods. Why was Absolom delivered to his enemies hanging by his beautiful hair (2 Sam 18: 9–10)? Answer: his pride in his own beauty brought him to this end.

[26] Jackson 1977: 38.

The victims of injury find something peculiarly gratifying in the malefactor being requited poetically as well as practically.

THE LANGUAGE OF ORACLES

It is probably right that this linguistic level of retaliation should sound unconvincing to the lawyers. It really belongs in the context of oracles, on which information is short. One can suppose that the speech of an oracle should not be in the same register as everyday speech; it is oxymoronic, its enigmatic sayings enhance the impression of tapping into deep resources of wisdom. His verbal wit contributed to Daniel's reputation as a brilliant judge. That a judgement should be funny when it requites the evil-doer with his own evil is only to be expected if we remember that bringing about distributive justice is the classically distinctive mark of comedy.

Some of these stories do not seem to have involved a formal oracular consultation: the Lord seems to have spoken out spontaneously in the story of Phinehas. When Moses said he would consult the Lord, as in the case of the blasphemer and the case of the wood-gatherer in Numbers, it has been understood that he used the priest's oracle, the Urim and Thummim. As we have described in an earlier chapter, if each tribe was associated with a number, a jewel, a virtue, a season, a wind, a configuration of the zodiac, and so on, a matrix for very complex consultation and prediction is present and could be produced at very short notice.[27]

Complex oracles only work because they have been coded to capture the human condition in a general framework of right- and wrongdoing. The Breastplate of Judgement would make a powerful framework for divination, enhanced by the echoing ambiguities of the Hebrew language and the cosmological references stored in the divinatory apparatus. Certain names derived from roots that give the words for relevant terms such as lawsuit, judgement, compensation, or quick repayment, may have been part of the regular repertoire of the oracle, ready to be churned out to validate a judgement.

[27] Séd 1981: 289.

This thought quells the charge of levity suggested by the names in Leviticus' talion stories. They would have been very serious, but we do not have the information to decode them.

A culture which plays with words and makes projections from language to space, where the construction of the text matches the construction of a tabernacle, and where this is a building with fixed orientations to the points of the compass—such a culture has developed a rich store of oracular resources. However, it was not available. The book itself says plainly why: 'A man or woman who is a medium or a wizard shall be put to death; they shall be stoned with stones, their blood shall be upon them' (Lev 20: 27). The interpretation of the talion stories suggests that the cultural storehouse on which Leviticus drew was very complex and sophisticated, albeit in a compact, archaic form. This makes it all the more plausible that the only two narratives in Leviticus are placed where they are to represent screens in a spatial analogue of the book itself. The sense is that the priestly writer is in the habit of using the logic of the concrete, his habit rests on the old expectation that oracular findings can reach into the truth of complex affairs, and that the language of oracles is inherently opaque. These cultural habits he has in common with other Pentateuch writers and editors, as they have them in common with the learned men of their region and period. But apart from this general notion about oracles, by the time that Leviticus was edited it is probable that no one knew how they worked.

The Leviticus writer has used talion to make a statement about exact restitution. The doctrine is in line with the precision of the rules of sacrifice. Crime and penalty are part of a pattern of reciprocity in which good things are repaid by good things and figure even more largely than violent crimes repaid in violence. Perfect reciprocity is the intellectual grounding for the covenant. To take the narrative lines about talion from Leviticus 24: 16–21 in isolation does indeed bring out the parallel with contemporary foreign law codes. To read them in this context does imply a harsh, unmerciful God. But though their style is aped, it is not sure that the parallel with foreign laws is fully intended. The full context of talion in Leviticus puts the negative reciprocity into balance with positive reciprocity, gift with gift, as well as crime with punishment. The other half of the comparison, the positive reciprocity, is the central theme in Leviticus. God's compassion and God's justice would be revealed to anyone allowed to pass through the screens and able to read the testament of the covenant hidden in the most holy place. Only the high priest can do that, but anyone can know what is there from reading the book.

❪ 11 ❫

Inside the House/Book of God

> One thing I have asked of the Lord, that I will seek after;
> that I may dwell in the house of the Lord all the days of
> my life, to behold the beauty of the Lord, and to inquire
> in his temple. (Psalm 27: 4)
>
> How lovely is thy dwelling place, O Lord of Hosts! . . .
> Blessed are those who dwell in thy house, ever singing
> thy praise! (Psalm 84: 1–4)

Exodus recounts how beautifully the tabernacle was made,
the psalmist extols the house of God. Leviticus honours it in
its own style. The book opens with God calling Moses at the
entrance to the tent of meeting, and the tabernacle remains
throughout not just the ground and pivot of all its teaching,
but the actual structure on which its literary form has been
projected.

The narratives have suggested an unexpected partitioning
of the book. They divide it into three unequal compartments
with laws filling the spaces between the stories. These compartments correspond to the relative size of the chambers in
the desert tabernacle built according to God's instructions in
Exodus. The result is to project the three parts of the book on
to the tripartite architecture of the tabernacle, itself modelled
on the three-zoned proportions of the holy mountain. When
the laws have been placed, as it were, in each part of the
building as prescribed by their position in the book, they turn
out to describe the contents or the actions that are supposed
to be performed in the appropriate compartment, or to
describe the requirements for entry into it. Other markers are
placed along the way to confirm the parallel.

MACRO MARKERS

References to Sinai seem to be scattered freely through the book, more or less randomly. It has hardly seemed necessary to enquire why the formulae occur in the order given, yet to suppose that their placings are arbitrary would be to give up any high esteem for the editor's control. On a closer look the distribution of references to Sinai supports the definition of three sections. The book starts when the people of Israel are at Sinai and after having built the tabernacle. The last chapter concludes with the name of Sinai. Only the first section and the third are marked by Sinai, as is shown in Table 11.1.

Table 11.1.   'Sinai' marks the narrative-defined sections

Section 1
Chapters 1–7. Implicit Sinai opening at the tent of meeting with the Lord speaking from Sinai, and double Sinai peroration 7: 38.

  Fire narrative, chapters 8–10.

Section 2
Chapters 11: 11–24: 9.

  Stoning narrative, 24:10–23.

Section 3
25.1. Sinai opening;
26. Sinai perorations, vv. 45, 46;
27. Sinai peroration, v. 34.

Sinai opens and ends the first section, it is not mentioned in the middle, but it opens and ends the third; thus Sinai marks the sections separated by the narratives. It is therefore safe to conclude that the name of Sinai is another marker, additional to the stories, like a set of brackets at the beginning and end of a section to guide the reader to recognize an *inclusio*, or ring.

   The references to Egypt in the middle part do not perform any similar structural function for bracketing off a panel. They are used for emphasis, often a grand peroration. Whereas the word Sinai is usually dropped in quite simply

('The Lord said to Moses on Mount Sinai', Lev 25: 1), the Egyptian reference is positively baroque: 'You shall not profane my holy name, but I will be hallowed among the people of Israel; I am the Lord who sanctify you, who brought you out of the land of Egypt to be your God: I am the Lord' (Lev 22: 32–3). This peroration is a warning signal to look out for what is going to happen: two chapters later the holy Name will have been profaned and the consequences for the profaner will be death by stoning. Without these divisions, the shape of the book looks crazy. There is one segment of seven chapters at the beginning, then the story at 8–10; one large segment of fourteen chapters until the second story at 24, and after that a small concluding segment of only three chapters. But the narratives and the Sinai references are flagging devices that signal the division of the book into three segments.

On the instructions given to Moses at Sinai the whole court was an oblong, 100 cubits long and 50 cubits wide, with the entrance at the east (Exod 20: 18). Exodus does not give instructions for locating the tabernacle proper within this large enclosure, but it gives the size of each part. The positioning of the three parts has been deduced from the size of the hangings, pillars and screens of the outer court and the holy of holies.[1] The front part is a large outer court, a square of 50 × 50 cubits, the place of sacrifice. A screen covered the entrance to the first sanctuary, which was a much narrower oblong area of 20 × 10 cubits. Beyond this, and divided from it by another screen, is the holy of holies, the inner sanctuary, a square of only 10 × 10 cubits, and inside the holy of holies, the ark of the covenant, 2½ × 1½ cubits. This leaves 20 cubits of length to make the surround at the back, which is usually occupied with profane things. We never hear of anything happening at the back or of anyone going round to it. To all intents and purposes there are three areas where ritual action takes place, the outer court, the sanctuary, and the inner chamber, the very small holy of holies. Moving from most accessible and common to most enclosed, interior, and holy of the three compartments, the first is very large and accessible, the next much smaller, and the last the smallest.

[1] Sarna 1991: 174.

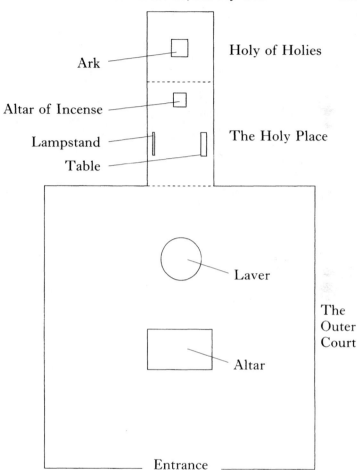

Figure 11.1.   Furnishings of the tabernacle
Source: Adapted from Sarna 1991: 155.

The furnishings of the compartments having been detailed in Exodus, Leviticus uses them to locate where we have got to in the tour of the tabernacle. It ordains what objects are to be placed in each compartment, and what is to be done with them. The separations made by the narratives are given full weight when we discover that the prescribed actions are being performed at the right places.

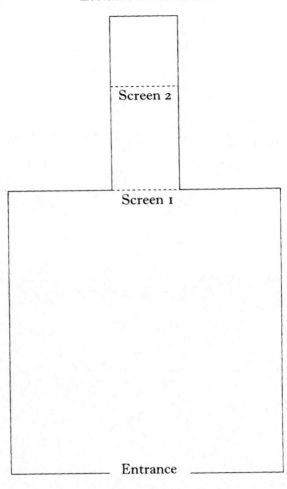

Figure 11.2. The proportions of the tabernacle
Source: Adapted from Milgrom 1991: 135.

THE OUTER COURT

Imagine the reader using the Book of Leviticus as a guide around the tabernacle. It starts at the entry, from where the Lord called Moses in the first line (Lev 1: 1). The visitor

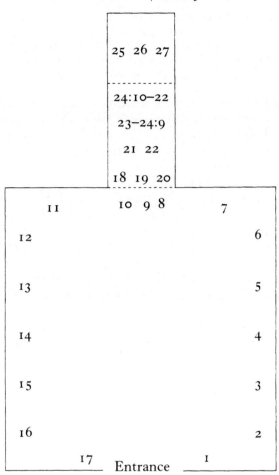

Figure 11.3. Leviticus projected on the grand plan of the tabernacle

starts, accordingly, at the entrance and walks down the right side, following chapters 1–7. We have noted already that these chapters make a literary ring, with a peroration in chapter 7, clinched by the double reference to Sinai.

This is the law of the burnt offering, of the cereal offering, of the sin offering, of the guilt offering, of the consecration, and of the peace offerings, which the Lord commanded Moses on Mount Sinai, on the day that he commanded the people of Israel to bring their offerings to the Lord, in the wilderness of Sinai. (Lev 7: 37–8)

In the outer court a fire always burns on the main altar of sacrifice and the people come to make their offerings. It contains the altar of burnt offering and the laver for the priests to wash in. Appropriately the first chapters, 1–7, give the rules for sacrifices made at the initiative of the laity, for sin, guilt, peace, or thanksgiving.

As figure 11.3 shows, the book so far has been following one side of the court of sacrifice. Walking in this direction the visitor encounters the screen that in the building separates the court from the sanctuary. In the book the narrative at chapters 8–10 corresponds to the first screen. The narrative ends calamitously, with the deaths of Aaron's sons who approached the sanctuary with unconsecrated (or unholy) fire in their incense burners.

At this point a guide always has to make a choice. Should he lead the way through the screen? The courtyard is very big: if the visitors go through the screen when they come to it, when will they ever see the other side of the courtyard? It would be advisable to complete the tour of the court so that they can appreciate the correspondences between the two

		10	9	8	
11		First screen			7
12					6
13					5
14					4
15					3
16					2
	17	Entrance		1	

Figure 11.4. The court of sacrifice

sides. But if they go right round they will be at the entrance again and they will have to be led back to the screen. In this case the guide, the Leviticus writer, has taken the visitors first down one side and then past the screen and along the opposite side of the outer court to the entrance, before returning to the guarded opening into the sanctuary. Changing direction on the plan of the tabernacle to complete the tour of the outer court gives better coverage. This strategy recognizes that chapters 11–16 are already aligned in parallel opposite chapters 1–7. The two sections, 1–7 and 11–17, are complementary in theme and ought to be read together. Chapters 1–7 are about how the people should bring their gifts to the altar for sacrifice and how their sins and defilements need atonement; chapters 11–15 give examples of defilement, chapter 16 describes how atonement is made. The bodily microcosm of the sacrificed animal in the first part is matched by a complementary microcosm in the second. The noble domestic animals to whom the covenant is extended stand opposite the zoo of animal kinds not to be eaten or touched. Thus the second half, 11–16, expands and completes the theme of the first half, 1–7.

Lastly, to confirm that this is the chosen route, when we get to chapter 16 we find that we have walked right round the outer court—here we are, back at the door where we came in. Our tour of the outer court is complete. Like Aaron, we will now make a backwards trajectory: first we find God telling Moses (Lev 16: 1) to teach Aaron how to proceed, when he is presumably still at the entrance to the court where he had been left at the end of chapter 10. The instructions tell him how to go into the most holy inner sanctuary, then running the story backwards, what animals to bring, then how to dress before entering it, then backwards again, to wash himself before dressing, and finally to make the sacrifice of atonement. David Damrosch calls this backwards sequence 'a rhetorical movement' by which Leviticus 11–25 seeks to reconstruct a metaphoric wholeness from the pieces of the metonymic narrative progressions it has taken apart.[2] Without disagreeing, it can also be said that the tracks that

[2] Damrosch 1987.

Aaron must make between the entry of the court of sacrifice, through the sanctuary to the holy place, and back again, guide the reader to each part of the tabernacle space. At the end of the chapter Aaron has washed and changed and come out of the tent of meeting into the court of the altar of sacrifice, here he offers the bull and the goat for sin offerings. The mention of his washing locates us at the outer court where the laver stands and where he will start off by bringing his animals, it is the place of the altar of sacrifice, as instructed in chapter 1 of Leviticus. The crossing and recrossing is a way of locating the point at which the book has arrived on the spatial projection of the tabernacle (Lev 16: 3–5).

In chapter 17 the lesson of the opening verses is repeated: that all animal slaughter must be brought to the tabernacle to be sacralized. The ring has already been closed, this is the latch which confirms the return to the point of origin. The beginning of chapter 17 echoes the words and reinforces the teaching of chapter 1.

Table 11.2.   Beginning and end of ring

End:	Beginning:
If any man of the house of Israel kills an ox or a lamb or a goat in the camp, or kills it outside the camp, and does not bring it to the door of the tent of meeting, to offer it as a gift to the Lord before the tabernacle of theLord, bloodguilt shall be imputed to that man. (Lev 17: 3–4)	Speak to the people of Israel and say to them, When any man of you brings offering to the Lord, you shall bring an offering of cattle from the herd or from the flock. . . . he shall offer it at the door of the tent of meeting . . . (Lev 1: 2–3)

We also find a benchmark telling us that we have completed the tour of the outer court: chapter 17 has the unusual double adddress which sets it apart: 'Say to Aaron and his sons, and to all the people of Israel, . . .' (17: 2). The chapter closes a ring, coming back to the beginning after summarizing much of what has gone before. It is a necessary part of the book's design that the biggest space of the tabernacle should correspond to the largest number of chapters, seven for each side. The reader now knows the way, the tour of the first of the three compartments is complete, the text can proceed straight through the screen at chapters 8–10 which divides the outer court from the sanctuary.

THE SANCTUARY

Remembering the analogies with Mount Sinai we should be ready for this middle compartment to contain something equivalent to the cloud on the mountain. It turns out that this is precisely where Moses was commanded to place the altar of incense (Exod 30: 6). This is where the table and the candelabra are placed on the narrow north–south axis of the building. Entry to this compartment is restricted, it is a holy place, dangerous even for consecrated priests unless they approach it with due precautions. We know from Exodus what the priests must do in here: Aaron and his sons must replenish the oil and keep the lights burning on the lampstand (Exod 30: 7–10) and replenish the show bread on the table, and eat it. Exodus has said how the sanctuary is to be furnished, with the lampstand (Exod 37: 17–24), the table for the show bread (Exod 37: 10–16), and the incense altar. Exodus has even said precisely where each article of furniture is to be placed:

And he put the table in the tent of meeting, on the north side of the tabernacle, outside the veil, and set the bread in order on it before the Lord; as the Lord had commanded Moses. And he put the lampstand in the tent of meeting, opposite the table on the south side of the tabernacle, and set up the lamps before the Lord; as the Lord had commanded Moses. And he put the golden altar in the tent of meeting before the veil, and burnt fragrant incense upon it; as the Lord had commanded Moses. (Exod 40: 22–7)

So the reader of Leviticus is correctly following the layout of the tabernacle, because there are two of the three named pieces of furniture here, on north and south. And this is the right place for Leviticus to explain two of the tasks which the priests must perform. The service of the candelabra is as follows:

Command the people of Israel to bring you pure oil from beaten olives for the lamp, that a light may be kept burning continually. Outside the veil of the testimony, in the tent of meeting, Aaron shall keep it in order from evening to morning before the Lord continually. (Lev 24: 2–4)

And the provisioning of bread for the table is described:

And you shall take fine flour, and bake twelve cakes of it; . . . and you shall set them in two rows, six in a row, upon the table of pure gold . . . Every sabbath day Aaron shall set it in order before the Lord continually on behalf of the people of Israel as a covenant for ever. (Lev 24: 5–8)

If the interpretation proposed were perfect, Leviticus would also provide a description in chapters 17–24 of the incense altar, or at least describe what the priests have to do for it. The claim is that incense is the equivalent in the tabernacle to cloud on the mountain and suet in the anatomy. But this is the one piece of furnishing of the tabernacle as given by Exodus which Leviticus ignores. All that can be said is that Leviticus 16: 11–14 says a lot about incense and mentions its altar. The instructions for supplying oil for the lampstand and bread for the table are located in the book in the part that corresponds to Exodus' instructions for the layout of the building. Their presence gives warning that the voyage round the desert tabernacle will shortly reach the second divider, since these two items are the very things which stand in the tabernacle in front of the screen which separates the most holy area from the rest (Exod 26: 33).

A second narrative is due, to correspond to the place of the second screen. And gratifyingly just here the narrative of the judgement on the blasphemer divides the book again. And it is no accident that the crime for which the blasphemer pays his life is to have dishonoured the name of the Lord, which was warned against in the Egypt peroration at the end of Leviticus 22. There is nothing haphazard about the placing of the story in this part of the book.

On the ground plan the sanctuary is a very small place to which entry is restricted, in the book plan it is less than seven chapters all told. The first thing facing the reader after the screen has been negotiated is the even smaller segment con-

sisting of a trio of chapters, 18, 19, and 20, about the cult and
righteousness. The reiterated Egypt peroration underlines
chapter 19 as one of the most important chapters in the book.
Why is it here in the middle of the tabernacle? Its central
position shows that these chapters on justice are the very
centre of the religion and therefore belong in the centre of the
tabernacle, and are the centre of the book of Leviticus. 'Shall
not the Judge of all the earth do right?' (Gen 19: 25). 'And I
will make justice the line and righteousness the plummet'
(Isa 28: 17).

In this section, which corresponds to the priests' part of
the tabernacle, the rules for a pure priesthood are given. The
two short chapters 21 and 22 form a little ring on their own,
and teach the rules for the marriage of the high priest, for
priests' obligations at funerals, for their families, and for
their physical condition of ritual purity. It is made very clear
that the laws of purity are much more restrictive for priests
than for other people and that breaches are much more
severely punished.

This section is also the fitting place to describe the calendrical feasts which are to be celebrated by a burnt offering.
Originally on reading Leviticus 1–7 it seemed arbitrary or
strange to confine the account of offerings by fire to free-will
offerings of individuals or groups without mentioning the
calendrical public sacrifices. A case of delayed completion,
the reason becomes clear in chapter 23, where the law of
offerings by fire is resumed in the list of the festivals
appointed by the Lord to divide the year. Chapters 1–7
taught the offerings made at the initiative of the laity, but
chapter 23 teaches about the offerings ordained by God for
his sabbaths. The latter rites are not a matter for lay initiative, but for the priests.

The other screen (Exod 26: 33) divides the sanctuary from
the innermost part, which contains the ark, which contains
the testament of the covenant (Exod 25: 17–22), guarded by
the cherubim. It is the abode of God on earth, the 'most holy
place', which can only be entered with correct precautions by
the high priest once a year. It is equivalent to the summit of
the mountain, where God descended to meet Moses, and to
the deep interior of the person where judgement and emotion

reside. It is the abode of God himself when he dwells among his people, the place of his glory and his covering cloud. Here (if entry were allowed) the reader would be standing in front of those awesome creatures who forever guard the entry to paradise. Here are the two cherubim, and under their covering wings the empty throne of God, which covers the ark (or coffer) and inside the ark, the testament of the covenant.

In this light the book is somewhat like a pilgrimage text. The worshippers make a journey of commemoration to a shrine and go round it with the sacred book as their guide, saying the words, marking out with their footsteps the very place of creation, or at least a space assigned by God to stand for his act of creation. Back into the problems of representation again, it is all taking place in the mind of the sixth- or fifth-century pilgrim, after the first destruction of the temple. There is no tabernacle, the faithful are not moving around in it, all the movement is in the book that they are reading, or hearing through their ears. Learning the book becomes a way of internalizing the tabernacle: it suggests a form of 'spiritual geography' that distinguishes the spiritual tabernacle from the physical tabernacle, in the same way as the spiritual Jerusalem was distinguished from the physical Jerusalem at the centre of the world. At the same time, moving round the tabernacle with the book, they are also moving round Mount Sinai, and even having access to parts of it that only Moses had.

As to the architectural space of the building and the space of the book, the pattern is a narrowing. It converges, movement in it flows through a funnel, burrows toward an interior point, or climbs to an inaccessible, hidden summit. It is concentrated and increasingly focused, it does not expand in all directions.[3] The model of the tabernacle is so deeply embedded in Leviticus that it contributes further to the differences with Deuteronomy on the subject of a central sanctuary. Leviticus' teaching on plural sanctuaries has a doctrinal basis too spiritual to have arisen as a strategy in a political impasse about rival holy places. A projectible universe constantly reconstituting itself in objects and places is the essence of its

---

[3] It is a cone, quite unlike the outward radiating circles of the Greek hearth and *agora*. Vernant 1983.

microcosmic thinking. The multiplication of tabernacles is implicit in the idea of replicable holy space. It would be a normal development of the philosophical microcosm which makes all sacred demarcations conform to the universal pattern. A side-effect of this habit of thought would be to allow the faithful to erect their sacred bounded spaces where they like. Or rather, the people do not need to be told any such thing, it will have been their age-old practice to sacralize space according to the divine proportions of the cosmos. The effect of microcosmic thinking is not to deny the importance of physical boundaries, but it makes them projectible. Correctly mapped on to space, their temple once consecrated will be as sacred as the original tabernacle, and they can build as many as they need.[4]

ATONEMENT

Discussing atonement was postponed until the pattern of the book had been laid out. The rule against eating blood is announced categorically in Leviticus 7: 22–7; only in chapter 19 is the blood doctrine given in its complete form. Leviticus prefaces the rule, 'You shall not eat anything with its blood' (Lev 19: 26) with, 'You shall not stand upon your brother's blood' (Lev 19: 16), or translated more accessibly, 'You shall not profit from your brother's blood.' Fulminations against eating blood, profiting from blood, blood of homicide, and illicit uses of blood, reverberate against the teaching of respect for life and the consecrated blood of sacrifice. This is the rhetoric of concrete logic, the initial rule expanded by a series of analogies.

The rite of animal sacrifice is the more awesome because of the strong teaching on animal blood in every other context. Blood must never be eaten, and Leviticus allows no unsacralized killing. Some commentators feel that in the English language the verb 'to eat' cannot be used for a liquid and so translate 'eat' with 'ingest', but their linguistic sensitivity is

---

[4] The reference to the tents of meeting in the plural in Psalm 74: 8 does not necessarily imply a date for the psalm, since Levitical teaching was likely to have been followed at the same time as Deuteronomic centralization.

misplaced. Eating, taking, partaking of blood fit the style better. The word for eating or consuming has many powerful and relevant meanings in Hebrew as well as in English, which are lost with 'ingest'. For any killing of a land animal apart from sacrifice the slayer must bear his iniquity himself, he will be cut off from his people, 'blood guilt shall be imputed to that man, he has shed blood' (17: 3–4). Levine points out the wordplay by which Leviticus writes about shedding animal blood in terms that are usually used for homicide, but he stops short of interpreting the laws about animals as lower-key representations of homicide laws.[5] There is no call to do so, since the language already serves well enough to dramatize the extreme gravity of the offence. Furthermore, Leviticus is about sacrifice and meat for food; the teaching on homicide is given elsewhere, in Genesis and in the Book of Numbers. The wider lessons are implicit. Genesis makes the reverse word-play, homicide described in terms of eating: God tells Cain that 'the ground . . . has opened its mouth to receive your brother's blood from your hand' (Gen 4: 11).

Given such telling verbal cross-references, it is not appropriate to try to determine precisely whether atonement is a form of ransoming, an expiation, a purification, or purgation. All these meanings are very close to each other, working by analogy from one context to the next. The word 'ransom' evokes the idea of covenant, a meaning never far beneath the surface in Leviticus. Serious breach of covenant deserves the death penalty; attack on the things belonging to the Lord is such a crime; eating meat with the blood in it is a very grave offence of the same order.

In the rite of atonement the blood of the sacrificed animal is used to anoint the altar, to sprinkle on it, and then it is poured out at the base. The body of the member of the congregation who must never eat meat with blood in it parallels again the altar which does not have blood burnt on it. The reason for not eating the blood is simply, 'For the life of the

---

[5] Levine assumes that Leviticus is at one with Deuteronomy on the latter's requirement that all animals for sacrifice be brought to the central shrine. Consequently he emphasizes the site, not the unsacralized killing: '. . . slaughter of animals at the wrong site is equated with the shedding of blood' (Levine 1989: 113

flesh is in the blood; and I have given it for you upon the altar to make atonement for your souls; for it is the blood that makes atonement, by reason of the life' (Lev 17: 11), and again: 'the life of every creature is the blood of it' (17: 14). Chapter 17 is nearly all about blood: 'I have given it to you to make atonement for your own lives.' Note again that this is the second half of Leviticus, but these enlargements of context and declarations of sameness (life = blood) are not causal explanations. They locate the rule in a series of associated classifications.

This is the context of Genesis and the creation that rationalizes the laws of purity. God made life, the life of all creatures belongs to God. If he had not given or assigned the blood of sacrifice for that specific purpose there could be no atonement. The blood doctrine is the context for the laws against touching the carcasses of animals defined as unable to be consecrated. Their blood (which carries the life) belongs to God, his laws protect them as the laws of a feudal lord protect the lives of his vassals.

On etymological grounds atonement is often described as a purification rite. It corrects a technical condition of being ritually unclean or impure. Even in English, the idea of purity goes deeper than washing clean. A 'pure' virgin is not necessarily a well-scrubbed girl. 'Pure' intentions are intentions unmixed with ulterior motives. Johannan Muffs suggests a technical meaning from Mesopotamian legal documents for 'pure', meaning 'quit', from the law of property and contract.[6] Purification also has the sense of refining in metallurgy.[7]

I have made you an assayer and tester among my people, that you may know and assay their ways. . . . they are bronze and iron, all of them act corruptly. The bellows blow fiercely, the lead is consumed by the fire; in vain the refining goes on, for the wicked are not removed. Refuse silver they are called, for the Lord has rejected them. (Jeremiah 6: 27–30)

[6] Muffs 1992: 89. 'Just as the sun is *zaki*, pure/quit, so the seller is quit', i.e. the seller relinquishes all claim to the object transferred. In this sense impure would mean some still adhering claim against the nominal possessor. Milgrom points out that a Hebrew related word means the same, *niggah* (Numbers 5: 31).

[7] Hoffman and Leibowitz-Schmidt 1994.

To describe the work of atonement as washing, lustration, purging, is appropriate for a rite that remedies uncleanness, as this does. But any major rite of purification does other things as well as remove the external effects of sin. By the strings of analogies it uses to form the idea of atonement Leviticus actually says less about the need to wash or purge than it says about 'covering'.

PEDIMENTAL COMPOSITION

Once past the first screen, which is the story of Aaron's sons' punishment, the reader is faced by a trilogy of chapters, 18 and 20 repeating each other, and between them chapter 19, which must be considered to be of central importance if only because of the way it is framed by the other two.

The two supporting chapters, 18 and 20, repeat each other like a song chorus or procession, chanting the same anathemas against the evil things that are done in the religions of Egypt and Canaan. They recall the ceremony described in Deuteronomy 27: 11–14 in which the twelve tribes are to be divided into two groups. Six of them are to stand upon Mount Gerizim, Simeon, Levi, Judah, Issachar, Joseph, and Benjamin, to bless the people, and the remaining six, Reuben, Gad, Asher, Zebulun, Dan, and Napthali, are to stand on Mount Ebal for the curse. Traditional commentators[8] have reconstructed the text and the scene in slightly varying ways. The Levites first face Mount Gerizim to call out a specific blessing, to which all the assembled tribes answer, Amen, and then turn round to face Mount Ebal, to call out the curse which is the converse of the blessing just given. The people answer, Amen, which is taken to constitute an oath not to commit the named sins. In effect Deuteronomy does not provide the text for the composite blessings/curses, but only gives twelve curses. Briefly, in Deuteronomy 27: 15–26, they are as follows: cursed be the man who makes a graven image, cursed be he who dishonours his father or mother, he who removes his neighbour's

---

[8] Tigay 1996: 252.

landmark, he who misleads a blind man, he who perverts justice, he who lies with his father's wife, he who lies with any kind of beast, he who lies with his sister, etc., he who lies with his mother-in-law, he who slays his neighbour in secret, he who takes a bribe to slay an innocent person, he who does not keep this law.

There is no obvious ordering of the curses, the sexual sins come mixed up with laws against taking bribes, moving landmarks, and misleading the blind. In the next chapter of Deuteronomy (28: 1–14), a further list of generalized blessings, in the form of promises of fertility and prosperity if the people keep the commandments, are followed by terrible disasters which will befall them if they do not, in 28: 15–68. The curses and blessings constitute the standard covenant formula for oaths concluding a treaty.

In chapters 18 and 20 Leviticus repeats the Deuteronomic formula with two interesting differences. First, in Deuteronomy the curses are drawn freely from the decalogue; prohibiting making molten or graven images is in the same list along with dishonouring father or mother, incest, murder, bribery, and corruption, whereas in the Leviticus version the laws in the two framing chapters 18 and 20 focus on idolatry and sexual offences. The first thing that the Leviticus writer has done is to rearrange the series of prohibitions, putting all the sexual offences into the outer chapters, the framing sections, and keeping all chapter 19's laws about righteous dealings in the middle, conspicuously in the place of honour. After Deuteronomy's comparatively haphazard list of curses in chapter 27 this is a very strong rearrangement. Second, the Leviticus writer further distinguishes its double list of sins from those anathematized in Deuteronomy by a preface that relates them to the cult. This also makes a strong difference to the reading. The Leviticus trilogy, chapters 18–20, is prefaced by a general injunction not to follow the statutes of Canaan and Egypt:

Say to the people of Israel, I am the Lord your God. You shall not do as they do in the land of Egypt, where you dwelt, and you shall not do as they do in the land of Canaan, to which I am bringing you. You shall not walk in their statutes. You shall do my ordinances and keep my statutes and walk in them. I am the Lord your God. You shall therefore keep my statutes and my ordinances, by doing which a man shall live: I am the Lord. (Lev 18: 2–5)

The Lord's ordinances are explicitly contrasted with the ordinances of the gods of Egypt and Canaan. Then follows the first of two matching sets of prohibitions. With slight variations in their sequencing but great overlap in content, the same peroration is repeated for each. There could not be a stronger framing of the central chapter at the apex of the pediment. Leviticus' scheme very deliberately puts the laws of righteous and honest dealings at the centre and the sexual sins at the periphery. Less a pedimental composition, these two chapters are more like two massively carved pillars on either side of a shrine, or like a proscenium arch. The laws on each side against incest, sodomy, and bestiality are backed by twice-repeated warnings that the land will vomit the people out if they follow these cults. The anathemas are not laws about everyday affairs. If they were intended to provide guidance for the organization of marriage, the choice of marriage partners, or about wrong and right conduct of family life and sex, they would have to be judged strangely inadequate. They say nothing about inheritance, divorce, or succession. The context is inescapably cultic. The perorations refer to defilement of the land, a grave situation which results from idolatry.

The formality of the context cannot be overlooked. These laws are about defilement by idolatry. They refer directly to filthy foreign cults. The verses start with Egypt and Canaan, so it is to be presumed that they refer to Egyptian and Canaanite cults. It was widely suggested in the Bible that Canaanite cults had male and female temple prostitutes (Deut 23: 18)[9] and the fact that there is no other evidence for it does not affect the interpretation based upon this belief. Incest is readily associated with the religion of the Egyptian Pharaohs. Foreign rites involving sexual congress with animals was cited for the surrounding regions. Herodotus said in connection with the cult of Pan:

The he-goat and Pan are both called Mendes in the Egyptian language. In this province, in my time, a monstrosity took place: a

9 See also 1 Kings 14: 24, 10, 22; 2 Chron 20: 35, 37.

Table 11.3. Example of pedimental composition

Leviticus 18	Leviticus 20
Prohibitions	*Prohibitions*
6–18. Incest with near kin and in-laws, father, mother, father's wife, sister, son's daughter, daughter's daughter, father's wife's daughter, father's sister, mother's sister, father's brother's wife, son's wife, brother's wife, a woman and her daughter, wife's sister	2–5. Devote children to Molech
	6–8. Mediums and Wizards
	9. Cursing father or mother
	10. Neighbour's wife
	11. Father's wife
	12. Daughter-in-law
	13. Sodomy
	14. A daughter and her mother
	15–16. Bestiality
19. Menstrual uncleanness	17. Sister
20. Neighbour's wife	18. Menstrual uncleanness
21. Devote children to Molech	19. Mother's or father's sister
22. Sodomy	20. Uncle's wife
23. Bestiality	21. Brother's wife
24–30. For all of these abominations the men of the land did, who were before you, so that the land became defiled; lest the land vomit you out, when you defile it, as it vomited out the nation that was before you.	22. You shall therefore keep all my statutes and all my ordinances, and do them, that the land where I am bringing you to dwell may not vomit you out. You shall not walk in the customs of the nation which which I am casting out before you.

he-goat coupled with a woman, plain, for all to see. This was done in the nature of a public exhibition.[10]

Always reserved about religious matters, he does not say that the monstrosity was part of a cult of Pan. Copulation with a stallion was part of a Vedic rite, also plain for all to see and a public exhibition.[11] Use of menstrual blood was associated with pacts with demons. The two supporting chapters both mention Molech worship, the second one emphasizes the cultic context by denouncing mediums and seers. The effect of using these unedifying sexual deviations framing chapter

[10] Herodotus 1987: 2.46   [11] Doniger 1990: 18–37.

19 is to show up the concepts of righteousness, liberty, and justice which it expounds in the middle. These chapters contrast the pure and noble character of the Hebrew God with the libidinous customs of the very strange false gods.

Chapters 18 and 20 have regularly been cited to condemn homosexual intercourse. The argument about their meaning has been given a new interest of recent years. 'Homosexuality has emerged as a central issue in organized religion in America, and most religious bodies have needed to examine their position toward it—often heatedly. Gay and lesbian Jews have themselves entered this discourse.[12] Homosexual Jews, grieved to find themselves excluded from their religion, have not only found arguments to reconcile their apparently divergent beliefs, they have founded thriving gay communities, with gay synagogues and other gay religious institutions. Their communities are able to find common cause with the people of Israel wrongfully oppressed. One of their arguments follows the lines of that presented above: the laws of Leviticus 18: 22 and 20: 13 are referring to temple prostitution. Following on this, the expression, Thou shalt not lie with a man as one lies with a woman, is in parallel with the prohibition against adultery with a neighbour's wife, both are intended to protect the married state.[13] Furthermore, the idea of homosexuality as a condition of a person was not envisaged: 'what Leviticus forbids is not homosexuality as understood today (in other words, a permanent orientation), but homosexual acts performed by heterosexuals (for example, the molestation described in Genesis 19: 4–5).[14] But another point arises from closely examining the two lists in chapters 18 and 20.

Recall that these lists are edited versions of the anathemas and curses of Deuteronomy 27 and 28. The effect has been to group together the cultic and sexual transgressions and to place them like a frame supporting chapter 19, which collects together the laws on righteousness. By a further subdivision, chapter 18 names the sins and chapter 20 names the punishments, and in chapter 20 the sins are grouped according to penalty. Offering children to Molech is punished by stoning, wizards and magicians are cut off. Then follow five sins punished by death, cursing father or mother, adultery, sex with father-in-law or daughter-in-law, homosexual acts, and bestiality. Whereas sex with a daughter and her mother is punished by burning, homosexual acts are set at the same level of gravity as adultery. A community which is determined to live by the law would take them equally seriously, and no one who would tolerate an adulterer in the community would be able consistently to persecute a homosexual.

Set between such hair-raising anathemas, chapter 19 is bound to seem tame. It can easily be overlooked because it surveys and enlarges upon some of the laws that Leviticus has given already. As the elaborate rhetorical framing suggests, it is in fact the most important chapter of the whole book, the chapter on the meaning of righteousness. The earlier laws remain cryptic and controversial if read separately, they need chapter 19 to bring them together. It starts off telling the people to honour their parents, keep the sabbaths, and not to turn to idols (verses 1–4). Then the doctrine of sacred left-overs from chapter 7: 16–18, is reiterated here (verses 5–8), contextualized, expanded, and enhanced by the laws on gleaning which follow on immediately. They require the compassionate farmer to make deliberate left-overs of his harvest for the sake of the poor (Lev 19: 9–10). The peroration of the chapter repeats the teaching which will be found in many other places:

You shall do no wrong in judgment, in measures of length or weight or quantity. You shall have just balances, just weights, a just ephah, and a just hin. (Lev 19: 35–6)

This chimes with Deuteronomy 25: 13–15:

You shall not have in your bag two kinds of weights, a large and a small. You shall not have in your house two kinds of measures, a large and a small. A full and just weight you shall have, a full and just measure you shall have.

And with Proverbs 11: 1 'A false balance is an abomination to the Lord, but a just weight is his delight' (also Proverbs, 16: 11; 20: 10, 23). The laws against stealing, lying, defrauding, swearing falsely, that were considered in Leviticus 5–6 in connection with sin offerings and guilt offerings, are repeated and concluded with the rule that astonishes Christians who did not think it could belong to the 'Old Testament': You shall love your neighbour as yourself (19: 18). Chapter 19 is not complete, it exemplifies the rhetorical principle of delayed completion by finding its counterpart only at the end, chapter 26. Only then do the pieces fall into place.

(12)

Inside the Holy of Holies

Weighing In

The 56 lb. weight. A solid iron
Unit of negation. Stamped and cast
With an inset, rung-thick, moulded, short crossbar
For a handle. Squared-off and harmless looking
Until you tried to lift it, then a socket-ripping
Life-belittling force—
Gravity's black box, the immovable
Stamp and squat and square-root of dead weight
Yet balance it
Against another one placed on a weighbridge—
And everything trembled, flowed with give and take.

Seamus Heaney[1]

When the second screen has been passed the reader is standing, as it were, inside the holy of holies. This is the apotheosis of the principle of containing forms. Jerusalem is the centre of the world, in the centre of Jerusalem is the tabernacle, in the centre of the tabernacle is the ark of the covenant. The virtual pilgrim with book in hand knows that he has arrived at this hidden place because in chapter 26 the Lord God proclaims his covenant no less than eight times (26: 9, 15, 25, 42 (three times), 44, 66). Another elaborate literary construction makes chapters 25 and 27 into a massive frame for honouring chapter 26.

THE GREAT PROCLAMATION OF LIBERTY

In the innermost, holiest part of the tabernacle, under the shadowing protective wings, the testament of the covenant

[1] Heaney 1996: 17 'Weighing In'.

lies in the coffer, or ark. At the very end of the book, the enigmatic analogies are finally expounded. This writer does not
make ineffable pronouncements; he is still talking the language of analogies. To discover the secret of what is inside
the ark, read what Leviticus says is contained in the coffer.
Read chapter 26 and find nothing less than the terms of the
covenant itself, strict reciprocity, honourable dealings, and
simple fairness. If Leviticus was the first to be written,[2]
chapter 19 gives the basis for the curses of Deuteronomy 27,
and likewise Leviticus chapter 26 provides the basis for the
blessings and curses of Deuteronomy 28. The two chapters
of Leviticus, 19 and 26, supply two consecutive chapters of
Deuteronomy, not consecutive here because separated by
their elaborate frames. Deuteronomy 28 starts with blessings, in verses 1–14, and goes on to horrendous curses which
underwrite the covenant of Moab; then much later Moses
reminds the people of Israel that if they return to his law God
will restore their fortunes (Deut 30: 1–14, and again 15–20).
Leviticus 26: 4–13 starts with blessings; it goes on to curses,
in verses 14–39, and then it concludes the series by having the
Lord turn round sweetly and say that he will never forget the
covenant he made with their forefathers (26: 40–5). It is a
treaty formula, but all that God has asked from his people for
their side of the treaty is that they keep the laws.

We now have two frames; like the two centre-pieces, they
have to be read together. The first frame has been summa-
rized, the cultic prohibitions in chapters 18 and 20 give a
sombre and punitive tone. The second frame, formed by
chapters 25 and 27, is in a joyous tone. Not to wait for them
is to miss this message. Chapter 25 gives the great proclama-
tion of liberty. It does not talk about liberty and justice in the
abstract, but as usual it uses analogies, making patterns in
time with movements across space: 'And you shall hallow the
fiftieth year, and proclaim liberty throughout the land to all
its inhabitants; it shall be a jubilee for you, when each of you
shall return to his property and each of you shall return to
his family' (Lev 25: 10 ff.). According to Moshe Weinfeld,
freedom and liberation were defined in both Mesopotamia

---

[2] This is the thesis of Milgrom 1991: 373–5.

and in Egypt by the idea of 'returning home or to one's home town'.

The original Mesopotamian term for freedom is *amargi*, which means 'returning to the mother (or: mother-home)', and similarly in Israel, the aim of the Jubilee is that everybody returns to his family and patrimony (Lev 25.10) . . . In Egypt Ramses IV (1155–1150 BCE) boasts that he caused those who had fled to return to their home-towns. The same language is used in the freedom proclamations of Ptolemaic Egypt . . .: 'everyone shall return to his own patrimony . . .'[3]

The idea is essentially to achieve justice and righteousness in the land. Freedom means that no one can be permanently enslaved, debts are to be cancelled, and land returned to its original owners in the jubilee year. To be able to promise this Leviticus has to insist that the land belongs to God, he is the owner, and the people are his tenants using it by right of a divine grant or contract.[4] Liberty in God's law is at last revealed as the culminating point to which the many times repeated reference to rescue from serfdom in Egypt have been leading.

Release of slaves and cancellation of debts incurred under the preceding regime were common practice for victorious conquerors, a magnanimity that cost them nothing while their rule was new and their power to enforce it recently demonstrated. But the law of Leviticus requires a redistribution every fifty years, something much more controversial and difficult to enforce for an established government. The jubilee doctrine, if it could have been enforced, would mean much for the welfare of the people. Effectively, it prohibits private accumulation and even accumulation by the temple treasury. It ensures that there will be no gross inequality of wealth-holding. No permanent underclass of enslaved families will feel aggrieved by the lineal transmission of privilege. Solidarity will not be undermined by resentment of perceived injustice. When Leviticus tells the people to walk in God's law, its insistence that the law will make them prosperous and able to resist their enemies is backed by this constitutional measure.

---

[3] Weinfeld 1985: 319.   [4] Levine 1993.

The first side of the frame, chapter 25, deals with person-to-person obligations, the release of slaves, their return to their homes, redemption of property, remission of secular debts. The second side, chapter 27, deals with the same topics from the point of view of debts to the Lord. God himself respects the jubilee law (Lev 27: 24) and he himself allows redemption of persons (Lev 27: 2–8), property (Lev 27: 14–15), and animals (Lev 27: 9–13). God himself, as a creditor, comes under the power of the jubilee laws. He proves his generosity by telling Moses the conditions under which persons, animals, or chattels which have been dedicated to his service can be redeemed. This is the grand pedimental frame over the ark of the covenant.

Chapter 27 also serves another rhetorical function. Ring composition is expected to end with a return to the beginning. Returning home is given a literary form when chapter 27 latches the ending on to the beginning. Recall that chapter 2: 3 starts with the meats reserved for the priests at a sacrifice (also 2: 10; 6: 29; 7: 6–10; 8: 31–6; 10: 12–20). At the end we see how Leviticus is in a large sense all about the things that have been consecrated and the things that belong to the Lord: blood, the priests, the land, and dedicated animals. From the time we left the outer court and passed the first screen into the sanctuary, which makes six chapters in all, two of them, 19 and 26, dominate the reading by the power of their pedimental framing. These two are about aspects of God's justice. Even going as far as we can go into the interior of the tabernacle, expecting to unveil its secrets, what we find is no secret: still, only and always, the justice of God and his fidelity to the covenants he made with Abraham and Isaac and Jacob.

READING LEVITICUS THROUGH GENESIS: COVERING

The chapters about physical impurity of humans who had to be cleansed by atonement were arranged to present the body in a series of covers, the covering of skin, the garment covering the skin, the house covering both. When we reach the end of the book we find that over the ark of the covenant is another cover, the throne where God sits (Exodus 30: 6). Without having to have recourse to philological arguments, this is the case for arguing that the atonement rite affords a cover for the people of Israel.

Pause for a moment and reflect on the range of reference in English for cover: to get insurance cover, to cover a debt, to stand cover for a friend. Soldiers take cover, every one does in a storm and game animals take cover from hunters. A shield covers the body, cover is a lid of a pot, of a manhole, covering is clothing. The idea of the garment as representing the person who wears it is a common biblical theme. The high priest's garment represented much more, the cosmos, the history of Israel, and the glory of God: 'For upon his long robe the whole world was depicted, and the glories of the fathers were engraved on the four rows of stones, and thy majesty on the diadem upon his head' (Wisdom of Solomon 18: 24).[5]

The way Leviticus emphasizes the theme of covering recalls the Genesis story of Adam and Eve making garments of fig leaves in the Garden of Eden. First Adam and Eve were naked, but after they had eaten the fruit, they sewed fig leaves together and made aprons. When the Lord God walked in the garden in the evening, Adam and Eve hid; on being questioned, Adam said: 'I heard thy voice . . . and I was afraid because I was naked', to which God replied: 'Who told you that you were naked?' Then, illogically to our mind, but in fact quite correctly, God deduced that Adam had broken his one command. How did God guess? Was it because of his omniscience, or was it from what Adam had said? And why did the story end with God making garments of skins for them to wear? If it was just to encourage their nascent modesty, leafy garments would have done.

As in English, the Hebrew word for 'naked' has several senses. In one meaning it implies sexual shame and modesty: in this story, 'they became one flesh . . . they were both naked and were not ashamed'. But when they had eaten the fruit their eyes were opened, and they recognized their nakedness. In this context the garment of fig leaves that they made is

---

[5] James Kugel drew my attention to these lines: Philo, *Special Laws*, 1.84; *Moses*, 2.117.

surely rightly translated as apron, or loincloth,[6] some covering for the pubic region.

In another sense, naked means being exposed, bare. Adam says that he was afraid because he was naked (Gen 3: 10), to which God replies: 'What's this? Why do you suddenly talk about being exposed? What is the danger in this sheltered place?' And then he comes, reasonably as we can now see, to the conclusion that Adam is indeed exposed to danger and expulsion. The sexual connotations are justified, but we should not overlook the meaning of exposure.

In the first part, the fig-leaf story is clearly talking about bodily appearance, sexual display and the covering of sex. The root for naked, exposed, bare, gives derivatives: to make naked, for sexual offences (in Lev 20: 18, 19); also to strip, to lay bare, and as a noun, the male genital organs. This is the sense of naked in Genesis 2, 'naked and not ashamed', and of Gen 9: 22–3 when Noah, lying asleep naked in his vineyard, was mocked by his impious son and covered up by his two good sons. (And Leviticus in chapters 18 and 20 prohibits exposing the nakedness of a kinsperson.)

Genesis expands this politically to mean exposed to view, to mockery, vulnerable to spies, wide open and undefended. Joseph said to his brothers: 'You are spies come to see the nakedness of the land' (Gen 42: 9, 12). It also suggests a bare place, devastated, a desert. Ezekiel takes up this sense in the image of Jerusalem as an abandoned woman: 'I will uncover thy nakedness to them, they shall see thee naked and bare' (Ezek 16: 37, 39). The same root gives the vocabulary for indecent exposure, a land laid waste, the skins of bodies, and for the many coverings of the tabernacle, sacred vessels, and bodies.[7] In English the word naked has a similar range, in addition to the sexual references we talk of naked power, naked truth, the heart bared, a bare land, an exposed site, deceit exposed and also a barefaced lie.

---

[6] Sarna 1989: 26.

[7] As a noun the dictionary gives skin (BDB: 736), the skin of the sacrificial victim (Exod 29: 14; Lev 4 and 5), or any skin (Lev 11: 32; 13: 48; Num 31: 20), for the coverings of sacred utensils (Num 4: 5–15), and of the tabernacle itself (see also Exod 25: 55) and of the ark (Exod 26: 35; 36; 39).

Return to the story: on the day that God made Adam (Gen 2: 4–8) the land had no planted fields, the ground was untilled, and watered by mists, it was a desolate and wild place. The first thing that God did was to plant a garden in Eden. After they had disobeyed the one command and had found that they were naked, God cursed roundly. He cursed the serpent, cursed the woman, cursed Adam, cursed the ground, and said: 'Thorns and thistles it shall bring forth to you' (Gen 3: 15–18). Realizing that Adam and Eve, naked outside the garden, would be vulnerable, God replaced their fig-leaf covering with more serviceable garments. The meaning has shifted from sexual shame to exposure and vulnerability. He clothed them (Gen 3: 21) to protect them from the thorns and thistles.[8] The garments of skin that God sewed for them are the first of the coverings in the store of allusions on which Leviticus draws: in the inside of the body the soft innermost parts have solid covers, the thick layers of suet fat over the kidneys and liver; outside the body there is the hide of the animal or the skin of a person, the garment over the skin over the fat over the innermost parts, the house on the garment on the skin, and so on.

READING SCAPEGOAT AND
SCAPEBIRD THROUGH GENESIS

Without reading the whole book it was difficult to interpret the rites of atonement that assimilated the cleansed leper to the ordained priest, or the sacrifice of one bird or goat and the releasing of the second. The place of teaching on God's justice has now been shown to be central. Impurity and sin, which in many interpretations of the book held the foreground, have taken their relatively minor place. A new reading of the scapegoat ceremony is possible. In scapegoat rites in other places, Greece for instance, the corresponding

---

[8] Since the covering idea, with all it implies for righteousness, is so important in the idea of atonement, it sounds biased to say that for the priestly school God instituted 'a cultic system detached from social arrangements or justice' (Knohl 1995: 141).

animal, or person, is roughly treated or killed. However, it must be firmly said that no violence is committed against the Leviticus scapegoat.

Reading the ceremony, Aaron has been washed and robed, and is furnished with a bull, two goats, and a ram. Then it appears that one of the goats is not to be sacrificed, but will be set free (Lev 16: 9). It is popularly assumed that it is destined to an unhappy fate. It is true that it is laden with the sins of the people, and carries them away. However, nothing says that the goat that is allowed to go forth to Azazel in the wilderness is condemned to death or even to humiliation and contempt. In Bible culture the wilderness is not always such a bad place to be. The standard interpretation jars with the kindly theology, the low-key reading of impurity, the deflection of accusations, the care for animal life. It pays no regard to the relation of Levitical rites to each other, or their relation to major themes of the Pentateuch. Remembering how the chapter depends on what has gone before, and remembering that the archaic style of writing places one analogy upon another in escalating degrees of importance, it is right to recall that the model for the scapegoat has already been anticipated.

Read it again: Aaron brings two goats and casts lots upon them. Their fates are uneven, for the goat on whom the lot for the Lord falls is to be killed as a sin offering, the other is to be sent alive into the wilderness. Surely the two goats, one sacrificed and one escaping with its life in the open field, parallel the two pairs of birds treated in the same way in the rites of cleansing from leprosy?

He shall take the living bird with the cedarwood and the scarlet stuff and the hyssop, and dip them and the living bird in the blood of the bird that was killed over the running water; and he shall sprinkle it seven times upon him who is to be cleansed of leprosy; then he shall pronounce him clean, and shall let the living bird go into the open field. (Lev 14: 6–7)

All this takes place at the door of the tent of meeting. Then the same for the cleansing of a house stricken with leprosy and cured, the two birds again, one of them killed, the other dipped in its blood: 'and he shall let the living bird go out of the city into the open field' (Lev 14: 53). There is also a curious one-sided anointing of the cured leper:

The priest shall take some of the blood of the guilt offering, and the priest shall put it on the tip of the right ear of him who is to be cleansed, and on the thumb of his right hand, and on the great toe of his right foot. Then the priest shall take some of the log of oil, and pour it into the palm of his own left hand, and dip his right finger in the oil that is in his left hand, and sprinkle some oil with his finger seven times before the Lord. (Lev 14: 14–16)

The same one-sided anointing is repeated with oil (Lev 14: 18). The precedent for this has already been given in chapter 8. At the consecration of Aaron and his sons, Moses has to anoint them with blood, on the tip of the right ear, the thumb of the right hand, and the big toe of the right foot (Lev 8: 23–4). Unlike the leper's rite, the anointing of the right side extremities with oil is left out for the priests, the anointing oil is sprinkled on them (Lev 8: 30). This rite of consecration is described first in Exodus 29: 20.

What is going on here? The rite is not as easy to perform as it sounds. Anointing someone on the right ear, thumb, and foot, with the right hand, is difficult standing face to face. The body has got two sides, one right, one left. Why is only the right side anointed? Two birds, two goats, the two sides of a person, in each pair only one is selected for consecration. Is the other side allowed to 'go free'? The goat is allowed to go forth, the verb that Moses was told to say to Pharaoh, 'Let my people go!' (Exod 10: 3), and used over and over again in Exodus. What happens to the goat once freed is not important to those who stay behind.

Two elements in the rite are more significant than the scapegoat's fate; one is the repeated parallel drawn between cleansed leper and consecrated priest. The teaching says something about degrees of purity. By the rite of atonement the cured leper is raised above the sick leper to a higher status on the ladder of purity; by the same rite the priest rises above the lay person to a higher ritual status. The parallel between priest and cured leper may be no more than part of the complex scheme of relative standing on the up–down dimension of honour or purity. But there is more to consider.

The repeated evocation of uneven complementarity, one element being chosen, the other freed, cannot be ignored. Following the example of Calum Carmichael, it is instructive to treat the biblical laws as if they were framed as an ongoing commentary on the biblical narratives.[9] In this perspective, recall the conspicuously uneven destinies of two brothers in Genesis. As between Isaac and Ishmael, the first accepted the constraints of the covenant, and the second was allowed to go free. When the Lord prophesies to Hagar that her son Ishmael would grow up to be a 'wild ass of a man' (Gen 16: 12), that meant unconstrained, nothing pejorative, but with some of the implications we might have for a lion 'born free'. There is no judgement against Ishmael, he is neither immoral nor destined to an unhappy or godless life. He is not condemned, he is free to roam the wilderness and will be a great prince. He is like the bird and the goat which were not chosen, while Isaac is parallel to the goat or the bird on which the lot of the Lord fell, destined to a sacred calling.

Likewise for two other brothers of that line: when Jacob cheated Esau of his birthright, Jacob came thereby under the constraints of the covenant. In a religious context being consecrated is the better destiny, but Esau still prospered and his house became a great kingdom. Other uneven pairs come to mind too; the thought of the Northen Kingdom is never far from biblical writing. Jacob and Israel, Judah and Joseph, Jerusalem and Samaria, the Leviticus writer may be credited with mourning the loss of the other half. His interests are not confined narrowly to the teaching of cultic practice. It is not far-fetched to read in this way the contrast of an animal chosen for consecration and another animal allowed to go free.

There is an echo of the injunction in Leviticus 19: 19 not to join grossly uneven pairs, whether cattle, seed, or textiles:

You shall not let your cattle breed with a different kind; you shall not sow your field with two kinds of seed; nor shall there come upon you a garment of cloth made of two kinds of stuff. (Lev 19: 19)

These rules against mixing are repeated in Deuteronomy:

[9] Carmichael 1985.

You shall not sow your vineyard with two kinds of seed . . .
You shall not plough with an ox and an ass together.
You shall not wear a mingled stuff, wool and linen together. (Deut 22: 9–11)

It is more in keeping with the ritual of one-sided anointing and with the way that Leviticus leans on Genesis to interpret these rules as teaching the old lesson about complementarity. The pairs are not so much uneven as different; respecting their difference is symbolic of completion and totality.[10] A body cannot be composed entirely of eyes, or hands.[11] Recall that parallelism is not just a way of writing, not just a stylistic device. It is only possible to write in parallels because it is a way of thinking, which is also a way of living in which it is impossible to organize except in terms of wholes and their halves, sometimes equal, more often unequal.

Leviticus' general reflection on God's justice reaches forward to the Book of Job. God's choice is unconstrained. His election is never deserved. The converse is also true: demerit does not explain misfortune; disease or barrenness is not the fault of the victim. This feature of Levitical teaching contrasts with the punishing theodicy of other religions.[12] The fate of the two goats was settled by lot. There is no way that a person could merit being chosen by God. He chose Israel freely, and his prophecies and promises became Israel's destiny.

[10] Saul Olyan's unpublished work brings out this deep structuralist aspect of the Bible's thought. 'Totality is communicated by a binary pairing understood to be all-encompassing; hierarchy is communicated when one member of an opposition is privileged over the other' (' "You shall keep my charge": boundaries, hierarchy and the Israelite cult').

[11] Paul, 1 Corinthians 12: 12 ff.

[12] For example, in the Dead Sea community the causes of disease might be attributed to transgression (Baumgarten, J., 1990).

REFERENCES

AVALOS, H. I., 'Medicine', in *The Oxford Encyclopedia of Archaeology in the Near East* (1997), 450–9.

BAEKE, V., 'The Wuli system of thought: the dead, the water spirits and witchcraft', in Luc de Heusch (ed.), *Objects: Signs of Africa* (Brussels, Snoek and Zoon, 1996), 58–92.

BASCOM, WILLIAM, *Ifa Divination* (Indiana University Press, 1969).

—— *Sixteen Cowries: Yoruba Divination from Africa to the New World* (Indiana University Press, 1980).

BAUMGARTEN, A. I., 'The temple scroll, toilet practices and the Essenes', *Jewish History* 10/1 (1996), 9–20.

BAUMGARTEN, JOSEPH M., 'The four Zadokite fragments on skin disease', *Journal of Jewish Studies* (1990), 153–65.

BAYLISS, M., 'The cult of dead kin in Assyria and Babylonia', *Iraq* (1973), 115–25.

BECK, B., 'The symbolic merger of body, space and cosmos in Hindu Tamil Nadu', Contributions to Indian sociology NS, 10 (1976), 213–44.

BERNSTEIN, B., 'A public language: some sociological implications of a linguistic form', *British Journal of Sociology* 10 (1959), 311–26. (Reprinted in *Class, Codes and Control*, i (1971).)

—— 'A socio-linguistic approach to social learning', in *Class, Codes and Control*, i: *Theoretical Studies towards a Sociology of Language* (Routledge and Kegan Paul, 1971), 118–39.

BLACK, JEREMY, and GREEN, A., *Gods, Demons and Symbols of Ancient Mesopotamia, an Illustrated Dictionary* (British Museum Press, 1992).

BLENKINSOPP, JOSEPH, 'Deuteronomy and the politics of post-mortem existence', *Vetus Testamentum* (1995), 1–16.

BURNS, ROBERT, 'I murder hate', in *The Life and Works of Robert Burns*, ed. Robert Chambers, rev. W. Wallace, iii (1896), 172.

BUSIA, K. A., *The Position of the Chief in the Modern Political System of the Ashanti* (International African Institute, Oxford University Press, 1951).

BUTTRICK, G. A., *et al.* (eds), *The Interpreter's Dictionary of the Bible* (Abingdon Press, 1962).

CAMPBELL, JOHN, *Honour, Family and Patronage* (Oxford University Press, 1964).

CARMICHAEL, CALUM, *Law and Narrative in the Bible* (Cornell University Press, 1985).

CARMICHAEL, CALUM, 'A strange sequence of rules: Leviticus 19.20–26', in J. Sawyer (ed.), *Reading Leviticus* (Sheffield, 1996), 182–206.

CARRUTHERS, MARY, *The Book of Memory: A Study of Memory in Medieval Culture* (Cambridge University Press, 1990).

CARTRY, M., and DE HEUSCH, L. (eds), *Systèmes de Pensée en Afrique Noire*, Cahier 2: *Le Sacrifice 1* (1976); Cahier 3: *Le Sacrifice 2* (1978); Cahier 4: *Le Sacrifice 3* (1979); Cahier 5: *Le Sacrifice 4* (1981); Cahier 6: *Le Sacrifice 5* (1983) (L'Ecole Pratique des Hautes Etudes, Section des Sciences Religieuses).

CASSIRER, ERNST, *An Essay on Man* (Yale University Press, 1944).
—— *Sprache und Mythos*, trans. Suzanne Langer, *Language and Myth* (Harper, 1945).
—— *The Myth of State* (Yale University Press, 1946).

CASSUTO, U., *A Commentary on the Book of Genesis* (original Hebrew, 1949), pt. 2: *From Noah to Abraham*, English trans. Israel Abrahams (Jerusalem, Magnes Press, 1964).

CHEMLA, K., 'La pertinence du concept de classification pour l'analyse de textes mathématiques chinois', *Extrême-Orient-Extrême-Occident* (1988), 61–87.

CHOURAQUI, ANDRÉ, *Il Crie . . . Lévitique* (J. C. Lattès, 1993).

CLIFFORD, RICHARD, *The Cosmic Mountain in Canaan and in the Old Testament* (Harvard University Press, 1972).

CLINES, DAVID J. A., 'The Wisdom Books', in Stephen Bigger (ed.), *Creating the Old Testament, the Emergence of the Hebrew Bible* (Blackwell, 1989), 269–91.

COHEN, L., and HESSE, MARY, *Inductive Appraisal of Scientific Theories* (Clarendon Press, 1980).

COHEN, PHILIP, *Ramban on the Torah* (Rubin, 1985).

COHN, ROBERT, *The Shape of Sacred Space: Four Biblical Studies* (AAR Studies in Religion 23, California, Scholars Press, 1981).

CONGER, G. P., *Microcosms in the History of Philosophy* (Columbia University Press, 1922).

CROSS, FRANK MOORE, *Canaanite Myth and Hebrew Epic: Essays in the History of the Religion of Israel* (Harvard University Press, 1973)

CRYER, FREDERICK, *Divination in Ancient Israel and its Near Eastern Environment* (JSOTS 142, Sheffield Academic Press, 1994).

DAHL, G., and HJORT, A., *Having Herds, Pastoral Herd Growth and Economy* (Stockholm, Dept. of Social Anthropology, 1976).

DAMROSCH, DAVID, 'Law and narrative in the priestly work', in *The Narrative Covenant: Transformations of Genre in the Growth of Biblical Literature* (Harper and Row, 1987), 261–97.

DAN, JOSEPH, 'The language of mystical prayer', *Studies in Spirituality* (1995), 40–60.

—— 'Jerusalem in Jewish spirituality', in Nitza Rosovsky (ed.), *City of the Great King: Jerusalem from David to the Present* (Harvard University Press, 1996).

DETIENNE, MARCEL, *Les maîtres de la Vérité dans la Grèce Archaique* (Paris, Maspero, 1967); trans. Janet Lloyd, *Masters of Truth in Archaic Greece* (Zone Books, 1996).

—— and VERNANT, J.-P., *La Cuisine du Sacrifice en Pays Grec* (Gallimard, 1979).

DEVISCH, R., 'Mediumistic divination among the Northern Yaka of Zaire', in P. M. Peek (ed.), *African Divination Systems: Ways of Knowing* (Indiana University Press, 1991), 112–32.

DONIGER, WENDY, 'The tail of the Indo-European horse sacrifices', *Incognita* 1/1 (1990), 18–37.

DOUGLAS, M., 'Animals in Lele religous symbolism', *Africa* 27 (1957).

—— *The Lele of the Kasai* (London, International African Institute, 1963).

—— 'The body of the world', *International Social Science Journal* 125, 395–9; in Eli Kazancigil (ed.), *Tales of Cities: The Culture and Political Economy of Urban Spaces* (Blackwell, UNESCO, 1990).

—— (1993a) 'Atonement in Leviticus', *Jewish Studies Quarterly* 1/2 (1993), 109–30.

—— (1993b) 'Rightness of Categories', in M. Douglas and D. Hull (eds), *How Classification Works* (Edinburgh University Press, 1993), 239–69.

—— (1993c) *In the Wilderness: the Doctrine of Defilement in the Book of Numbers* (Sheffield Academic Press, 1993).

—— (1993d) 'The place of Balaam in the Book of Numbers', *Man: Journal of the Royal Anthropological Institute* 28/3, (1993), 411–30.

—— 'Poetic structure in Leviticus', in D. Wright, D. Freedman, and A. Hurvitz (eds), *Pomegranates and Golden Bells* (Eisenbrauns, 1995), 239–56.

—— 'Sacred Contagion', in John Sawyer (ed.), *Leviticus* (Sheffield Academic Press, 1996), 86–106.

DOUGLAS, MARY, and NEY, STEVEN, *Missing Persons: a Criticism of Personhood in the Social Sciences* (California University Press, 1998).

DOUGLAS, M., and HULL, D. (eds), *How Classification Works* (Edinburgh, 1993).

DURAND, J.-L., 'La Bête Grècque, Propositions pour une Topologie des Corps à manger', in M. Detienne and J.-P. Vernant, *La Cuisine du Sacrifice en Pays Grec* (Gallimard, 1979), 133–81.

—— *Sacrifice et Labeur en Grèce Ancienne: Essai d'Anthropologie Religieuse* (Editions de la Decouverte, 1986).

EDMONDS, J. M., *The Greek Bucolic Poets*, Loeb Classical Library (Heinemann, 1912).

EDWARDS, ADRIAN, 'On the non-existence of an ancestor cult among the Tiv', *Anthropos* 78 (1984), 77–112.

ERMAN, A., and RANKE, H., *La Civilisation Égyptienne* (Payot, 1963).

EVANS-PRITCHARD, E. E., *Witchcraft, Oracles and Magic among the Azande* (Clarendon Press, 1937).

—— *Nuer Religion* (Clarendon Press, 1956).

FERNANDEZ, J., *Fang Architectonics* (Ishi, 1977).

—— *Bwiti: An Ethnography of the Religious Imagination in Africa* (Princeton University Press, 1982).

FORD, MARK, 'Living with Equations', *Times Literary Supplement* (12 Dec. 1997), 11.

FOSTER, BENJAMIN, *Before the Muses, an Anthology of Akkadian Literature* (CDL Press, 1993).

FOSTER, R. F., 'History and identity in modern Ireland', The Eighth Annual Bindoff Lecture, The Department of History, Queen Mary and Westfield College, London (1997).

FOURIE, L., 'Preliminary notes on certain customs of the Hei-/om Bushmen', *Journal of Southwest Africa Scientific Society* 1 (Windhoek, S. Africa, 1926).

FOX, JAMES, 'Roman Jakobson and the comparative study of parallelism', in C. Lisse (ed.), *Roman Jakobson: Echoes of His Scholarship* (The Peter de Ridder Press, 1977).

FRANKFORT, HENRI, *Kingship and the Gods: A Study of Ancient Near Eastern Religion as the Integration of Society and Nature* (University of Chicago Press, 1948).

FREUD, SIGMUND, *Jokes and their Relation to the Unconscious* (1905); trans. James Strachey (Routledge and Kegan Paul, 1960).

GARSIEL, MOSHE, 'Puns upon names as a literary device in 1 K:1–2', *Biblica*, 72/3 (1991), 379–86.

GASTER, T. H., 'Sacrifices and Offerings in the Old Testament', in G. A. Buttrick *et al.* (eds), *The Interpreter's Dictionary of the Bible*, iv (Abingdon Press, 1962), 147–59.

GELLER, M., 'Taboo in Mesopotamia', A review article, *JCS* 42/1 (1990),105–17.

GELLER, STEPHEN,'Blood cult: toward a literary theology of the priestly work of the Pentateuch', *Prooftexts* 12 (1992), 97–124.

GELLNER, E., *Saints of the Atlas* (Weidenfeld and Nicolson, (1969).

GINSBURG, CARLO, *Night Battles, Witchraft and Agrarian Cults in the 16th and 17th Centuries* (Routledge, 1983).

GLOVER, MICHAEL, *Wellington as Military Commander* (Batsford, 1968).

GLOVER, RICHARD, *Peninsular Preparation: the Reform of the British Army 1795–1809* (Cambridge University Press, 1988).

GOLDBERG, HARVEY E., 'Cambridge in the land of Canaan: descent, alliance, circumcision, and instruction in the Bible', *JANES* 24 (1996), 9–34.

GOODMAN, NELSON, *Languages of Art* (Bobbs Merril, 1968).

GOODY, J., *Death, Property and the Ancestors* (Tavistock Publications, 1962).

GRAHAM, A. C., *Disputes of the Tao: Philosophical Argument in Ancient China* (Open Court, 1989).

GRANET, MARCEL, *The Religion of the Chinese People* (Blackwell, 1975).

GRAPPE, C., and MARX, A., *Le sacrifice, vocation et subversion du sacrifice dans les deux testaments* (Essais bibliques, 29, Labor et Fides, 1998).

GUTZWILLER, KATHRYN, *Theocritus Pastoral Analogies: the Formation of a Genre* (University of Wisconsin Press, 1991).

HACKING, IAN, *Representing and Intervening: Introductory Topics in the Philosophy of Natural Science* (Cambridge University Press, 1983).

HALL, D., and AMES, R., *Thinking Through Confucius* (SUNY, 1987).
—— —— *Anticipating China* (SUNY, 1995).

HALLIDAY, W. R., *Greek Divination: a Study of its Methods and Principles* (Macmillan, 1913)

HANSON, K. C., 'The Herodians and Mediterranean kinship; part I: Genealogy and Descent', *Biblical Theology Bulletin* 19 (1989), 75–84.

HARAN, MENAHEM, *Temples and Temple Service in Ancient Israel* (Oxford University Press, 1978).

HARDIE, P. (ed.), *Classical Closure: Reading the End in Greek and Latin Literature* (Princeton University Press, 1997).

HARRINGTON, H. K., 'Interpreting Leviticus in the Second Temple Period: struggling with ambiguity', in J. Sawyer (ed.), *Reading Leviticus* (Sheffield Academic Press, 1996).

258   *References*

HARTOG, FRANCOIS, *The Mirror of Herodotus: The Representation of the Other in the Writing of History* (The New Historicism, Studies in Cultural Poetics, University of California Press, 1988).

HEANEY, SEAMUS, *The Spirit Level* (Faber and Faber, 1996).

HEIDER, GEORGE, *The Cult of Molech, a Reassessment* (Sheffield Academic Press, 1985).

HERODOTUS, *The History*, trans. by David Grene (University of Chicago Press, 1987).

HESSE, MARY, *Models and Analogies in Science*, The Newman History and Philosophy of Science Series (Sheed and Ward, 1963).

—— *The Structure of Scientific Inference* (University of California Press, 1974).

—— *Revolutions and Reconstructions in the Philosophy of Science* (Harvester Press, 1980).

HICKS, F. C. N., *The Fullness of Sacrifice*, 3rd edn (SPCK, 1953).

HOFFMAN, RONALD, and LEIBOWITZ-SCHMIDT, SHIRA, 'Pure/Impure', *New England Review* 16/1 (1994), 41–64.

HOUSTON, WALTER, *Purity and Monotheism: Clean and Unclean Animals in Biblical Law* (JSOTS 140, Sheffield Academic Press, 1993).

HUFFMAN, HERBERT B., 'Priestly divination in Israel', in Carol Meyers and M. O'Connor (eds), *The Word of the Lord Shall Go Forth: Essays in Honour of David Noel Freedman* (Eisenbrauns, Winona Lake, Indiana, 1983), 355–9.

JACKSON, BERNARD, 'Susanna and the singular history of singular witnesses', in *Acta Juridica: Studies in Honour of Ben Beinart*, ii (1977).

JACOBSON-WIDDING, ANITA, 'The shadow as an expression of individuality in Congolese conceptions of personhood', in Michael Jackson and Ivan Karp (eds), *Personhood and Agency* (Uppsala, Acta Universitatis Upsaliensis, 1990), 31–58.

JAIN, KAILASH CHAND, *Lord Mahavira and his Times* (Delhi, Motilal Banarsidass Publishers, 1974).

JAKOBSON, ROMAN and POMORSKA, K., *Dialogues* (Paris, Flammarion, 1980); English edn. (Cambridge University Press, 1983).

JAMIESON-DRAKE, D. W., *Scribes and Schools in Monarchic Judah: a Socio-archeological Approach* (The Social World of Biblical Antiquity, Series 9, Sheffield Academic Press, 1991).

JANTZEN, J., *The Quest for Therapy in Lower Zaire* (University of California Press, 1978).

JAPHET, SARA, 'The prohibition of the habitation of women: the temple scroll's attitude toward sexual impurity and its biblical precedents', *JANES* 22 (1993), 69–87.

JASTROW, MARCUS, *Dictionary of Talmud Babli. Jerushalmi. Midrashtic Literature and Targuimim*, 2 vols. (Pardes Publishing House, 1950).

JAULIN, ROBERT, *La Geomancie, Analyse Formelle*, Cahiers de l'Homme (Paris, Mouton, 1966).

JUNOD, H. A., *The Life of a South African Tribe* (Macmillan, 1927).

KASS, L. R., *The Hungry Soul, Eating and the Perfection of Our Nature* (Free Press, 1994).

KNOHL, ISRAEL, *The Sanctuary of Silence* (Augsburg Fortress, 1995).

KOCHAN, LIONEL, *Beyond the Graven Image* (Macmillan, 1997).

KUGEL, JAMES, *The Idea of Biblical Poetry* (Yale University Press, 1981).

KUHN, THOMAS, 'Second thoughts on paradigms', in F. Suppes (ed.), *The Structure of Scientific Theories* (University of Illinois Press, 1974).

KUPER, A., *The Invention of Primitive Society: Transformations of an Illusion* (Routledge, 1988).

LABAT, R., *Traité Akkadien de Diagnostics et Pronostics Medicaux*, Tablette 18, Serie 3 (Leiden, Brill, 1951).

LANGER, SUZANNE K., *Philosophy in a New Key: A Study in the Symbolism of Reason, Rite and Art* (Harvard University Press, 1942).

—— *Feeling and Form* (Charles Scribner and Sons, 1953).

LEVINE, BARUCH, *The JPS Commentary, Leviticus* (Jewish Publication Society, 1989).

—— 'On the semantics of land tenure in biblical literature: the term *"ahuzzah"* ', in *The Tablet and the Scroll—Studies* (1993), 134–9.

—— and DE TARRAGON, J-M., 'Dead kings and Raphaim: the patrons of the Ugaritic dynasty', *Journal of the American Oriental Society* 104 (1984), 649–59.

LÉVI-STRAUSS, CLAUDE, *Totemism* (trans. from the French, *Le Totemisme*, by Rodney Needham) (Beacon Press, 1963).

—— (1966a) *The Savage Mind* (trans. from the French, *La Pensée Sauvage* (Plon, 1962) (Weidenfeld and Nicolson, 1966).

—— *Mythologiques*, i: *Le Cru et le Cuit* (Plon, 1964); ii (1966b): *Du Miel aux Cendres* (Plon, 1966); iii: *L'Origine des Manières de Table* (Plon, 1968).

LLOYD, GEOFFREY, 'Greek democracy, philosophy and science', in John Dunn (ed.), *Democracy, The Unfinished Journey, 508 BC to AD 1933* (Oxford University Press, 1992), 41–56.

—— *Adversaries and Authorities* (Cambridge University Press, 1996).

LLOYD-JONES, H., *The Justice of Zeus*, addenda to 2nd edn (University of California Press, 1983), 179–83.

LOHFINK, NORBERT, *Theology of the Pentateuch: Themes of the Priestly Narrative and Deuteronomy* (Augsburg Fortress, 1994).

MACCOBY, HYAM, 'Leviticus and abomination', *Times Literary Supplement* (11 September 1998), 17.

MAGONET, JONATHAN, *Form and Meaning: Studies in Literary Techniques in the Book of Jonah* (Almond Press, 1983).

—— ' "But if it is a girl, she is unclean for twice seven days . . .", the riddle of Leviticus 12.5', in J. Sawyer (ed.), *Reading Leviticus* (Sheffield, 1996), 144–52.

MAIMONIDES, Moses, *Guide for the Perplexed* (London, 1881).

MALAMAT, ABRAHAM, ' "Love your neighbour as yourself", what it really means', *Biblical Archeological Review* (July/August 1990), 50–1.

MARX, ALFRED, *Les Offrandes Végétales dans l'Ancien Testament, Du Tribut au Repas Eschatalogique* (Brill, 1994).

MATORY, J.L., *Sex and the Empire that Is No More* (University of Minnesota Press, 1994).

MAURUS, B. RABANUS, *Patrologiae Cursus Completus*, i, ed. J.-P. Migne (Bibliothecae Cleri Universae, Paris, 1831).

MAYER, ADRIAN C. (ed.), *Culture, Nature and Morality* (Oxford University Press, 1981).

MEYER, ADOLPH, *Wesen und Geschichte der Theorie vom Mikr-un Makrokosmos* (Bernen Studien zur Philoosophie, 25, 1900).

MICHELL, GEORGE, *The Hindu Temple* (Paul Elek, 1977).

MILGROM, JACOB, 'The biblical diet laws as an ethical system', *Interpretation* 17 (1963), 288–301.

—— *Cult and Conscience: the Asham and the Priestly Doctrine of Repentance* (Brill, 1976).

—— 'Israel's sanctuary: the priestly "Picture of Dorian Gray" ', in *Studies in Cultic Theology and Terminology*, Studies in Judaism in Late Antiquity, ed. Jacob Neusner, 36 (Brill, 1983), 390–400.

—— 'Rationale for cultic law: the case of impurity', *Semeia* 45 (1989),103–9.

—— *Numbers*, JPS Commentary (Jewish Publication Society, 1990).

—— *Leviticus 1–16*, The Anchor Bible (Doubleday, 1991).

—— 'Two biblical Hebrew priestly terms: Seqes and Tame' *MAARAV* 8 (1992), 107–16.

—— 'The changing concept of holiness', in John Sawyer (ed.), *Reading Leviticus* (Sheffield, 1996), 65–75.

MISHNAH, THE, Sixth Division, *Tohoroth* (Cleanness), 4–6. Translated with notes by H. Danby (Clarendon Press, 1933).

MUFFS, JOCHANAN, *Love and Joy: Law, Language and Religion in Ancient Israel* (JTS, Harvard University Press, 1992).

MURRAY, ROBERT, *The Cosmic Covenant*, Heythrop Monographs, 7 (Sheed and Ward, 1992).

MYRES, JOHN L., *Herodotus, Father of History* (Clarendon Press, 1953).

NEUSNER, JACOB, 'History and Structure, the Case of the Mishnah' *JAAR* 45/2 (1977), 161–92.

—— (ed.), *Studies in Cultic Theology and Terminology*, Studies in Judaism in Late Antiquity (Brill, 1983).

NICHOLAS, H., (ed.), *Dispatches and Letters of Lord Nelson*, vii (London, 1846).

NICOLAS, GUY, *Dynamique Social et Appréhension du Monde au Sein d'une Société Hausa*, Muséum National d'Histoire Naturelle, Travaux et Mémoires de l'Institut d'Ethnologie, 78 (Paris, Musée de l'Homme, 1975).

NOTH, M., *Numbers: a Commentary* (SCM Press, 1968).

O'CONNOR, M., 'Cardinal direction terms in biblical Hebrew', *Semitic Studies* 2 (1991), 1140–57.

—— 'The body in the Bible: anatomy and morphology', in V. Klimoski and M. C. Athans (eds.), *In the Service of the Church: Essays on Theology and Ministry in Honor of Reverend Charles Froehle* (University of St Thomas, St Paul, Minnesota, 1993).

PARKIN, DAVID (ed.), *The Anthropology of Evil* (Blackwell, 1985).

PATAI, RALPH, *Man and Temple* (Thomas Nelson, 1947).

PEEK, P., 'Cultural systems within divination systems', editorial introduction to Part 3, *African Divining Systems, Ways of Knowing* (Indiana University Press, 1991).

PHILO, with English translation, ed. F. H. Colson, viii: *The Special Laws* (Harvard University Press, 1939).

POPE, MARVIN, 'Cult of the dead at Ugarit', in Gordon Young (ed.), *Ugarit in Retrospect* (Eisenbrauns, 1981), 159–79.

PORTEN, B., *The Jews in Egypt*, ch. 13: 'The Diaspora', The Cambridge History of Judaism, i (Cambridge University Press, 1984), 372–400.

POUILLOUX, J., 'Asoka, Roi Indien. Inscription bilingue gréco-araméenne (3e s. avant J.C.)', in *Choix d'Inscriptions Grecques* (Belles Lettres, 1960).

RABANUS, *De Laudibus Crucis,* Patrologiae Tomus CVII (Paris, J.-P. Migne ed., 1831), 167 fig. 5.

RADCLIFFE-BROWN, A. R., 'Religion and society, the Henry Myers Lecture, 1945', in *Structure and Function in Primitive Society* (Cohen and West, 1952), 153–77.

RADDAY, Y. T., 'Chiasmus in biblical narrative', in J. W. Welch, (ed.), *Chiasmus in Antiquity* (Hildesheim, Gerstenberg Verlag, 1981).

RENDSBURG, GARY A., 'The inclusio in Leviticus XI', *Vetus Testamentum,* 43/3 (1993), 418–19.

ROBERTS, D., DUNN, F. M., and FOWLER, D. (eds), *Classical Closure: Reading the End in Greek and Latin Literature* (Princeton University Press, 1997).

SAGGS, H. W. F., *The Encounter with the Divine in Mesopotamia and Israel* (Athlone Press, 1978).

SANDERS, E. P., *Jewish Law from Jesus to the Mishnah, Five Studies* (SCM Press, 1990).

SARNA, N. M., *The JPS Torah Commentary, Genesis* (Philadelphia, The Jewish Publication Society, 1989).

—— *The JPS Torah Commentary, Exodus* (Philadelphia, The Jewish Publication Society, 1991).

SAWYER, JOHN F. A., 'Root meanings in Hebrew', *Journal of Semitic Studies* 12/1 (1967), 37–50.

—— 'A note on the etymology of Sara'at', *Vetus Testamentum* 26/2 (1976), 241–5.

—— 'The authorship and structure of the Book of Job', *Studia Biblica* 1 (1978), 251–7.

—— 'Biblical alternatives to monotheism', *Theology* 87 (1984), 172–80.

—— 'The language of Leviticus', in J. Sawyer (ed.), *Reading Leviticus* (Sheffield, 1996), 15–20.

SCHAPERA, I., 'The sin of Cain', *Journal of the Royal Anthropological Institute* 85 (1955), 33–43.

SCHMITT, JOHN J., 'Gender correctness and biblical metaphors, the case of God's relation to Israel', *Biblical Theology Bulletin* 26 (1996), 1–11.

SCHWARTZ, BARUCH J., 'The bearing of sin in the priestly litera-ture', in *Pomegranates and Golden Bells: Studies in Honour of Jacob Milgrom* (Eisenbrauns, 1995), 3–21.

SÉD, NICOLAS, 'Les hymnes sur le paradis de Saint Ephrem et les traditions juives', *Le Muséon, Revue d'Études Orientales*, 81 (1968), 455–501.

—— *Etudes Juives: La Mystique Cosmologique Juive* (Mouton, 1981).

SHARON, DIANE M., 'The doom of paradise: literary patterns in accounts of paradise and mortality in the Hebrew Bible and the ancient Near East', in *Genesis, The Feminist Companion to the Bible*, Second Series (Sheffield Academic Press, 1998), 63–79.

SHOKEID, MOSHE, *A Gay Synagogue in New York* (Columbia University Press, 1995).

SIFRA, with translation and commentary by Rabbi Dr Morris Ginsberg, MA, Ph.D (published by the Gainsford Family, rights reserved Leshon Limudim Ltd, POB 4282 Jerusalem, 1994).

SIVAN, EMMANUEL, 'To remember is to forget: Israel's 1948 War', *Journal of Contemporary History* 28 (1993), 341–59.

SKEHAN, PATRICK, 'The seven columns of Wisdom's house in Proverbs 1–9', *CBQ* 9 (1947), 190–8.

SMITH, MORTON, 'The common theology of the Ancient Near East', *JBL* 71 (1952), 135 ff.

—— *Palestinian Parties and Politics that Shaped the Old Testament* (Columbia University Press, 1971).

SMITH, W. ROBERTSON, (1889) *The Religion of the Semites, the Fundamental Institutions* (Shocken Books, 1972).

SNAITH, N. H., *Leviticus and Numbers* (Thomas Nelson, 1967).

SPRONK, KLAUS, *Beatific Afterlife in the Ancient Near East* (Kevelaer and Neukirchen-Vluyn, 1986).

STAAL, FRITZ, *Agni, the Vedic Ritual of the Fire Altar*, 2 vols. (Asian Humanities Press, 1983).

STOL, M., *Epilepsy in Babylonia*, Cuneiform Monographs, 2 (STYX Publications, Groningen, 1993).

STUART, CHARLES, *Demons and the Devil: Moral Imagination in Modern Greek Culture* (Princeton University Press, 1991).

TALMON, S., 'Calendar reckoning of the sect from the Judaean Desert', in Chaim Rabin and Y. Yadin (eds), *Scripta Hierosolymitana*, iv: *Aspects of the Dead Sea Scrolls* (Jerusalem, Magnes Press, 1965).

TIGAY, J., *Deuteronomy, the People's Torah* (Jewish Publication Society, 1996).

TURNER, V. W., *The Forest of Symbols: Aspects of Ndembu Ritual* (Cornell University Press, 1967).

—— *Image and Pilgrimage* (Columbia University Press, 1978).

VAN DAM, CORNELIS, *The Urim and Thummim: A Means of Revelation in Israel* (Eisenbrauns, 1997).

VAN DE MEER, L. B., *The Bronze Liver of Piacenza: Analysis of a Polytheistic Structure* (J. C. Gieben, 1987).

VERDIER, YVONNE, *Façons de Dire, Façons de Faire: La laveuse, la Couturière, la Cuisinière* (Gallimard, 1987).

VERIN, P., and RAJAONARIMA, N., 'Divination in Madagascar', in P. Peek (ed.), *African Divining Systems* (Indiana University Press, 1991).

VERNANT, J-P., 'Hestia-Hermes: the religious expression of space and movement in Ancient Greece', in *Myth and Thought among the Greeks* (Routledge and Kegan Paul, 1983), 127–75.

WATSON, RICHARD, *The Life of the Rev. John Wesley, A.M, Sometime Fellow of Lincoln College, Oxford and Founder of the Methodist Societies* (New York, Thomas George Jnr, 1885).

WEINFELD, MOSHE, *Deuteronomy and the Deuteronomic School* (Clarendon Press, 1972).

—— 'Jeremiah and the spiritual metamorphosis of Israel', *Zeitschrift fur die Alttestamentliche Wissenschaft* 88/1 (1976), 2–56.

—— *Justice and Righteousness in Israel and the Nations: Equality and Freedom in Israel in the light of Ancient Near Eastern Concepts of Social Justice* (Jerusalem, 1984).

—— 'Freedom proclamations in Egypt and in the Ancient Near East', in *The Bible and Christianity* (Israel, Magnes Press, 1985).

WRIGHT, D., FREEDMAN, D., and HURVITZ, A. (eds), *Pomegranates and Golden Bells* (Eisenbrauns, 1995).

YAN, LI, and SHIVAN, DU, *Chinese Mathematics: a Concise History* (Oxford Science Publications, 1987).

YATES, FRANCES, *The Theatre of the World* (Routledge and Kegan Paul, 1969).

Zohar Hadash, Midrash Eklah, cited in Ralph Patai, *Man and Temple* (Thomas Nelson, 1947) as: Ps. 137.5; edit. Warsaw, n.d.: 183.

ZONG-QI, CAI, 'Synthetic parallelism as a cultural expression: a cross-cultural and cross-disciplinary study', *Tamking Review* 20/2 (1989), 151–67.

INDEX OF BIBLE REFERENCES

GENERAL INDEX